C000295402

Steve Kemme

THE OUTSIDER
The Life and Work of
Lafcadio Hearn
The Man Who Introduced Voodoo, Creole Cooking and Japanese Ghosts to the World

TUTTLE Publishing

Tokyo | Rutland, Vermont | Singapore

Dedication

FOR MY WIFE, Karen, whose love and courage always inspire me.

Contents

Foreword

*O*n April 2, 1876, in an interview article for the *Cincinnati Commercial* titled "Story of a Slave," 25-year-old Lafcadio Hearn (also known by his Japanese name Yakumo Koizumi) described the years of suffering endured by an emancipated woman named Henrietta Wood. One-hundred and forty-five years later, in 2021, the *Washington Post* noted how Hearn, who had been married to Alethea "Mattie" Foley, a formerly enslaved woman in Cincinnati, had with this article made an important contribution to a broader understanding of "slavery and freedom," an example of his tolerance and exceptional sensitivity to "the voices of fleeting lives."

Hearn travelled widely to hear these voices. He was born in Greece, lived in Ireland and England and travelled to the United States and the French Caribbean island of Martinique, where he was fascinated by the folk beliefs, ghost stories, and music of Black and mixed-race people. Similarly, after he went to Japan, he was eager to learn about the folklore and ghost stories and the sounds of insects that were beloved by the Japanese.

As a great-grandson of Hearn, I am thrilled and proud that my friend Steve Kemme, a longtime reporter for the *Cincinnati Enquirer* and a distinguished Hearn scholar, has published this new biography of Hearn. Mr. Kemme is the president of the Lafcadio Hearn Society/USA and has long appreciated Hearn's warm gaze towards ordinary people. In 2019, he kindly took part in the "Lafcadio Hearn Reading Performance" for "The Open Mind of Lafcadio Hearn in the USA" held at the Cincinnati Art Museum to commemorate the 150th anniversary of Hearn's arrival in America.

I have visited the beautiful city of Cincinnati several times. With each visit, I have been warmly welcomed by Mr. Kemme and others who help keep Hearn's memory alive. This city, situated on the border with the South, offers a unique, multilayered experience of history and culture, encompassing memories of the Civil War and the regret and sorrow of the enslaved Black people. It was this geographical and cultural marginality that attracted Hearn to Cincinnati and the city must have had a significant meaning for Hearn as a place to start his career as a writer and cultivate his open-mindedness.

After residing in Cincinnati for eight years, Hearn relocated to New Orleans, where he discovered a paradise of orange and lemon-colored sunshine. There he became deeply absorbed in the creative and vibrant Creole culture that flourished in the city, formed by a fusion of French, Spanish, African, and indigenous cultures. While he lived in New Orleans, Hearn published the book *Gombo Zhèbes* (1885), a dictionary of Creole proverbs, with an introduction emphasizing the importance of preserving folklore. He also published *La Cuisine Creole* (1885), the world's first collection of Creole recipes, which revealed his love and interest in the mixed culture of New Orleans, a book that is still widely read today.

In New Orleans, Hearn frequently visited with Marie Laveau, known as the Voodoo Queen, and worked diligently to document the West African origins of the Voodoo religion which had deep roots in the city. This interest in Voodoo continued even after he moved to Martinique, where he collected supernatural tales about zombies from a maid named Cyrillia, who lived among the zombie believers. He incorporated them into his reportage travelogue, *Two Years in the French West Indies* (1890).

In New Orleans and Martinique, Hearn contracted malaria and typhoid fever, respectively, and at one point found himself near death. Fortunately, he survived thanks to the dedicated care of friends who lived nearby. The experience changed him. Hearn would write at least six works on infectious diseases based on his experience and practiced handwashing and gargling to prevent infection. The courage and gentleness displayed by so many people during such a difficult time deepened his respect for the ordinary people he lived among.

In 1890, Hearn arrived in Japan, a country he had longed to visit, as a reporter for *Harper's* in New York. Not long after his arrival, he split with *Harper's* and found work as an English teacher in Matsue, a castle town in western Japan. The region, Izumo, where Matsue is located, was steeped in myth and was dotted with ancient Shinto shrines. Hearn was fascinated by the devout people who prayed to the rising sun and moon while clapping their hands. He loved Matsue, calling the place "The Chief City of the Province of the Gods."

In Matsue, he met Setsu Koizumi, the daughter of a Samurai family, whom he later married. After becoming a naturalized Japanese citizen, Hearn changed his name to "Yakumo Koizumi." His first name, "Yakumo," was derived from a *makurakotoba* (a poetic epithet) of the Izumo region used in the earliest Japanese waka poem.

Hearn's life in Japan, where animism was still prevalent, fostered his keen interest in traditional tales of the supernatural passed down by the people. He retold around a hundred of these stories, and his book, *Kwaidan* (1904), is considered his literary masterpiece of the genre. This work has been translated into many languages, once into Inuit and more recently into Irish and Catalan. Hearn believed that "the ghostly represents always some shadow of truth," which led him to view Japanese popular culture with a warm and understanding perspective. He was a writer who gleaned much insight from the culture of the invisible, including *yōkai*, ghosts, and infectious diseases.

Where does Hearn's "open-mindedness" come from? First and foremost, it is born from his diverse cultural origins and rich cross-cultural experiences. In addition, his values, which were not limited by Christianity or Western-centric thinking, and his ability to perceive culture using all his senses. Hearn was particularly affected by his hearing, which developed to compensate for the loss of sight in his left eye. At a time when only Western classical music was considered "music" and all other music was dismissed as "noise," he traveled to New Orleans to study music that later formed the genre called jazz. He stated, "I have always been much impressed and charmed by primitive music." In Japan, he was impressed by the Bon Odori songs of Shimoichi village, Tottori Prefecture, and depicted his life in Matsue from the perspective of the soundscape. By first respecting others and approaching interaction with an open mind, the essence of culture may have naturally come into view for him.

The idea of an "open mind" as it pertains to Hearn was proposed by Takis Efstathiou, an avid Greek reader of Hearn who actively promotes the idea. In 2009, the American College of Greece in Athens hosted a contemporary art exhibition with the theme "The Open Mind of Lafcadio Hearn." More than forty artists exhibited their works along with writings that conveyed Hearn's spirit. The exhibition was well-received and led to another show with the same theme at Matsue Castle in 2010, which later traveled to New York and New Orleans. Since 2014, we have held a series of events in Greece, Ireland, and the U.S. to further explore Hearn's open mind. It has included symposiums, exhibitions of materials, and readings and musical performances by Matsue-born actor Shiro Sano and guitarist Kyoji Yamamoto. By combining literature and art, we have conveyed Hearn's spirit through diverse artistic expressions.

The success of these events seems to owe a lot to people's empathy for Hearn's philosophy of tolerance. After more than a decade of activity, I am surprised and pleased to see that the project is being introduced and appreciated in various ways. In Matsue, an ordinance passed in March 2021 includes "Yakumo Koizumi" as one of Matsue's seven key elements of cultural power. The city aims to be "a town where everyone recognizes various values through an 'open mind' that respects diversity." Although Hearn's life ended in 1904, his works and spirit continue to be appreciated, studied and celebrated in Matsue, a place he deeply loved, and throughout the world.

Bon Koizumi

Introduction

*F*OR A DIMINUTIVE MAN with a soft, flute-like voice, Lafcadio Hearn often made a strong impression on those he met—and not always for the best. His wit, intelligence and kindness drew many people to him, while his impatience, irreverence and temper drove some away. Hearn severed many of his close, longstanding friendships because of perceived slights or misunderstandings. He invariably clashed with his editors, even those who loved and championed his work.

His method of writing was as eccentric as his personality. Hearn cut a strange-looking figure as he sat at his writing table to work. The 5-foot-3 half-blind man wrote while hunched way over his desk, his good eye an inch or two from the paper. He sometimes became so absorbed in his work that to get his attention, his wife had to stand next to him and shout.

By any standards, Hearn led a singularly unusual life. Born Patrick Lafcadio Hearn to a Greek mother and an Irish father in 1850, he was abandoned by his parents, raised by a great-aunt in Dublin and immigrated to the United States at the age of 19. At that point, he decided to be known as Lafcadio (given to him because his birthplace was the Greek island of Lefkada) instead of Patrick. After living in Cincinnati, New Orleans and Martinique, he moved to Japan at the age of 40 in 1890. He married a Japanese woman, had four children, changed his name to Yakumo Koizumi and lived as much as possible according to Japanese and Buddhist traditions.

A nomad at heart, he lived most comfortably in the realm of the imagination and the intellect. He used his acute powers of observation, his keen mind and his prodigious writing talent to produce a distinctive body of work that attracted international accolades. He was regarded as one of the late 19th century's finest prose stylists.

Today, Hearn is best known for his writings about Japan. But some of his work in the earlier periods of his life contain as much value and deserve just as much attention as his Japanese books.

Like an archaeologist digging into the earth for remnants of ancient civilizations, Hearn vigorously delved into the histories, rituals, myths and folktales of the vanishing worlds he encountered in his far-flung travels. Before moving to Japan, Hearn wrote insightfully about the post-Civil War African-Americans in Cincinnati, the Creoles in New Orleans, and the social and cultural fabric of every-day life in Martinique. Hearn realized the sub-cultures he chronicled were disappearing. He could see that outside cultural influences and commercialism endangered their long-term existence. That knowledge motivated Hearn and gave him a heightened sense about the urgency and significance of his work.

Although Hearn's a literary icon in Japan, he's unknown to the general public in the United States and Europe. Even in the literary world, he's not much more than a cult figure. I decided to write this book to encourage more people to read and appreciate his wide-ranging work. Besides writing newspaper stories for 15 years, he wrote 12 books about Japan, one book about the West Indies, two novels and English translations of French fiction writers such as Charles Baudelaire, Theophile Gautier and Pierre Loti. Few authors boast as varied a bibliography.

My initial attraction to Hearn stemmed from both personal and literary reasons. I grew up in Cincinnati and in 1982 began writing for the *Cincinnati Enquirer*, the same newspaper that had launched Hearn's career more than 100 years earlier. I feel fortunate to count him as one of my journalism ancestors.

Hearn overcame enormous obstacles throughout his life. Abandoned as a child by his Irish father and his Greek mother, he was raised by a great-aunt in Dublin, Ireland. When he was 16, he sustained a playground injury that caused permanent blindness in his left eye and disfigured his face. For the rest of his life, he was extremely self-conscious about his appearance. He almost always made sure he was photographed with the left side of his face hidden from the camera. To be an effective reporter, he had to overcome his anxiety about his appearance. The white film that had formed over his blind eye gave him a grotesque appearance, which often drew stares. I could identify with the fear and shame his disfigurement caused him—not because I was self-conscious about my appearance, but because I was sensitive about my speech.

In high school, I developed a serious stuttering problem. My stuttering had been slightly noticeable in the last two years or so of grade school. But when I started high school, it worsened to the point that I wouldn't talk on the telephone and would try my best to avoid talking in class. If a teacher called on me, I would act like I didn't know the answer and say nothing. Or I would give a wrong answer I knew I could say without stuttering. I worried that my speech problem would interfere with my college education and prevent me from having a writing career. Through several years of speech therapy, I managed to learn to control my stuttering and to stop avoiding speaking situations. I worked as a newspaper reporter for 37 years, devoting roughly half of my average work day talking to people in person or on the telephone. Even as my speech improved through years of speech therapy, there were times when I was afraid of stuttering when I interviewed prominent people. As Hearn wanted to hide his disfigured eye, I wanted to hide my speech impediment. But my desire to do my work helped prevent my fear from stopping me. I spent the last 30 years of my newspaper career with the *Enquirer* writing news and feature stories.

I didn't begin reading Hearn until the early 1990s. I first saw his name in a 1990 review of an anthology of some of his Cincinnati newspaper writings. The book featured a tantalizing title, *Period of the Gruesome*. Jon Hughes, then a journalism professor at the University of Cincinnati, had researched and assembled a collection featuring many of the sensational and lurid crime stories Hearn had written when he worked as a reporter in Cincinnati from 1872 to 1877. He wrote first for the *Enquirer* and then for another daily, the *Cincinnati Commercial*.

The review of this book appeared in 1990 in the *Enquirer*. Owen Findsen, an *Enquirer* art critic with a passion for local history, wrote the review.

A few years later, I was browsing in a used book store when I saw a book with Hearn's name on it. It was called *The Selected Writings of Lafcadio Hearn* (1949, Citadel Press), edited by Henry Goodman with an introduction by the literary critic Malcolm Cowley. The 566-page book contained selections from each period of his career: Cincinnati, 1872–1877; New Orleans, 1877–1887; Martinique, 1887–1889; and Japan, 1890–1904. I bought the book for a few dollars and soon began reading it.

The anthology opened with his book, *Kwaidan*, which contained ancient Japanese folk tales that Hearn expanded and rewrote in his own literary style. I found these stories, which usually were rooted in Japanese history and religion, completely captivating. Hearn had taken the bare bones of these tales and fleshed them out, giving them new life. In powerful, lyrical prose, Hearn infused these stories of the supernatural with drama, suspense and humanity. In his skillful hands, they became more than simple ghost stories meant to frighten. They revealed part of the essence of Japan's soul.

I eagerly read the rest of the anthology. While his Cincinnati pieces—when he was learning how to write—struck me as being too flowery and undisciplined, I was impressed by young Hearn's broad range of topics and his earnest attempts to draw readers into his stories. I also couldn't help but laugh in amazement at the sheer audacity of the startling, graphic details he included in his crime stories.

I could see in the selections from his New Orleans and Martinique years that Hearn's writing had progressed quite a bit from his Cincinnati period. It flowed more smoothly and his descriptions were sharper. The writing in his Martinique sketches was so vivid, I felt like I was on the island with him, walking by his side on the winding streets of St. Pierre down to the bay for his daily morning swim.

The anthology's other tales and essays from his Japanese period totally engrossed me. I began buying his books and anthologies in used book stores and online and read several biographies. I acquired *Children of the Levee* (University of Kentucky Press, 1957), a collection edited by O.W. Frost of his Cincinnati writings about African-Americans living there. These stories, which had been published in the *Enquirer* and the *Commercial* in the mid-1870s, reflect Hearn's sympathetic attitude toward non-whites. They contain some of his best writing during that early part of his career. He paid a price for his friendly relationship with Black people. In 1875, the *Enquirer* fired him partly because he married a Black woman, Alethea "Mattie" Foley, at a time when Ohio banned interracial marriage. The *Com-*

mercial quickly hired him, but his relationship with his illegal wife soon ended.

The more I learned about Hearn, the more I admired his intelligence, courage and compassion. He had a limitless curiosity, a quality that drove him to explore the world through reading and traveling. He sought stories in dangerous, crime-ridden sections of Cincinnati, in Creole enclaves and the bayous of New Orleans and in small islands in the Gulf of Mexico. In Martinique, he climbed a volcanic mountain and walked through dense forests. In Japan, he traveled to remote villages, sea caves and the summit of Mount Fuji.

He learned as much as he could about the people, the culture, the religions, the rituals and the folklore of each of the widely disparate places he lived. In contrast with the prevailing racism and cultural myopia of his day, Hearn wrote empathetically about those outside the mainstream, especially people of color. When he wrote about Black people, he occasionally lapsed into a patronizing tone. But he never fell prey to the racial stereotypes common in that period. He spent much of his career revealing the humanity and beauty in people mainstream society ignored or belittled. He pointed out social injustices and urged reforms.

Hearn was as passionate and fearless a writer as he was a traveler. This man who grew up an orphan and an outcast loved exploring the unfamiliar and far-flung. He wrote with his head and his heart. Since his death at the age of 54 in 1904, his reputation has fluctuated with changing literary trends and political developments. Through these ups and downs, Hearn's work has shown a resiliency and strength that reflect the depth and character of the man. With racism and xenophobia finding firmer footholds in the United States and other parts of the world today, Hearn's example of openness to people of different races, countries, cultures and faiths is both heartening and badly needed. He continues to enthrall and inspire. I hope this biography does likewise.

CHAPTER 1

Greek-Irish Roots

*O*N THE RAINY afternoon of September 26, 2004, dozens of people gathered in Zoshigaya Cemetery in Tokyo at the gravesite of someone none of them had ever met. The visitors came from all parts of Japan and from nations throughout the world to pay homage to Lafcadio Hearn, a writer of Greek-Irish heritage who achieved his greatest fame while living and working in Japan for the last 14 years of his life.

Hearn, a nomad at heart, had found a home in a country among people of a different race, language and culture. He adopted the Japanese name, Yakumo Koizumi. In his books and articles, he had revealed to the outside world the meaning and richness of Japan's ancient traditions and their place in the country's daily life. He also reminded the Japanese of aspects of their culture that were beginning to fade as the country tried to modernize and become more open to Western cultural and economic influences. From his arrival in Japan in 1890 until his death in 1904, Hearn's delved into Japanese life and culture in a way no other Westerner had and wrote about it in a way that captivated his readers in the United States and in other English-speaking countries.

During this solemn ceremony commemorating the centennial of Hearn's death, the visitors at the cemetery formed a single line. One by one, they walked to the grave, bowed respectfully and placed a burning incense stick at the foot of the grave. Hearn's 79-year-old grandson, Toki Koizumi, stood under an umbrella in the mist-like rain for much of the afternoon and graciously thanked each visitor. The tombstone and an upright stone marker on his grave bore the inscriptions, "Koizumi Yakumo—1850–1904" and the posthumous Buddhist name given to him to honor his spirituality, which translates in English to

"Believing man similar to undefiled flower blooming like eight rising clouds, who dwells in mansion of right enlightenment."[1]

This ceremony was part of a nine-day, four-city symposium focusing on Hearn's life and writings. It was a major event that illustrated the deep respect and love Hearn's adopted country had for him. Hundreds of people came to Tokyo for the opening sessions. The symposium moved from Tokyo to Kyoto to Matsue and to Kumamoto, all cities where Hearn had lived. Hearn's great-grandson, Bon Koizumi, a college folklore professor, led about 40 symposium-goers on a bus trip from Himeji to Matsue, following the same 150-mile route Hearn took by rickshaw in 1890.

Considering origins, Patrick Lafcadio Hearn was an unlikely person to become a literary icon in Japan. His ancestral roots trace back to a much smaller island more than 6,000 miles from Japan. Known for its rough terrain, steep cliffs and harsh winds, Kythira is the most remote of the seven Greek islands in the Ionian Sea. For centuries, it was on an important naval trade route and had been invaded and overtaken at various times since the Middle Ages by a succession of conquerors, including the Turks, the Venetians, the French, the Russians and the British. The island also held a prominent place in Greek mythology. It was said to be the island of Aphrodite, the goddess of love.

But when the British army sent Charles Bush Hearn, an Anglo-Irish officer-surgeon, to the sparsely populated island in April 1848, it was no longer called Kythira. The British had changed its name to Cerigo after seizing it in 1815. In 1848, the Ionian islands began rebelling and announced their desire to become a part of Greece, not Great Britain. As a result, Great Britain established a strong military presence in the islands in an attempt to hold onto them. The constantly shifting military needs caused British authorities to move troops from one island to the next.[2]

Cerigo was the fourth Greek island Hearn had been dispatched to since being commissioned into the army six years ago. Moving from place to place didn't bother the hardy 30-year-old man. As a member of a family with a long tradition of military service, he accepted the

---

[1] The author attended this ceremony.
[2] O. W. Frost, *Young Hearn* (Tokyo: Hokuseido Press, 1958), 6-11.

demands of army life and enjoyed sailing the seas and traveling to distant ports of call.

Hearn took his transfer to Cerigo in stride. But Cerigo was more isolated and desolate than the other Greek islands where he had been stationed. Ships seldom stopped at Cerigo's harbor because of strong seas from the south that sometimes made anchoring difficult. Hearn's military detachment lived in a small Venetian castle at the top of a high rocky summit above the bay of Kapsali. A steep, winding path from the castle led to the nearby town of Cerigo.

During one of Hearn's meanderings through the town, he met Rosa Antonia Cassimati, a pretty, raven-haired 25-year-old woman with dark, enchanting eyes. Cassimati and Hearn, a handsome man with dark, curly hair and thick eyebrows, were immediately smitten with each other. On this island of the Greek goddess of love, Hearn had found romance. The two lovers could hardly have been more dissimilar. Hearn was a well-educated, worldly, outgoing Irish Anglican. Cassimati, a member of the Greek Orthodox Church, was a naive, sheltered young woman who couldn't read nor write—activities that Cerigo society discouraged women from pursuing. She spoke Romaic and Italian, but could manage only broken English. Besides, her family was of noble Ionian rank and didn't want any family member becoming romantically involved with a foreigner, much less a man who was an officer in the despised occupying army. Hearn also upset the family by appearing with Rosa in public. In Cerigo, women weren't even supposed to accompany their husbands on public walks. But the powerful attraction the dashing Hearn and the beguiling Cassimati felt for each other made them ignore her family's objections and continue seeing each other.

Her family's displeasure with their relationship turned to rage later in 1848 when Cassimati told them she was pregnant. Her brother reputedly beat and stabbed Hearn for defiling his sister. Rosa hid Charles in a barn and nursed him back to health.[3]

In June 1849, Hearn was transferred to another Greek island, Lefkada, also called Lefkas and Leucadia. A month later, on July 24, Cassimati gave birth to their son, George Robert Hearn. In November of that year, Hearn received a promotion to Staff Surgeon, Second

---

[3] Ibid., 4-6.

Class, and was ordered to report to England for assignment.

In defiance of Cassimati's family, before leaving for England, Hearn married Rosa on November 25 in the Greek Orthodox Church. With Rosa five months pregnant with their second child, Hearn left Lefkada on February 27, 1850, to report to England for reassignment. Hearn never told the army that he had a wife and son. Because George Robert had been born out of wedlock, he feared army officials would view his relationship with Rosa as scandalous and deny him promotions. Rosa stayed in Lefkada, where she gave birth to their second son on June 27, 1850. Charles was in Ireland then on a brief visit before he receiving an assignment to the West Indies. The boy was given a name that reflected both his Irish and his Greek heritage—Patrick Lafcadio, the second name honoring the island of his birth. He was known as Patrick to his family and friends. He didn't begin using Lafcadio as his first name until he emigrated to the United States when he was 19. He was baptized in the Greek Orthodox Church. Sadly, the Hearns' first son, George Robert, died two months after Lafcadio was born. With her husband away, Rosa had to bear the grief alone.[4]

During the next two years, Charles Hearn served in the West Indies on the island of Dominica and then on Grenada. The British army didn't permit officers to bring their wives with them on assignments. On June 30, 1852, he finally reported the existence of his wife and son to the War Office in London. He took that action to enable Rosa to inherit his estate if he died.

At that time, Hearn directed Rosa to Dublin, where she and Lafcadio could live with his family while he was away. With the assistance of Charles Hearn's brother, Richard Holmes Hearn, Rosa and Lafcadio made the long journey to Ireland. Accompanied by Hearn's brother, Richard, and an English woman who served as Rosa's interpreter, Rosa and two-year-old Lafcadio arrived in Dublin on August 1, 1852. They moved in with Charles Hearn's mother, Elizabeth Holmes Hearn. Her daughter, Jane, and her son-in-law, Henry Clocough Stephens, also lived the rented house.

The Hearn family had lived in Ireland since the 17th century and boasted a long line of military men, a tradition Charles upheld. The family had a slim but interesting connection to British royalty and to

---

[4]Elizabeth Stevenson, *Lafcadio Hearn* (New York: Macmillan, 1961), 5.

the great English poet, Andrew Pope. Elizabeth Hearn's mother was the great-niece of Dr. John Arbuthnot, a physician to Queen Anne and the subject of Pope's poem "Epistle to Dr. Arbuthnot."

This proud Anglo-Irish family didn't quite know what to make of Rosa, who spoke no English and clung fiercely to her Greek Orthodox faith, or of little Patrick Lafcadio, who had shoulder-length hair and wore two gold earrings. Neither Rosa nor the Hearn family made much effort to adapt to each other. Charles' widowed aunt, Sarah Brenane, was the only member of the family to develop a rapport with Rosa, who was overwhelmed by the strange culture and language and detested the cold climate.

Brenane knew what it felt like to be an outsider. She had violated her family's staunch Anglican Church background when she married a Catholic man and converted to Catholicism. Charles Hearn's great grandfather, the Venerable Daniel Hearn (1693–1766) had been a high-ranking Anglican official. He had served as Archdeacon of Cashel, Rector of St. Anne's, Dublin, and private chaplain to Lionel Sackville, the Duke of Dorset. Because of the Hearns' strong ties to the Anglican Church, they considered themselves more English than Irish.[5]

Sarah Brenane kindly reached out to Rosa and Lafcadio. She invited Rosa and Lafcadio to visit her house and took them on rides in her grand carriage. Despite her efforts, Rosa was deeply unhappy in Dublin and began exhibiting signs of mental illness. She suffered bouts of depression and displayed violent fits of anger. Once she attempted suicide by trying to throw herself out of an upper story window in the Hearn house.

Charles Hearn's return to Dublin on October 8, 1853, marked the first time he had ever seen his son. Lafcadio carried into adulthood vague memories of this first encounter with his father.

"I remember my father taking me on horseback when coming into town with his regiment," Lafcadio recalled much later. "I remember being at dinner with a number of men in red coats and striped trousers, and crawling about under the table and pinching their legs."[6]

---

[5] Frost, "The Hearn Family," *Young Hearn*, 1-34.
[6] From Lafcadio Hearn to his brother, James Hearn, 1890, in "Lafcadio Hearn's Brother," by Tracy Kneeland, *Atlantic Monthly*, January 1923, http://www.lafcadiohearn. net/jameshearn.html.

But Charles' arrival in Dublin after such a long absence brought his marriage to Rosa to the point of crisis. Realizing he no longer loved her, Rosa suffered some kind of nervous breakdown, displaying manic fits and temper tantrums. She convalesced at a mental asylum in Dundrum, a village about 110 miles southwest of Dublin. She received visits from Charles. After her mental health improved, she set up her own house near the Portobello Barracks in Rathmines, a Dublin suburb. Charles, who was stationed at the barracks, hired Catherine "Kate" Ronane, an Irish nursemaid, to stay with Rosa and help care for her and Lafcadio. Rosa was still mentally unstable. She sometimes threw temper tantrums and had to be physically restrained. After a six-month stay in Dublin, Charles left in March 1854 to go to Crimea, where his regiment was fighting. Terribly homesick and pregnant with their third child, Rosa left Dublin in the early summer ostensibly to visit her family in Greece. Lafcadio remained in Dublin under the care of Sarah Brenane, who paid for the trip and sent a nurse along to care for Rosa and her soon-to-be-born baby. On the way to Cerigo, Rosa gave birth to Daniel James Hearn on the island of Cephalonia. When she was physically able, she completed her journey to Cerigo with her infant son.[7]

After the Crimean War, Charles returned to Dublin on July 23, 1856. But before the ship arrived in Dublin, a fellow officer told him that Alicia Goslin, a woman he had been in love with two years before he met Rosa, was a widow and was living in Dublin.

Charles and Alicia, an attractive Irish woman, may have been engaged to be married when he left the country on army duty in 1846. While he was away, she eventually stopped writing to him and married a judge, Arthur Crawford. Arthur died while they were living in Australia, and she and her two children returned to Dublin.

Hearn was neither surprised nor disappointed to discover that Rosa had not returned from Cerigo. After reconnecting with Alicia, he began taking steps to have his marriage annulled. He achieved it by seizing upon a legal technicality. Being illiterate, Rosa hadn't signed the marriage contract, creating the legal loophole Charles used to terminate their union.[8]

---

[7] Frost, *Young Hearn*, 27-28.
[8] Ibid., 30.

Lafcadio recalled being taken by his father to Alicia's house: "One day my father came to my aunt's house to take me out for a walk. He took me into some very quiet street, where the houses were very high—with long flights of steps going up to the front door. Then a lady came down to meet us, all white-robed, with very bright hair— quite slender. I thought her beautiful as an angel, perhaps partly because she kissed me and petted me, and gave me a beautiful book and a toy gun. But my aunt found it out, and took away the book and the gun, and said that was a very wicked woman and my father a very wicked man."[9]

Crawford became Charles' second wife in July 1857. His divorce of Rosa and marriage to Alicia infuriated Sarah Brenane. She demanded that he repay all the money she had lent him and she removed his name from her will.

Rosa started a new life for herself in Cerigo. She married Giovanni Cavallini, who later became governor under the British at Cerigotto, a small island near Cerigo, and then served as Vice-Consul for Austria-Hungary. But Cavallini wanted nothing to do with her two sons and made her agree before they married that she leave Lafcadio and James in the care of others and legally give up custody of the two boys. Lafcadio, six years old, remained with Brenane, and James, two years old, was sent away permanently to a school in England, where he remained until he reached adulthood. James emigrated to the United States. Neither brother knew the fate of the other until they corresponded by letters during the later part of Lafcadio's life.

Charles and Rosa gave up their legal parental rights to both sons. Lafcadio never saw either of them again. Over the next few years, Charles sent a letters to Lafcadio from India, telling him about the tigers, elephants and serpents he saw there. To make the letters easier for his son to read, Charles printed the words instead of writing in cursive. Lafcadio never answered the letters, even though his aunt didn't forbid or discourage him from doing it. Brenane and her servants persistently defended Rosa, telling the boy not to believe anything unkind he might hear about his mother. They assured him that she loved him and his brother very much and couldn't help the way things had turned out. Lafcadio was convinced that his mother

---

[9]From Lafcadio Hearn to his brother, James Hearn, 1890, in "Lafcadio Hearn's Brother."

believed he and his brother would be well cared for.

"I was to be my grandaunt's heir and she was quite rich; my father had made some promises regarding you," he wrote many years later to his brother, James. "As for her never making inquiries afterword, I doubt it…Neither could I blame her nor cease to love her, were I to hear she had committed any fault. Her circumstances were very peculiar and cruel, and her nature probably intensely confiding and impulsive, with (Charles Hearn)."[10]

Lafcadio was not as forgiving of his father. Undoubtedly influenced by his aunt's condemnation of Charles, Lafcadio harbored a deep disdain for his father for the rest of his life.

"I can remember seeing father only four times," he wrote to his brother. "He never caressed me; I always felt afraid of him. He was rather taciturn…I cannot feel much in my life common with his. I suspect I do not love him." By contrast, he cherished the memory of his mother, particularly her "dark and beautiful face—with large brown eyes like a wild deer's."

Each of his parents' lives with their new spouses ended in tragedy. Charles and his second wife, Alicia, had three daughters. In 1861, Alicia died of fever in India, and in 1866, Charles died of malaria in the Gulf of Suez on a return trip to Dublin. Rosa had four children with her second husband. She ventured to Dublin once to see her two boys, but the Hearn family refused to tell her where they were. Crushed, she went back to Cerigo without having seen them. That debacle caused her unstable mental condition to worsen. She became so obsessed by religion, and her behavior grew so erratic that her husband committed her to the National Mental Institution of Corfu. Rosa spent the last ten years of her life there, dying on December 12, 1882, at the age of 59.

Although Lafcadio's Aunt Sarah never legally adopted him, she eagerly accepted the responsibility of raising him. She loved the boy and wanted to make him her heir, fulfilling the wish of her dying husband that she find someone worthy to inherit their wealth. She was determined to raise Lafcadio to be a devout Catholic and to provide for him the best education she could afford.

Her three-story house was located in the upper-middle class Dub-

---

[10]Ibid.

lin suburb of Rathmines. She employed a parlor maid and footmen. The house's interior décor was formal and contained high ceilings, four-poster beds and carpeted stairways. Brenane was well-intentioned, but had no experience in raising children and had no concept of how to engage or play with them. She probably wasn't prepared to deal with the emotional damage Lafcadio suffered from his parents' abandonment. Aunt Sarah usually referred to her nephew as "The Child," seldom by his name. She decided the best way to help him overcome his fear of the dark was to lock him in his bedroom at night with no light on. He would scream so that someone would come in, turn the light on and talk to him. But after a while, Aunt Sarah and the servants stopped responding to his screams because they thought he was just trying to delay going to bed.

During the day, his nursemaid Kate Ronane would regale him with fairy tales and ghost stories. Hearn was enthralled by these stories and later credited them with forming his lifelong attraction to folk tales. They stirred his imagination and scared him in a pleasant way. But in his dark bedroom behind a locked door, Lafcadio often had frightening dreams. He would awaken, believing ghosts and goblins and "shadowy, dark-robed figures capable of self-distortion" lurked in the corners of the room, in the fireplace, "capable of growing up to the ceiling, and then across it, and then lengthening themselves, head-downwards, along the opposite wall…Before going to sleep I would always cover up my head to prevent them from looking at me; and I used to scream when I felt them pulling at the bedclothes."[11]

Some of Hearn's happiest childhood moments in Ireland had been spent during family summer vacations at the seaside town of Tramore on the south coast of Ireland, at a resort at Bangor, North Wales, or at the large country home of his cousins in the town of Cong on the north shore of Lake Corrib. On these summer vacations, Hearn developed his lifelong love of swimming and the sea. Besides swimming, he fished, went boating and listened to the sea adventures told by an old boatman who befriended him.

In Cong, young Hearn and Brenane would stay at the home of one of his favorite aunts, Catherine Elwood. During these visits to

---

[11] Elizabeth Bisland, *The Life and Letters of Lafcadio Hearn,* vol. 1 (Boston: Houghton Mifflin Co., 1906), 16.

Cong, Hearn first felt the powerful emotional impact of music. He loved listening to his Aunt Catherine sing and play the piano. He also enjoyed the music of another Cong resident, gypsy singer and harpist, Dan Fitzpatrick, whose rich, baritone voice once touched him so deeply that he became misty-eyed. Music stirred young Hearn's emotions more than any of the other arts. Although he expressed no desire to learn to play a musical instrument or to learn musical notation, he had an intuitive appreciation for the beauty of music.[12]

Another source of delight for him was his Aunt Sarah's library. As a child, he had begun avidly reading the many books in his great-aunt's library, partly to overcome the boredom from a lack of play-mates. In this large, book-filled room, he was happily free to explore, liberated from the supervision of adults.

While in his early teens, he discovered a book filled with pictures of Greek gods and goddesses, nymphs, fauns, satyrs and dryads. Many of the figures in this book were partially or completely nude. Hearn preferred these figures, which exuded beauty, health and energy, to the somber Catholic saints depicted on the holy cards he had been given. He frequently returned to this book to enjoy the pictures and to read the exciting stories surrounding the gods and goddesses.

But some time later, he was shocked when he opened this book and found that clothing had been drawn over some of the gods and goddesses to cover breasts, thighs, butts and other body parts. Hearn's tutor, concerned about the boy's interest in this book, had decided to censor what he considered objectionable images. He also counseled the boy on the evils of pantheism. But to Hearn, the gorgeous, sensuous world of the Greek gods and goddesses seemed far more appealing than the nightmarish hell-and-damnation theology he associated with Catholicism. Pantheism had roused his awareness of the beauty of nature. The tutor's lecture failed to discourage Hearn's attraction to this decidedly non-Christian view of the universe.

"Now after I had learned to know and to love the elder gods, the world again began to glow about me," he later wrote of this pivotal

---

[12]John Moran, "Early Influences on Lafcadio Hearn," *Proceedings: International Symposium on "The Open Mind of Lafcadio Hearn: His Spirit from the West to the East, July 5-6, 2014,"* Shingo Nagaoka, editor-in-chief. Tokyo: The Planning Committee for the Memorial Events in Greece to Commemorate the 110th Anniversary of Lafcadio Hearn's Death, 2014.

point in his life. "Glooms that had brooded over it slowly thinned away. The terror was not yet gone; but I now wanted only reasons to disbelieve all that I feared and hated. In the sunshine, in the green of the fields, in the blue of the sky, I found a gladness before unknown. Within myself new thoughts, new imaginings, dim longing for I knew not what were quickening and thrilling. I looked for beauty, and everywhere I found it; in passing faces—in attitudes and motions—in the poise of plants and trees—in long white clouds—in faint-blue lines of far-off hills. At moments the simple pleasure of life would frighten me. But at other times there would come to me a new and strange sadness—a shadowy and inexplicable pain. I had entered my renaissance."[13]

But this blossoming enlightenment didn't immediately lead to a happier life. When he was 12, his aunt sent him to a private Catholic school. Hearn's early biographers said the school was the Institution Ecclésiastique at Yvetot, France, near Rouen. The school accepted English-speaking students, although they were a distinct minority. But there's no evidence that he ever registered there.[14] Whatever school Hearn attended that year, he chafed under the Catholic school's rigorous daily regimen. Students were roused from bed in time to attend a 5 a.m. Mass in the chapel and spent most of the day in classes and study periods. Meal times were short and included religious and French history readings. The day ended at 9 p.m. with prayers in the chapel. Although Hearn detested the school, it sparked his deep interest in French literature, which greatly influenced his writing career.

The next school year, his aunt enrolled him at St. Cuthbert's College in Ushaw, England. Around this time, Brenane moved into the home of Henry and Agnes Molyneux in Redhill, England. She had entrusted Henry Molyneux, a young relative of Brenane's husband, with the financial management of her estate. The Molyneuxs had become her primary family, and before the move, had invited her to stay for long stretches at their home.

---

[13] Bisland, *Life and Letters*, 32.

[14] Bernadette Lemoine, "Lafcadio Hearn as an Ambassador of French Literature in the United States and Japan," a presentation given at the Matsue International Symposium Commenorating the Centennial of the Death of Yakumo Koizumi," September, 2004, and published in *Revue de Litterature Comparee*, March, 2006, https://www.cairn.info/revue-de-litterature-comparee-2006-3-page-299.htm#.

St. Cuthbert's, a Catholic school, suited Hearn no better than the previous school had. He perturbed his teachers by his persistent questioning of Catholic doctrine and by his championing of pantheism. When he was confessing his sins to a priest, he admitted that he was guilty of wanting a beautiful woman to come to him so that he might give in to her temptations.

The normally nonplussed priest rose angrily to his feet and shouted, "Let me warn you! Let me warn you of all things! Never wish that! You might be more sorry for it than you can possibly believe!"

Later recalling this incident, Hearn wrote, "Now when he thus spoke, his earnestness filled me with a fearful joy;—for I thought all that I wished for might be realized—so serious he looked. And, after that, oh! How I prayed for some pretty gracious devil to come to me, and take my soul in exchange for—! But the merciless succubi all continued to remain in hell!"[15]

His contentious statements and, most of all, his mischievous but harmless pranks, made him popular among his fellow students, who called him Paddy. Most of his teachers grew to like him even as they punished him for his misbehavior. His aunt, however, was not amused by his antics at the school. Reports about him from the school intensified her doubts that he would become the model Catholic family heir she had hoped for.

Monsignor Joseph Corbishly, who was a classmate of Hearn's at Upshaw and later became president of the school, remembered him as "so very curious a boy, so wild in the tumult of his thoughts, that you felt he might do anything in different surroundings."[16]

Despite his shenanigans at St. Cuthbert, Hearn developed a strong interest in writing, English literature and French. His writing skills especially impressed his teachers. He won several English composition contests at the school.[17] It may have been during these teenage years when he began to see a dichotomy in his life—positive personality traits he believed came from his mother and negative ones from his father.

Hearn believed his affinity for the sea as well as for the arts

[15]Bisland, *Life and Letters,* vol. 1, 33.

[16]Nina H. Kennard, *Lafcadio Hearn* (New York: D. Appleton, 1912), 45.

[17]Stevenson, *Lafcadio Hearn*, 22.

stemmed from his mother, the Greek side of his personality. "Whatever there is of good in me came from that dark race-soul of which we know so little," he wrote years later to his brother, James. "My love of right, my hate of wrong;—my admiration for what is beautiful or true;—my admiration for what is beautiful or true;—my capacity for faith in man or woman;—my sensitiveness to artistic things which gives me whatever little success I have,—even that language-power whose physical sign is in both of us,—came from Her.... It is the mother who makes us,—makes at least all that makes the nobler man: not his strength or powers of calculation, but his heart and power to love. And I would rather have her portrait than a fortune."[18] Only much later in his life did he concede that he had benefitted from his Irish heritage. The Irish myths and legends he had heard and read about and the Irish penchant for story-telling enriched his youth and contributed to his development into a writer.

In his fourth year at St. Cuthbert's, the 16-year-old Hearn suffered a devastating injury that plagued him for the rest of his life. A boy was swinging around a rope with a knotted end during a playground game when the rope slipped out of his hand. The knotted end struck Hearn's left eye. Several operations failed to restore the sight in that eye. Eventually a white scar tissue formed and covered the cornea. The extra strain he placed on his right eye caused it to protrude noticeably, further marring his facial appearance and increasing his self-consciousness.

After a long recovery at home, Hearn returned to St. Cuthbert's. But his teachers and classmates noticed immediately that he was no longer the lively, witty, amusing rebel he had been before his injury. His sensitivity about his appearance drained much of the joy from his life. He often covered his blind eye with his left hand when talking to people. In almost all subsequent photos of Hearn, he turns toward his left, hiding his grotesque-looking white eye from view.

To add to his miseries, the financial problems of his aunt and the Molyneuxs forced him to withdraw from St. Cuthbert's in October 1867 before completing his final year. Unable to afford a university education and unwilling to live in the same house as Molyneux, he spent a year in London living with his Aunt Sarah's former maid,

---

[18]From Lafcadio Hearn to his brother, James Hearn, 1890, in "Lafcadio Hearn's Brother."

Catherine Delaney, and her family. Brenane sent the Delaneys a small amount of money to help cover her nephew's upkeep.[19]

Lonely and ashamed of his disfigured face, Hearn led an aimless existence in London. He read poetry and fiction, visited libraries and the British Museum, and roamed London's streets, especially in the poor sections of town, which fascinated him. Occasionally, he would disappear from the Delaneys' house in East End for weeks at a time, sometimes staying in workhouses, often hungry, tired and disgusted with his life.

By this time, Molyneux, a devout Catholic, had displaced Hearn in Brenane's affections. Hearn's rebellious behavior and disdain for Catholicism greatly disappointed her. In the spring of 1869, Molyneux decided to rid himself of Hearn for good. With the 75-year-old Brenane in failing physical and mental health, he didn't have to seek her approval of his plan to send Hearn, then 19, to the United States to fashion a life for himself. Without telling Hearn of the plan, Molyneux bought him a one-way boat ticket to New York City. Hearn learned about this when Molyneux handed him the ticket with a small sum of money and told him he was to go to Cincinnati, where his sister, Frances Anne, and her husband, Thomas Cullinan, would help him.[20] Hearn saw this as an opportunity to escape from his unpleasant home situation in London and take advantage of the opportunities in the New World. He was as anxious to banish Molyneux from his life as Molyneux was to get rid of him.

But Hearn still felt hurt by the tacit rejection of his great-aunt. He had struggled with the emotional trauma of being abandoned by his mother and his father. Now the great-aunt who had raised him and provided him with an education had cast him out of her life. With the boat ticket and the money, Hearn walked out of Molyneux's office and prepared to cross the Atlantic to begin anew.

---

[19]Frost, *Young Hearn*, 65-66
[20]Ibid., 67.

CHAPTER 2

Struggles in Cincinnati

*P*ATRICK LAFCADIO HEARN boarded the immigrant steamship, the S.S. *Cella* in London. On September 2, 1869, the
ship landed at a New York City port, and the 19-year-old Hearn
stepped onto American soil to begin searching for a better life.[1] For
a period of anywhere from several weeks to several months, Hearn
lived in New York. Nothing concrete is known about his stay there,
other than he found the city to be overwhelmingly big and baffling.
He decided to come to come to Cincinnati and see what assistance he
might receive from Henry Molyneux's brother-in-law.

One day, probably in early 1870, a train packed with immigrants
pulled into the Little Miami train station just east of Cincinnati's bus-
tling Ohio River Landing. Hearn, short, thin and dressed in shabby,
frayed black clothes, stepped down from one of the third-class cars.
He wore thick-lensed glasses partly to hide his whitish blind left eye
and his protruding brown right eye.

Nearly penniless, Hearn hadn't eaten much during the five-day
train ride from New York City. Two days earlier, a pretty, young Nor-
wegian woman sitting across from him in the train car noticed he
looked hungry and offered him a large slice of brown bread with an
inch-thick cut of yellow cheese. He eagerly devoured it, forgetting to
thank her. When a bit later, he tried to thank her, she misunderstood
what he had said and took offense. She spoke to him sharply, causing
him to blush with shame and embarrassment. An older man sitting
next to him assured her the young man had only tried to thank her

---

[1]From copies of the ship's records provided to the author by Hearn aficionado Dr.
Kinji Tanaka, of Mason, Ohio. Dr. Tanaka is president of the Japan Research Center
of Greater Cincinnati.

for the bread and cheese. The explanation satisfied her. She calmed down and turned to look out her window at the passing landscape. But Hearn, mortified, didn't dare speak to her for the rest of the trip.[2]

Standing with his luggage at the train station and still feeling the sting of the woman's rebuke, Hearn felt even more lonely and apprehensive. Hearn had arrived in America's largest inland city, with little money, no job, no skills, no friends and no family.

In coming to make Cincinnati his new home, Hearn was following the example of legions of other European immigrants who had swelled the city's population during the previous 40 years. Economic hardships, unemployment, religious oppression and civil unrest drove many Europeans to the United States.

By the end of the American Civil War, Cincinnati had established itself as one of the nation's most prosperous and fastest-growing cities. It had matured from a large, roughhewn frontier town that had been famously ridiculed in Frances (Fanny) Trollope's "Domestic Manners in America" (1848) into a thriving metropolis of nearly a quarter of a million inhabitants, the nation's eighth largest city. Cincinnati, which still was considered a part of the American West, had earned a reputation as an important center of manufacturing and commerce. Cincinnati had grown culturally as well as economically. It boasted grand venues for the arts, impressive libraries, institutions of higher learning, an ever-expanding public school system, fine hotels and panoramic views from the hills surrounding the city's basin area bordered on the south by the Ohio River.

Cincinnati, dubbed early in its history as "The Queen City of the West," offered abundant job opportunities. Germans comprised the first large wave of immigration in Cincinnati. The city's population nearly doubled in the 1830s, rising from 24,831 in 1830 to 46,382 in 1840. During that decade, the German population leaped from about 1,242 or 5 percent of the total number of residents to 12,986 or 28 percent. By 1860, 48,313 or 30 percent of the 161,044 city residents were German. Largely because of a post-Civil War surge in immigration, Cincinnati's German population rose to about 70,000.[3]

---

[2]Elizabeth Bisland, *The Life and Letters of Lafcadio Hearn,* vol. 1 (Boston: Houghton Mifflin Co., 1906), 48-49.

[3]George E. Stevens, *The Queen City in 1869* (Cincinnati, OH: George S. Blanchard & Co., 1869), 72-74.

Cincinnati's extensive range of businesses that manufactured iron products, furniture, clothing, soap and candles, and countless other items drew many German artisans, mechanics and laborers.

The Irish were the second largest group to migrate to the city during this period. The Irish potato famine from 1845 to 1852 devastated the largely agricultural nation. Irish families depended heavily on potatoes for their subsistence. The potato blight that decimated the crop in 1845 plunged Ireland into an abyss of starvation and disease. During this time, Ireland lost a quarter of its population—half to emigration and half to death.

Because it bordered a slave state and played a major role in the Underground Railroad, Cincinnati attracted thousands of African-Americans seeking freedom before and during the Civil War. Harriet Beecher Stowe based much of her momentous 1852 novel, "Uncle Tom's Cabin," upon what she learned about slavery while living in Cincinnati from 1832 to 1850. She moved to Cincinnati with her parents and siblings from Connecticut to Cincinnati so her father, Lyman Beecher, an evangelical minister, could become the first president of Lane Seminary. That seminary quickly evolved into a center of abolitionist thought and free speech. An 1834 series of debates on abolitionism at Lane drew national attention and intensified divisions over the slavery issue.

By 1869, the city had a substantial African-American population. Many Black people lived in the poorer, crime-ridden areas near the riverfront and just east of downtown. In Toni Morrison's 1988 Pulitzer-Prize-winning novel, "Beloved," the family that's haunted by its past resides in one of Cincinnati's Black neighborhoods, a short horse-carriage ride from downtown, just after the Civil War. Her novel is set in the same period when Hearn was living in Cincinnati.

In the years immediately after the Civil War, Cincinnati enjoyed an economic boom. During the war, Cincinnati businesses could no longer sell their industrial projects, meats, clothing and other goods to the South, which had been a source of substantial revenue for the city. Indeed, some Cincinnatians had opposed the war because of the anticipated loss of business. But once the war ended, the Southern market reopened, although it wasn't as robust as before because of the defeated South's dire economic condition.

For all its virtues, Cincinnati suffered from the typical ills of urban life that also plagued other Northern industrial and commer-cial centers. As the most densely populated city in the United States, Cincinnati was crowded, dirty and stinking. The city's pork-packing plants, tanneries and soap-making and glue-making factories pro-duced a stench that became even more oppressive during the hot summer weather. The daily herding of pigs through the streets to slaughterhouses contributed to the general filth in many of the city's crowded residential areas in the basin. Cincinnati richly deserved its nickname, Porkopolis.[4]

For residents who couldn't afford a horse-and-buggy, there was no easy respite from the foul-aired, grimy city basin. The hills were too steep and high for anyone but the young or hardy to climb on foot. That didn't change until the first of the city's inclined-plane railways transporting passengers to the hilltops was built 1872, three years after Hearn's arrival.

For a newcomer, Cincinnati was a far less imposing place than New York City. But for a painfully shy, insecure young immigrant with no job experience, surviving in Cincinnati proved to be a daunt-ing challenge. Hearn, who had decided to begin his life in the New World by using Lafcadio as his first name instead of Patrick, struggled terribly in his first few months in the city.

Soon after arriving, Hearn went to the apartment of Molyneaux's brother-in-law, Thomas Cullinan, hoping for the promised assis-tance. Cullinan had been expecting Hearn to appear at his door, but he wasn't looking forward to it. He lived in a crowded neighborhood west of Mill Creek and downtown. With a large family to support, he had no inclination to serve as a mentor or a benefactor to some stranger from England. The shy, scruffy-looking youth made a bad first impression on Cullinan, who felt no obligation to help this shirttail relative of his wife. Immediately sensing he wasn't welcome, Hearn took an instant disliking to Cullinan. After a brief, chilly con-versation, Cullinan gave Hearn the $5 Brenane had sent for him. He passed along similar amounts of money from Aunt Sarah when Hearn stopped by two other times during the next few months. Hearn re-sented having to come to Cullinan for his aunt's handouts, and after his third visit, he didn't go there any more.

---

[4]Stevens, *The Queen City in 1869*, 76-82.

Hearn tried and failed at many different jobs during his first months in Cincinnati. One of his first jobs was peddling small hand-mirrors on the streets. He lasted only one day. After carrying a tray of these mirrors around the city for hours, Hearn, having sold nothing, returned to the Syrian man who had hired him. As Hearn set the tray on the curb, the mirrors slid off into the street. When the Syrian saw that one of the mirrors had broken, he screamed and cursed at Hearn, causing a crowd of amused spectators to gather around them. The red-faced Hearn quickly fled to his boarding house room.

But he wasn't able to stay in the boarding house for long. His unproductive day of misadventures left him with no way to pay his rent. His unsympathetic landlord seized Hearn's few possessions and threw him out of the house. Those lost possessions included his only photograph of his father.

With just the clothes he was wearing and no money, Hearn began living on the streets and desperately searching for work. Like a street waif in a Charles Dickens novel, Hearn slept in dry-goods boxes and sheltered doorways. For a while, he slept in an unused boiler in a vacant lot.

An English coachman took pity on him one cold night and allowed him to sleep in a hayloft above where the horses were kept and told him he would bring him food in the morning. As Hearn lay naked on his bed of hay with his head resting on his rolled-up clothes, he looked up through the cracks in the roof at the stars. Destitute in a foreign country with no friends, he sadly reflected on his pitiful circumstances. He thought of the horses sleeping below him. Although they were mere animals, they at least had worked for their shelter. He had received his through charity. They were worth about $1,500 each. He ruefully wondered if he were worth that much. "They are of use in the world," he thought. "Of what use am I?"[5]

Through the kindness of the English coachmen, Hearn slept in that hayloft on many other nights. The coachmen snuck food out of their master's house and gave it to him.

Hearn's self-pride and his disdain for Thomas Cullinan kept him from returning to Cullinan's house for money from his Aunt Sarah. He preferred living on the streets to suffering the humiliation of going

---

[5]Bisland, *Life and Letters*, vol. I, 37-38.

to Cullinan for handouts.

He referred later to this difficult time as "the wolf's side of life…I found myself dropped into the enormous machinery of life I knew nothing about," he wrote. "I had to sleep for nights in the street, for which the police scolded me…"[6]

He obtained an accounting job in a business office, but soon quit when he discovered he didn't have the mathematical acumen to perform the work adequately. He took a job as a messenger boy in a telegraph office. But at 19, he was much older than the other messenger boys and looked comically out of place. During his first week on the job, some of the boys teased him. The hypersensitive Hearn walked out without asking for the wages due him. A few friends who had been trying to help him find work became angry when he quit this job for such a flimsy reason, and they refused to give him any more assistance.

Finally, he got a job as a boarding house servant. In exchange for food and sleeping space on the floor of the smoking room, he lit fires, shoveled coal and performed other menial tasks. He held that job for a year-and-a-half. It left him plenty of time for reading and writing, activities he pursued with increasing vigor and seriousness. He had some stories published in cheap weekly newspapers that paid nothing.

To earn some money, he did various odd jobs, such as canvassing and writing showcards. They paid enough for him to buy second-hand clothes and smoking tobacco, but not much else.

During Hearn's first year in Cincinnati, a Scottish printer introduced him to Henry Watkin, a tall 46-year-old man with a bushy beard who owned a small printing shop downtown on the east side of Walnut Street between Fifth and Sixth streets. Born in England, Watkin had emigrated to the United States in 1845 at the age of 23. He came to Cincinnati two years later.

"Well, my young man, how do you expect to earn a living?," Watkin said to Hearn.

"I don't know."

"Have you any trade?"

"No, sir."

"Can you do anything at all?"

---

[6]Nina H. Kennard, *Lafcadio Hearn* (New York: D. Appleton, 1912), 67-68.

"Yes, sir; I might write."

"Umph! Better learn some bread-winning trade and put off writing until later."[7]

Like Hearn, Watkin had been an immigrant trying to forge a new life in America. He knew the sense of alienation and loneliness that could overwhelm someone living in a strange country with no family or friends. Both men had come from England, even though Hearn grew up in Ireland. But there was an even more visceral connection between them. Like Hearn, Watkin had sustained a serious childhood eye injury that permanently impaired his vision. He well understood the difficulties Hearn's eye problems caused him in various kinds of work and in everyday life. He also sympathized with Hearn's sensitivity about his odd appearance.

Eventually, Watkin offered to teach Hearn the basics of typesetting, provide him with three meals a day and let him sleep in one of the shop's back rooms on a bed of paper shavings from the book-trimming department. In return, Hearn ran errands, swept the floors, and generally kept the shop clean and orderly.

The two men, one 26 years older than the other, quickly developed a strong rapport. They shared an open-minded curiosity about the world and a love for literature and philosophy.

Watkin was a mostly self-educated man with a leaning toward agnosticism, utopianism, cooperative socialism and quasi-scientific thought. He began working as a printer for the *Cincinnati Daily Gazette* in 1847 and left in 1853 to establish his own bookstore and printing shop. He married Laura Fry, who came from a family of master woodcarvers. Her father, Henry L. Fry, and her brother, William H. Fry, helped launch and foster an art-carved furniture movement in Cincinnati.

The slow-speaking, amiable Watkin had become interested in utopian societies when he still lived in England. He read books by such utopian socialists as Charles Fourier, Robert Owens and Comte de Saint-Simon. Watkin was especially enamored with the writings of the Frenchman, Fourier.

A staunch opponent of the emerging industrial societies in Eu-

---

[7]Milton Bronner, ed., from "Introduction," *Letters from the Raven* (New York: Bretano's, 1907), 23-24.

rope and the United States, Fourier advocated the creation of cooperative communities in which individuals would constantly change roles and serve the common welfare. Some elements of Fourier's futuristic vision were wildly absurd. For instance, he believed that tens of thousands of years into the future, the ideal world he would help create would enter an era of Perfect Harmony. He predicted six moons would revolve around the earth and that the Earth's seas would consist of lemonade, not water.[8]

Despite these and other bizarre features of Fourierism, the more practical economic and socialistic aspects of the movement appealed to some freethinking people in Europe and America. At least 23 communes based on Fourier's principles formed in the United States during the 19th century in reaction to the perceived evils of capitalism and industrialism. The most famous was Brook Farm, which was created in the 1840s in Massachusetts. Nathaniel Hawthorne lived there briefly. He decided that milking cows at dawn, planting crops and shoveling cow dung wasn't his idea of utopia.

In 1844, followers of Fourier founded a utopian settlement in Ohio, about 40 miles up the Ohio River from Cincinnati. Appropriately called Utopia, it existed as a cooperative farm community for only two years before dissolving. Utopia, however, still exists there, but only as a tiny unincorporated crossroads community with an Ohio historical marker posted on US 52 informing visitors of its early history.

Although Watkin conceded that some aspects of Fourier's philosophy were ridiculous, he believed strongly in the virtues of forming communities based on cooperative principles. Watkin was a founding member of a building cooperative that created a railroad suburban community in 1870 called Bond Hill, located several miles north of Cincinnati. Near the home Watkin shared with his wife and their daughter, Bond Hill welcomed all ethnic groups and banned the sale of liquor. After ten years or so, as the community grew and disagreements developed among residents, it began drifting from the ideals of its founders. It later was annexed by Cincinnati.

At the time Hearn began his apprenticeship, Watkin lived in the print shop because there wasn't room for his wife and daughter, who

---

[8]Jonathan Cott, *Wandering Ghost: The Odyssey of Lafcadio Hearn* (New York: Knopf, 1991), 35.

were living outside Cincinnati. He and Hearn soon developed a close friendship, talking far into the nights about philosophers, writers, Greek gods, religion, and their personal dreams and problems. They would read each other passages from books or poems they particularly liked. Hearn often read stories to Watkin from the *Atlantic Monthly*. Watkin had a shelf of books in his shop that he and Hearn read and discussed. He introduced Hearn to the work of E. T. A. Hoffman, a German Romantic writer, composer and caricaturist whose novella, "The Nutcracker and the Mouse King," formed the basis for Tchaikovsky's iconic opera, "The Nutcracker." Hoffman, who died in 1822, shared similarities with Edgar Allan Poe. Like Poe, he wrote horror stories and tales of the supernatural focusing on the hideous, grotesque side of human nature. Hearn, already a Poe aficionado, loved Hoffman's eerie, haunting fiction.

They also enthusiastically discussed the writings of Herbert Spencer, an English philosopher who became extremely popular in the later quarter of the 19th century. Several years before Charles Darwin published his *On the Origin of Species* in 1859, Spencer advanced a theory of evolution that he applied to all entities in the universe—not just biological forms of life, but also the human intellect and societies. He believed everything progressed in an unwavering upward arc from simplicity to complexity and perfection. Watkin had become enamored with Spencer and encouraged Hearn to read his works. Hearn wholeheartedly embraced Spencer's ideas, which seemed to offer a scientific basis for a more optimistic outlook on the world and, in Hearn's view, an alternative to conventional Western religious beliefs.

Watkin's quiet, affable temperament and innate understanding of human nature enabled him to provide an emotional ballast for the mercurial, insecure younger man. Watkin quickly became Hearn's father figure. But unlike his real father, who had been remote and cold, Watkin showed an affection for him and a deep interest in both the important and the more routine aspects of his daily life. With the middle-aged Englishman, Hearn could be serious and playful. This odd pair were indeed kindred spirits. Hearn often addressed him as "Dad" or "Old Dad," and Watkin sometimes called Hearn "The Raven," in recognition of his love for Poe's writings and for the aspects of Poe's personality—moodiness and a preoccupation with the morbid—that Hearn shared. Even when Hearn was no longer living in Watkin's shop, he would stop by almost every day to chat. When Watkin wasn't there, instead of a simple note, Hearn sometimes drew humorous sketches of a raven and left them at the door. One such sketch intended to let Watkin know he had left the shop to get a haircut contained the hand-written message, "Gone to get my sable plumage plucked."[9]

After Watkin's print shop, Hearn's next favorite place to spend time was the downtown Cincinnati Public Library. Hearn's initial trips to the library would have been at its location on the second floor of the Ohio Mechanics Institute at Sixth and Vine streets. In 1870, the library moved to a new location a few doors to the north on the west side of Vine. The first of three new buildings on the site that were to comprise the main library opened on December 9, 1870. The other two buildings—the middle one and the cathedral-like main hall—opened on February 25, 1874. The four-story library, with a checkerboard tile floor, contained 60,000 volumes with a capacity for 500,000. Light streamed through the library's massive skylight roof and its many windows.[10]

Several times each week, Hearn walked beneath the busts of William Shakespeare, Benjamin Franklin and John Milton as he entered the library, then considered one of the finest in the nation. With its five levels of books jamming the shelves, the library became his university. He spent countless hours there every week reading not only English-language writers but also the French Romantic authors.

Another influential person Hearn met in his first couple of years in Cincinnati was Thomas Vickers, a Unitarian minister. Impressed with Hearn's intense reading regimen and his lively intellect, Vickers occasionally hired him to perform clerical and secretarial duties. In 1874, Vickers became Librarian of the Cincinnati Public Library and continued to encourage Hearn in his writing and intellectual pursuits.

In 1870 and 1871, Hearn wrote articles for the *Boston Independent*, a free-thought weekly newspaper that he probably first heard about from Watkin. Hearn wrote under the pseudonym, "Fiat Lux," a Latin phrase meaning, "Let there be light." The stories concerned primarily religious and philosophical issues, including Eastern phi-

---

[9]Bronner, ed., *Letters from the Raven*, 30.

[10]Jeff Suess, "Charming 'Old Main,'" *Cincinnati Enquirer*, January 19, 2004, L5.

losophy, a topic he would continue to study for the rest of his life.

At Watkin's recommendation, Hearn was hired in the summer of 1872 to work as assistant editor and handy man for the *Cincinnati Trade List*. It was a new weekly journal founded by Capt. Leonard Barney, the paper's editor and a friend of Watkin. Hearn's duties included editing copy, serving as a mailing clerk, soliciting advertisements (a task he hated), and running errands. He also wrote a few stories that Barney agreed to publish.

Later that year, he became a proofreader for the Robert Clarke Company, book dealers and publishers of Americana. He tried unsuccessfully to persuade his employer to adopt British methods of punctuation. But his obsession with punctuation did earn him the nickname, "Old Semicolon," a moniker that followed him when he went to work later for the *Cincinnati Enquirer*. In his own writing, Hearn often used semicolons in places where most people would have used commas or periods. He also adopted the idiosyncratic practice of pairing a semicolon or a comma with a dash to separate clauses in his sentences.

Although Hearn liked seeing his stories in the *Cincinnati Trade List*, the little weekly newspaper couldn't satisfy his ambition to write longer, more complex stories about a wide variety of topics for a larger reading audience. The idea of approaching an editor at one of the city's five English-language daily newspapers about freelance writing made him uneasy. He felt uncomfortable talking to important people.

But his desire to enlarge his writing opportunities overcame his innate shyness. He decided to go to one of the daily newspaper offices, present one of his stories to the editor and find out if the editor thought it worthy of publication. It was a big step for Hearn. But he knew he had to do it if he would ever fulfill his dream of becoming a writer.

In the autumn of 1872, with his heart pounding, Hearn climbed the stairs to the *Enquirer's* editorial offices in a building located on Vine Street right next to the public library he had made his second home. One of the pockets inside his shabby coat contained a manuscript he intended to present to the newspaper's managing editor, John Cockerill. He nervously stood in the hallway outside Cockerill's office, trying to muster the courage to knock on the door. Suddenly, the door flung open, and there stood Cockerill, a dark-haired, distinguished-looking man.

Looking up at Cockerill, the 22-year-old diminutive Hearn meekly asked him if he paid for stories from non-staff writers. Cockerill
told him his budget for outside contributors was limited, but he would
consider whatever stories Hearn had to submit. He invited Hearn inside his office. With a trembling hand, Hearn pulled the manuscript
from inside his coat, laid it on Cockerill's desk and scurried away
without another word.

"Later in the day," Cockerill recalled years later, "I looked over the
contribution which he had left. I was astonished to find it charming-
ly written in the purest and strongest English, and full of ideas that
were bright and forceful. I printed the article, and the next day the
writer called for his money, which, as I remember, I paid from my
own exchequer. I became interested in him, for it seemed strange to
me that a person of such appearance should show such writing talent
and marks of education."[11]

Two of Hearn's biographers believe the story Hearn showed Cockerill on that day in late October 1872 was a long critical review of
Lord Alfred Tennyson's newly published "Idylls of the King."[12] But no
one knows for certain. Neither Cockerill nor Hearn ever mentioned
in letters or in publications the identity of that inaugural story. His
review of Tennyson's Idylls of the King was published in three parts,
on November 24, December 1 and December 9. But before the first
part of the Tennyson piece ran, the *Enquirer* published two other
stories by Hearn—"London Sights" on November 4 and "The Blues"
on November 15.

"London Sights," a long, observant portrait of a poor, working-class section of London, was more likely to have been what Hearn
first presented to Cockerill than "The Blues," a short melancholy
meditation on the winter's first snowfall. In "London Sights," Hearn
displays a knack for observing and selecting compelling details and
for writing in an interesting literary style. Surely, that piece would have
caught Cockerill's attention and alerted him to a promising new talent.

"Few things stir Whitechapel so quickly as a fight," Hearn writes.
"'Make a ring!' 'Go at 'em, yer blokes!' sounds up from every side,

[11]John A. Cockerill, "Lafcadio Hearn: The Author of Kokoro," *Current Literature* Vol.
    XIX, June, 1896.

[12]Elizabeth Stevenson, *Lafcadio Hearn* (New York: Macmillan, 1961), 37.; Cott, *Wan-
    dering Ghost*, 38.

and at it they go. Two Parisians and two Berliners talk themselves black in the face, but two Londoners are in their shirt-sleeves and at one another's eyes in a wink, and woe to the unhappy creature who refuses to satisfy the popular or who thinks to prevent it. So quick is the instinct to fisticuffs among them that they hardly stop to think where their hats and coats will be safest, for it is a melancholy truth that even those who cry very loudly for satisfaction are only too ready to make off with the garments of the fighters."[13]

This story reflects his intimate knowledge of working-class Londoners and their environs, no doubt gleaned from the many days he spent roaming through the city's rough neighborhoods. Even at this early stage of his career, he displays in the scraps of dialogue in this story his ability to render dialects accurately in print.

The meeting of Hearn and Cockerill occurred at an especially propitious time in each man's life. As a neophyte writer, Hearn badly needed a powerful editor like Cockerill to take an interest in his work and to become his mentor. For his part, Cockerill needed talented writers to aid the *Enquirer* in gaining ground in its fierce battle with Cincinnati's other four English-language newspapers for readers and revenue.

Cockerill, born in 1845 in the tiny rural community of Locust Grove, about 70 miles east of Cincinnati, had risen rapidly in the newspaper business. Unlike Hearn, Cockerill came from a stable and financially secure family. His father, Joseph Cockerill, had been a teacher and a lawyer before being elected to the Ohio legislature and then to U.S. Congress. Growing up in a household that valued education and encouraged discussions about national and international news events, young John earned high grades in school. At 13, Cockerill began working part-time on the local weekly newspaper, the *West Union Scion*. The precocious boy quickly learned how to typeset and soon began writing short items for the paper.

But the outbreak of the Civil War interrupted his education and his budding journalism career. Shortly after the war's first battle erupted at Fort Sumter, Cockerill's father and brother entered the Union Army, his father as a colonel and his brother, Armistead, as a lieutenant. John, 15 years old, tried to enlist, but was turned down

---

[13]Lafcadio Hearn, "London Sights," *Cincinnati Enquirer*, 5.

because of his age and short stature. He talked the authorities into admitting him as a drummer boy. At one point during the Battle of Shiloh, he set down his drum and took up a musket.

He was discharged in late 1862 and immediately resumed his journalism career. He and a business partner published a newspaper, the *Democratic Union*, to compete with the paper he had once worked for. Two years later, Cockerill became editor of a weekly in Hamilton, Ohio, called the *True Telegraph*. By 1867, at the age of 21, he was the paper's publisher-editor. After a stint in 1868 as the *Enquirer's* Hamilton correspondent, Cockerill became co-publisher of the *Dayton Daily Ledger* with the extremely controversial Clement Vallandigham, who had been arrested in 1863 for expressing strong sympathies for the Confederacy, sent to federal prison and then banished to the Confederate states. The former Ohio Congressman had opposed the abolition of slavery and supported the right of the Southern states to secede. Cockerill became the "fill-in editor" at the Ledger while Vallandigham took refuge in Canada from U.S. officials who wanted to prosecute him for treason and ran for Congress in absentia. Vallandigham won the Democratic Party's nomination. But he lost the election, and Cockerel lost the money Vallandigham had talked him into investing in the newspaper.[14]

The *Enquirer* re-hired Cockerill as a reporter. His work as a reporter and then as city editor impressed publisher John McLean so much that he named him managing editor in 1872. McLean, like Cockerill, was young, ambitious and aggressive. He believed Cockerill was the man to reshape the drab, struggling *Enquirer* into a hard-hitting, attention-grabbing newspaper.

Perhaps influenced by the no-nonsense leadership he witnessed in the military, Cockerill wasted no time in establishing a strong newsroom presence. He set high standards and drove his reporters and editors relentlessly, frequently shouting and cursing to get the results he wanted. His sardonic barbs stung. But he was a wise enough supervisor to temper his hard-charging management style with generous doses of praise and encouragement when merited. Cockerill

---

[14]Joanne Smith, "John A. Cockerill," *American Newspaper Journalists, 1873-1900*. Ed, Perry J. Ashley. Detroit: Gale Research, 1883. *Dictionary of Literary Biography*, Vol. 23. Literature Resource Center. Web. 28 February 2013.

understood Hearn's fragile temperament, calling him "as sensitive as a flower. An unkind word from anybody was as serious to him as a cut from a whiplash."[15] Cockerill mentored Hearn with a firm but gentle hand.

Hearn later recounted the respect and fear Cockerill instilled in the *Enquirer* staff: "He was a hard master, a tremendous worker, and a born journalist. I think none of us liked him, but we all admired his ability to run things. He used to swear at us, work us half to death (never sparing himself), and he had a rough skill in sarcasm that we were all afraid of."[16]

Cockerill's greatest accomplishments occurred after McLean forced him to leave Cincinnati in 1877. Jealous of the credit Cockerill was receiving for the *Enquirer's* soaring circulation, McLean arranged for him to take a leave from the *Enquirer* to cover the Russo-Turkish War. During his absence, McLean served as managing editor. When Cockerill's foreign assignment ended and he returned to Cincinnati, he realized that McLean planned to continue in the managing editor's position.

So Cockerill went to Washington, D.C., to help launch the *Washington Post*. He soon joined forces with publisher Joseph Pulitzer to create a more edgy, sensational brand of journalism at the *St. Louis Post-Dispatch* and later at the *New York World*. At the *World*, Cockerill encouraged and guided reporter Nellie Bly in her undercover investigative work that brought her and her newspaper international acclaim. Cockerill has been credited with concocting some of the ideas for her investigative stories, possibly even her famed infiltration of an insane asylum by posing as a patient to expose its shocking abuses.

But in 1872, the *Cincinnati Enquirer's* newly appointed managing editor was focused on establishing himself in a less exalted yet important journalism realm. He had a mission to lead a daily news operation in one of America's biggest cities.

In recognition of Cockerill's authoritative manner and his military experience, the *Enquirer* staff called him "the Colonel," a title he disapproved of because it was inaccurate. He repeatedly reminded ev-

---

[15]Cockerill, "Lafcadio Hearn: The Author of Kokoro," *Current Literature* Vol. XIX, June, 1896.
[16]Bisland, *Life and Letters,* vol. I, 53-54.

eryone that his father had been a colonel in the Civil War and he had been a mere private. But the title stuck in Cincinnati and everywhere else he worked after that.

Even though Hearn was just starting his writing career, he had a lot to offer the *Enquirer*. He brought to the newspaper a keen and scholarly intellect, a nascent literary style, a European education and background, a knowledge of world cultures, an appreciation of the arts and an insatiable curiosity.

For the rest of 1872 and throughout 1873, Hearn contributed stories to the *Enquirer* while continuing to work as a proofreader for the Robert Clarke Company. During this period, he wrote about a multitude of topics. Some were his own ideas, others Cockerill's. He wrote about homeless shelters, the suicide of a recluse, a camp of gypsies, the stabbing death of a butcher, the high price of beer, past and current customs of celebrating St. Valentine's Day, Russian imperial marriages, the origin of certain words, famous men's deathbed statements, amusing epitaphs, lectures about the Scottish poet Robert Burns and Shakespeare's "MacBeth," a lecture by the author and poet Bret Harte and a comical eyewitness account of a woman being arrested for disrupting a play.

Hearn was essentially what modern journalism calls a general-assignment reporter, writing news and feature stories. Cockerill didn't send him to cover stories that would require him to interview government officials or prominent people of Cincinnati high society because he knew Hearn was too bashful to talk to them. But Hearn had no reticence about talking to ordinary people for stories.

In a story published on November 29, 1872, Hearn demonstrated his affinity for the downtrodden and his antipathy toward the more fortunate who are insensitive to their plight.[17] In "Sleeping on the Bricks," Hearn describes a shelter for the homeless located in a basement room of the police headquarters on Hammond Street. About 20 men and boys, most them afflicted with lice, slept on the brick floor, getting as close as possible to the stove in the center of the room.

"The noise of opening the door, mingled with the howl of the cold wind without, stirred one of the half-naked sleepers, who turned over, scratched himself, and went to sleep again. The city authorities, while

---

[17] Hearn, "Sleeping on the Bricks," *Cincinnati Enquirer*, November 29, 1872, 5-6.

they turn no one away from their doors, give them no bed. There are some benches around the wall, and they are soon filled; and, after the first half-dozen, the brick floor is their only resting-place. Men and boys, from ten upward, are to be found here; wretches who but for this shelter would lie in the streets, or, perhaps, earn a bed behind iron bars…When all are in, they lie so close together, that one can hardly put a foot between them."

He contrasts this shelter with homeless shelters in London, where he undoubtedly stayed during his sojourns in the poor sections of that city. At the London shelters, the homeless were bathed, their clothes were held over burning sulphur to remove their stench and they were given breakfast the next morning as well as an opportunity to work to pay for those services. Hearn chastises the Cincinnati Christian Association, forerunner of the Young Men's Christian Association, for its inadequate philanthropic efforts. He writes that on the same night he was observing this homeless shelter, the members of the Christian Association were dining and singing songs in their "warm well-lighted rooms." If they were sincere about their philanthropy, Hearn writes, they should spend more time helping the people who desperately need it.

Two of his *Enquirer* stories during this period foreshadowed his penchant for writing about the gruesome. The death of 200 horses in a two-week period from an unknown disease prompted a very graphic Hearn story, informing readers how the bodies of the dead horses are skinned, cut apart and disemboweled for parts used to make soap, sausage casings and other items.[18] Another Hearn story described an autopsy performed on a man to determine whether he died from meningitis or a beating. The man's body was dug up after being buried for more than a week, and the coroner performed the autopsy in front of a jury empaneled to rule on the case.

With Poe-like luridness, Hearn spares no details in his story: "Dr. Edwin Rives, who handled the instruments, cut a neat slit from the top of the ribs down the center, the thick, green skin parting as the knife passed through, laying open the insides. He then raised the skin from the rib-bones, laying it back and carefully separating the ligaments, took out, one after another, the lungs, liver, heart and kid-

---

[18]Hearn, "The Last of the Horse," *Cincinnati Enquirer*, November 27, 1872, 1.

neys...After notes had been taken on these they were slapped back and the opening sewed up with cotton cord. By this time the ground was spattered with the drippings and the basins filled with bloody water, while the Doctor's cuffs, which professional pride forbade rolling up, were fringed with the disgusting mess."[19]

Hearn displayed the same rigorous attention to detail when he covered two days of the month-long Cincinnati Industrial Exposition in 1873. This festival began in 1869 primarily as a showcase for products from the city's businesses. But the inaugural event was so successful that it became an annual event. By 1873, it drew more than 500,000 people and featured new machinery, furniture and textile products from all parts of the country, exhibited paintings and sculptures by living artists from around the world and offered daily concerts. The exposition was one of Cincinnati's premiere money-making events and raised the city's national profile. It was held on the site now occupied by Music Hall.

Hearn's stories about the exposition are filled with interesting observations about all that was on display, including ancient Greek and Roman coins, the concerts, farm machinery, new-fangled washing machines and a new kind of railroad track joints. He particularly excelled in writing about the exposition's huge fine arts exhibit. In praising the oil painting of a child, Hearn writes: "In drawing, color and design it is exquisite; the little arms are full, round and permeated with a glow of health; while the innocent, self-willed head is faithfully and vigorously rendered. It makes one young again to look at this picture. How infinitely superior is this little figure, with its worn shoes, soiled hose, dirty pinafore and faded frock, to the usual manner of painting a child in elegant boottees, [sic] silk stockings and the air of an infant milliner, brand-new, and just taken out of a box!"[20]

Hearn wrote more than 40 stories for the *Enquirer* during 1873 while working full-time for the Robert Clarke Company. His productivity and the versatility and quality of his writing prompted Cockerill to hire him as a full-time staff reporter in early 1874. He gave Hearn a desk in the corner of his office to allow him to focus on

[19]Hearn, "Dug-Up," April 16, 1873, 8.
[20]Hearn, "Fourth Industrial Exposition," *Cincinnati Enquirer*, September 22, 1873, 4 and 5.

writing special stories for the Sunday editions, whose readership was much higher than the weekday editions. Bent over, with his good eye an inch or two from the page, Hearn wrote with total concentration.

"He was delighted to work, and I was pleased to have him work," Cockerill said, "for his style was beautiful, and the tone he imported to the newspaper was considerable. Hour after hour he would sit at his table, his great bulbous eyes resting as close to the paper as his nose would permit, scratching away with beaver-like diligence, and giving me no more annoyance than a bronze ornament."[21]

But before long, Hearn's writing would create plenty of noise outside the *Enquirer* newsroom.

---

[21]Cockerill, "Lafcadio Hearn: The Author of Kokoro," *Current Literature* Vol. XIX, June, 1896.

CHAPTER 3

Budding Reporter

*A*FTER HEARN achieved a firm foothold in the daily newspaper business, he was able to support himself solely by his writing. He had earned the admiration of his editor, with his stories regularly featured in the *Enquirer's* Sunday edition. He gained confidence in his writing and in his ability to support himself. Although he still felt uncomfortable in the presence of Cincinnati's high society, he no longer felt like a failure. His intellectual growth through avid reading and his development as a fledgling daily newspaper reporter bolstered his self-image and made him feel like a worthy and productive member of society.

Like most daily newspaper reporters of this era, Hearn worked long hours for relatively low pay. The *Enquirer* paid him a starting salary of $10 a week. He usually worked 14 to 16 hours a day, seven days a week, arriving at the newsroom around 1 p.m. and leaving for home an hour or two before dawn. He preferred writing in the early morning hours when the newsroom was quieter.

He expressed his journalism credo in a short, alternately serious and amusing piece published in the *Enquirer* on April 25, 1875. Referring both to newspaper reporters in general and to himself in particular, Hearn writes: "The good that men do he loves to blazon to the world; and when he exposes their evil deeds, it is to warn others to avoid the ragged edges of despair. If he sometimes exposes ugly social sores, he oftener instructs, amuses and cheers the world of humanity. He is altogether too useful to be dispensed with—this curious bird, this witty bird, this laughing bird, this singular bird, this newspaper reporter."[1]

---

[1] Lafcadio Hearn, "The Reporter," *Cincinnati Enquirer*, April 25, 1875, 9.

Although Hearn derived an impish delight from imagining people eating breakfast while reading his graphically lurid stories, he took his responsibilities as a journalist very seriously. During his tenure at the *Enquirer*, he worked diligently to uncover medical quacks, free-love advocates, all kinds of swindlers and all forms of religious hypocrisy.

Hearn wrote about the sordid activities of Madame Sidney Augustine, a fortune-teller who performed abortions in a small back room of her downtown brick house and ran a prostitution operation in the same house. He followed up a May 22, 1873, story about her arrest with a story the next day offering more details about the police investigation, including the discovery of a dead fetus wrapped in a black silk dress of Augustine's.[2] It was found under two feet of muck in a privy on her property. Hearn interviewed neighbors and a hospitalized woman whose abortion sparked the police investigation.

William Raphael, an astrologer and charlatan physician, tried to bribe Hearn not to write about the arrest of him and his wife for medical fraud and sex crimes. Hearn, of course, declined and wrote the story, concluding with an account of Raphael's attempt to bribe him.

He wrote about a "baby farm," a money-making operation run by a doctor who boarded unwanted babies for money and then tried to have them adopted for a fee. But babies who failed to be adopted quickly or whose mothers stopped sending weekly boarding payments to the doctor were scandalously neglected and sometimes died.[3]

One of Hearn's favorite targets was spiritualism, a movement whose followers believed it was possible to communicate with the spirits of the dead. This movement, which peaked between the mid-19th and early-20th centuries, produced legions of scam artists—or "humbugs," as they were called then—who would charge money to hold seances, show photographs they claimed depicted spirits, predict the future, make objects move without touching them and perform countless other displays of their supposed supernatural mental powers.

But Hearn had an unsettling experience when someone he described as a spiritualist friend invited him to a séance and gave him

---

[2]Hearn, "Mme. Sidney Augustine," *Cincinnati Enquirer*, May 23, 1873, 4.
[3]Hearn, "Baby-Farming," *Cincinnati Enquirer*, December 13, 1874, 1.

permission to examine the room in her house where it would take place. He had written in the *Enquirer* the week before about a previous seance with this medium. The medium had told Hearn then that the spirit would not appear because Hearn was "too physically and psychically filthy."

In Hearn's January 24, 1874, story about this second visit (titled "Among the Spirits"), he comically describes purifying himself by taking numerous baths, abstaining from tobacco, wearing a clean shirt and refraining from foul language during the week before the second seance.[4] After making sure the doors to the séance room were locked and fastened with pen-knives, Hearn obliged the medium's request and nailed her dress to the floor with a tack. Shortly after the séance began, Hearn felt someone's fingers tap his knee and thigh. A tapping noise ensued, and the medium began talking to a spirit who was invisible but spoke through a trumpet in a hoarse whisper. The spirit identified himself as Hearn's father, gave his correct name and called Hearn by the name of Patrick, as Lafcadio's father did when he was alive.

The voice claiming to be Hearn's father asked him for forgiveness.

"I have nothing to forgive," Hearn replied.

"You have, indeed," the voice said faintly. The voice said insistently, "I wronged you: forgive me."

Hearn asked the spirit to write down the circumstances he was referring to. The spirit said he would write it down with a pencil and paper lying on the table, but the spirit left before doing it.

At the end of the story, Hearn states the séance occurred exactly as he reported and that he has no explanation for how the "Voice" knew his dead father's name and certain aspects of his family history. Hearn doesn't name this medium friend in either story because, he says, her husband is a prominent Cincinnatian. Even though he couldn't figure out how the medium had fooled him, it didn't affect his staunch skepticism of spiritualism.

In a later story headlined, "The Progress of Spiritualism" (November 29, 1874), Hearn ridicules the spiritualists' contention that the dead and other objects could be made to materialize. "(Spiritualism) will doubtless add immensely to human happiness," he writes sar-

---

[4]Hearn, "Among the Spirits," *Cincinnati Enquirer*, January 25, 1874, 8.

castically. "If the spirits can 'materialize' a pipe and a suit of clothes and can dance among the people of the world, they can 'materialize' a bridge over the Ohio River…and a plate of 'roast beef rare,' and a cord of wood, to do which things would add to human happiness."[5]

Hearn wrote *Enquirer* stories lampooning the free-love advocates who sprang from the utopian and Transcendentalism movements sweeping the eastern half of the country. Transcendentalists believed in the glories of nature, the innate goodness of human beings and the corrupt nature of society's institutions. Free-love disciples attacked marriage as an unnatural state that hampered the growth and freedom of individuals. Hearn despised the free-love movement because it violated his essentially romantic nature and he felt it debased and endangered women.

In several stories, he derides free-love advocates as purveyors of "licentious social doctrine" and "that peculiar paganism." In particular, he homes in on Ohio native free-love pioneers Victoria (Claflin) Woodhull and her sister, Tennessee Claflin. In New York, they published the *Woodhull & Claflin Weekly*, which promoted women's voting rights and labor reform as well as free love. Woodhull became the United States' first female presidential candidate in 1872, receiving no electoral votes.

That same year, the controversial weekly sparked a national sensation by publishing a story accusing Henry Ward Beecher, one of America's most renowned clergymen and the brother of Harriet Beecher Stowe, of adultery. After Beecher's church exonerated him, the husband of his alleged lover filed a civil lawsuit charging him with adultery. Cincinnatians had a special interest in this scandal because the Stowes had lived in the city from 1832 to 1850, and the *Enquirer* assigned Hearn to pursue a local angle.

Shortly before the trial was to begin, Hearn interviewed two people, a book store owner and a banker who said they knew the Claflins when they lived in Cincinnati in the 1850s. Hearn tells most of the August 3, 1874, story in dialogue.[6] The banker, who also had seen them on business trips to New York, offers the most interesting details, saying that as a teenager, Tennessee helped support the family

---

[5] Hearn, "The Progress of Spiritualism," *Cincinnati Enquirer*, November 29, 1874, 4.
[6] Hearn, "The Sensational Sisters," *Cincinnati Enquirer*, August 3, 1874, 4.

by telling fortunes. He says that after they moved to New York, the Claflin sisters would encourage their fortune-telling clients to reveal shameful secrets to them and then later the sisters would blackmail them. The banker says he believed their accusations against Beecher were true. Hearn's use of extensive dialogue, as he does in "The Sensational Sisters," is one of the literary techniques he experimented with in Cincinnati. He worked hard to refine this technique during his first two years with the *Enquirer*.

One of his other literary experiments in Cincinnati involved injecting himself into the story, usually referring to himself as "the reporter" or "our reporter," as he did in "Among the Spirits." He didn't use the first-person "I" in his Cincinnati stories because newspaper style forbade it. Instead, he substituted "this reporter" or the first-person plural pronoun "we" for "I." In a few humorous stories, he referred to himself by such nicknames as "the Dismal Man," and "the Ghoul."

Becoming a part of his stories helped him achieve three primary goals—to entertain, to shock and to educate his readers. Often, he did all three in one story. Although he sometimes portrayed himself as a mischievous rascal trying to startle and amuse, he usually had a serious purpose when he wrote his Cincinnati stories. He wanted to reform society, to reveal Cincinnati's underbelly and force the powerful and prosperous citizens to acknowledge and learn about the needy social outcasts and the social evils being widely ignored. Placing himself in the story, he believed, would add personality and color to what might otherwise be a dry newspaper story. Some of his early attempts at using this technique weren't always effective, but he kept doing it and improving it.

Hearn became so adept at this self-referential kind of story and did it so frequently that he is considered one of the forerunners of New Journalism, a style of participatory journalism popularized by Gay Talese, Norman Mailer, Hunter S. Thompson and others in the 1960s and 1970s. Hearn's first attempts at this kind of story, which often used extensive dialogue, were awkward and ineffective. He continued honing this technique after he left Cincinnati in 1877 for a 10-year stint in New Orleans. He perfected it later in the French West Indies and in Japan.

One of his first *Enquirer* stories using this self-referential technique was a feature on October 29, 1872, about Cincinnati's weather clerk, whose office was situated on the top floor of Pike's Opera House.[7] Hearn offers lengthy factual descriptions of the various scientific instruments in the weather station. The last part of the story is a stilted dialogue between Hearn ("Reporter") and the weather clerk ("Observer"). At the end of the story, the weather clerk, who is never named, chides Hearn because the *Enquirer* was the only one of the five English-language Cincinnati daily newspapers that didn't publish his monthly weather reports.

"…we have been looking for the *Enquirer* to follow suit," the weather clerk says, "but, as yet, we have been unable to find the right man…" Hearn ends the story with a whimsical touch, writing: "At this point, seeing Observer was getting a little personal, our reporter made his exit unassisted."

He had been contributing to the *Enquirer* for about eight months when he wrote a feature story about the railroad's "pay-car" trips.[8] To distribute weekly wages to its many employees working along a certain route, a railroad paymaster would travel in a single passenger coach pulled by an engine and stop along the route wherever its employees worked. At each stop, employees would come to the car to pick up the envelopes containing their money.

Hearn arranged to accompany the pay-car on its weekly trip from Cincinnati to Richmond, Indiana and Hamilton and Dayton, Ohio, to write about the 150-mile day-long trip and the railroad employees he encountered. He opens the story with a conversation between himself, referred to as "the *Enquirer* man," and B.D. Stevenson, the railroad paymaster. As in the weather station story, Hearn cast himself as a comical target of mild abuse.

The story opens with a playful dialogue between Hearn and Stevenson, who agrees to take Hearn along. "But none of your nonsense if you go along with me," he warns Hearn. "You reporter fellows can do the right thing, if you want to, but the trouble is that you don't very often want to. I don't desire any of your extras, and don't care whether you write any thing [sic] about the trip or not. You look sort of hungry, as if you didn't have a very good boarding-house, and I thought I

---

[7] Hearn, "Our Local Weather-Clerk," *Cincinnati Enquirer*, October 29, 1872. 5.

[8] Hearn, "A Pay-Car Trip. How Railroad Men Get Their Money," *Cincinnati Enquirer*, June 18, 1873, 1.

would like to take you out into the country a little ways and give you a square meal and a few mouthfuls of fresh air by way of relish. That's my only motive in inviting you. But if you do write about the trip, I don't want you to say any thing except what you actually see." Hearn assures him he is much more honest than "the wicked reporters of the other city papers."

Partly because of his grim experiences in London and his first months in Cincinnati, Hearn identified strongly with society's down-trodden. He felt compelled to explore and write about their plight. He usually didn't propose specific solutions to help them, but he hoped that by exposing their dire situations, his stories would stir government officials and other leaders to do something to improve their lives.

Early in his *Cincinnati Enquirer* career, Hearn wrote a story about a filthy, rat-infested house where a woman almost died from a miscarriage and where one of the house's owners recruited young girls to be prostitutes. In his first two paragraphs of this story, Hearn declared the rationale behind his muckraking journalism:

"Cincinnati may brag of having the handsomest this and the largest that in the world, but she is mighty quiet in regard to her possession of some of the most miserable and disgusting features. Her quiet may come, however, from her ignorance, for it is much better and comforting to think that good men and women of this city who sit with folded hands, and believe themselves to be Christian, have no idea that there are such foul scabs on the city's face as now and then become uncovered to the light of day."[9]

Hearn considered it his solemn journalistic duty to shine the light on these "foul scabs on the city's face." He often accomplished this by revealing not only the injustices suffered by society's outcasts but also by showing the humanity of Cincinnati's have-nots. He sometimes placed himself in these stories to make the readers feel as though they themselves were interacting with the subjects of his stories.

In long stories, he chronicled the daily lives of washerwomen, chambermaids, seamstresses and rag-pickers. He includes himself in these stories, relating his conversations with them and describing their working and living environments. In a story about seamstress-es, he pokes fun at himself. "The reporter chosen for this expedi-

---

[9]Hearn, "A Nasty Nest," *Cincinnati Enquirer*, July 27, 1873, 4.

tion unfortunately happens to be the ugliest local in the office (the good-looking ones were all engaged on other work that day); and his spectacled visage, which bears a grotesque resemblance to the countenance of an owl, called forth a number of very uncomplimentary remarks from Ethiopian maidens during his progress through the negro quarter. Boys pelted him with snowballs and a dog attacked him."[10] This light, self-deprecating passage seems out of place in an otherwise somber, earnest story about a class of women who were grossly underpaid for their work.

The seamstresses, who live and work "in hundreds of those dingy little frame hovels, situated in the most dilapidated suburbs of Cincinnati," earned $2 to $3 for working 60 to 80 hours a week. In recounting his conversations with the seamstresses, Hearn carefully captures the nuances of their speech. He asks one seamstress about the prices she receives from the stores for the clothes she makes.

"'Ah, the divil take the prices! Shure we don't get any prices at all now. I used to have a whole roomful of girls working for me; but since prices has come down, I haven't the face to offer them work for the little I could pay them. There's the work we used to get forty cints for, we only get twinty-five for now.'"

In his July 26, 1874, story about rag-pickers, Hearn visits several rag merchants in Cincinnati and uses dialogue to convey their information about the rag business and the desperate men and women who eke out a living gathering rags from dumps and selling them to the merchants.[11] In an effort to personalize his story, Hearn goes to a dump, which he describes as "a Golgotha of foul bones and refuse; a great grave-yard for worn out pots and kettles and smashed glasses, and rotten vegetables and animal filth, and shattered household utensils and abominations unutterable."

He tries to interview an elderly female rag-picker who is kneeling in a trash pile searching for rags. He describes her physical appearance in extremely unflattering terms—"a huge vulture nose, great black eyes, deep-set, and flowing with a brilliancy that seemed phosphorescent, a high, bold, frowning forehead, crowned with a filthy

---

[10] Hearn, "Slow Starvation," *Cincinnati Enquirer*, February 15, 1874, 5.
[11] Hearn, "Les Chiffoniers. Rags, Wretchedness and Rascality," *Cincinnati Enquirer*, July 26, 1874, 5.

turban, long, thin bloodless lips and a long massive chin, all begrimed to deep blackness by the filth of the dumps."

Reluctantly, the woman answers a few of his questions, telling him she earns no more than two or three dollars a week. She says she had to give up laundry washing a year ago after injuring her right hand. Hearn asks her if there's any other better-paying work she might do. "I don't want to talk about it," she says sharply. "You can't do me any good anyhow, and I'm too busy to bother with you."

Hearn asks one of the rag merchants to give him thumbnail sketches of his rag-pickers. The story ends with a list of the brief, sometimes complimentary and sometimes cruelly candid descriptions of 18 rag-pickers along with their names. For example: "GENERAL HARVEY THOMAS.—Colored, one hundred year [sic] old. Keeps his person clean and neat. Fought at the Battle of New Orleans; fourteen years at the business; is shrewd, and successful in business." "MARY WINKER.—"Fifty years old. Sixteen years at the rag business. Drunk, disorderly and filthy." "MRS. MILLER.—Her husband and grown-up son refuse to support her. Over fifty-five years of age, and fourteen at rag-picking."

Through these kinds of stories, Hearn forced his readers to meet in print people they would shun if they saw them on the streets. In revealing Cincinnati's underbelly, he gave voice to the underclass wracked by poverty. In this same vein, he once took *Enquirer* readers inside the Hamilton County Jail, providing a vivid picture of jail's interior, including individual cells and the men and women who occupied them.[12]

"Some of the prisoners squat on their cot beds, pulled in the middle of their cells," he writes in the story, "and with hands under their haunches watch the stray bits of sunlight by the hour, moving only to lie down or to eat. They live this way week after week, moody and gaunt, while others trim their cells up until by comparison they are little palaces. One ingenious young man, who is in for counterfeiting money, has with scolloped [sic] and ornamented newspapers festooned the ceiling of his den, and covered the walls with prints, framed with like trimming, until it has lost much of his prison look."

---

[12] Hearn, "Within the Bars; How Prisoners Look, Live and Conduct Themselves," *Cincinnati Enquirer,* March 16, 1873, 8.

Hearn used participatory journalism to entertain as well as to enlighten. On the afternoon of January 21, 1874, Hearn pulled off one of his most outrageous journalism stunts. Edith O'Gorman, a notorious anti-Catholic speaker and author, had come to Cincinnati to talk about the shameful things she had supposedly experienced and witnessed during her brief time as a Catholic nun before her brother helped her escape from the convent. Because part of this talk would cover sex-related matters, her matinee lecture on January 21 at Pike's Hall was restricted to women only.

The week before, Hearn had covered a lecture entitled "The Catholic Power in America" O'Gorman had presented in a Cincinnati chapel to an audience of men and women. She had been jeered and pelted with snowballs by protesters as she walked from her carriage to the chapel. There was nothing racy in that lecture, according to Hearn's story. Her long harangue about the frightening political power of the Catholic Church and the flaws of democracy left Hearn unimpressed. "A great many of her statements are transparently untruthful," he writes, "and her lecture was neither interesting nor well delivered."[13]

Determined to hear and report on her women-only lecture, Hearn donned a blond wig, a dress, ladies' gloves and buttoned boots. After stumbling on his dress as he went up the stairs leading to the hall's entrance, Hearn sat down in the auditorium and tried to be as unobtrusive as possible. When a woman yelled, "There's a man!," his heart sank. But then he realized the woman and those near her were looking at another man dressed as a woman, not him. Describing the unfortunate fellow, Hearn observes, "…from the mustache and the general look of her we knew we were safe."

Most of this story centers on his amusing appearance, his fear of being discovered, his feigned shock at O'Gorman's scandalous allegations ("…oh, she made your reporter blush, and wish that he had stayed away.") and the reactions of the other members of the audience. The story contains very little of O'Gorman's lecture because most of it was too salacious for a family newspaper. "A trusting public expects information," Hearn writes, "but modesty forbids."[14]

---

[13] Hearn, "That 'Nun'; Miss Edith O'Houligan in the Show Business. The King of Stuff that Some People Pay for Listening to," *Cincinnati Enquirer,* January 15, 1874, 2.

[14] Hearn, "Feminine Curiosity. A Female Blackguard's Lecture to Prurient Sisters. The 'Escaped Nun's' Matinee at Pike's Hall," *Cincinnati Enquirer*, January 22, 1874, 2.

But modesty didn't stop Hearn from writing about a female model who occasionally posed nude for several Cincinnati artists. All the artists raved to Hearn about the stunning beauty of this young woman. The more they rhapsodized about her, the more Hearn ached to see her posing and to write about her.

He talked an artist he doesn't name in his story[15] to let him come to his studio when this woman was posing. One Hearn's biographer believes the artist was Frank Duveneck, whom he says playfully taunted Hearn with talk of her beauty, while another biographer says it probably was Henry Farny, another good artist/friend of Hearn's. The studio described in Hearn's story about the nude model bears some similarities to Farny's studio, which Hearn described in a March 22, 1874, story about Farny and two other Cincinnati artists.[16] Whoever the artist was, he provided Hearn with a delicious opportunity to tease Cincinnati readers with a topic sure to shock Victorian sensibilities. The October 18, 1874, story's headline read: "Beauty Undraped; What a Wicked Reporter Saw in an Artist's Studio." The model, 19 or 20 years old and six feet tall, had long, flowing blond hair and a very pleasing statuesque figure. "Why, my dear fellow," the artist says to Hearn, "she's the most splendid girl that's ever stripped in a studio."

The artist tells Hearn that he can't reveal the model's name in the story and must not write anything that would cast doubts on her moral character. "She has a good name, and deserves a good name as an honest, innocent girl," the artist says.

Hearn spends half of the story building the suspense and anticipation for the moment when he casts his eyes upon this voluptuous model. He climbs the stairs to the studio and taps on the door five times with his thumb-nail, his identifying signal he and the artist had worked out ahead of time. Hearn enters. As the nude model reclines on a sofa, two artists are sketching, and Hearn's artist/friend is painting with oils. Hearn is awe-struck by what he sees:

"She lay at full length upon a long sofa, unclad and unadorned save by the matchless gifts of nature, her white limbs lightly crossed, both hands clasped over her graceful little head, and her luxurious

---

[15] Hearn, "Beauty Undraped; What a Wicked Reporter Saw in an Artist's Studio," *Cincinnati Enquirer*, October 18, 1874, 1.

[16] Hearn, "Our Artists," *Cincinnati Enquirer*, March 22, 1874, 7.

blonde hair streaming loose beneath her in a river of tawny gold. As the lounge had been placed with its back to the door, the approach of the visitor had not been perceived. But for the burning blush that dyed her face and throat crimson at the moment of rencounter, and the scarcely perceptible heaving of her snowy bosom, she might have been taken for a waxen model of the Paphian Aphrodite. She was unusually tall—taller even than most men—yet as exquisitely proportioned as an Oriental dancing-girl. The complexion of her limbs and body was something marvelous in color—a pearly opaline, that no brush could mimic on canvas. It had the sheen and smoothness of polished marble, yet seemed to glow as if the blue veins that gleamed through its delicate transparency 'ran lightning.' Her limbs were marvelously round, and on the under side flushed, daintily pink, like the heart of a sea-shell, yet formed so as to convey the sense of strength combined with grace; and her throat and shoulders and bosom were a living realization of that matchless symmetry admired by the world in the marble of Greek art for more than a thousand years."

After absorbing the full impact of her beauty, Hearn collapses in an easy chair and puffs on a cigar, coolly observing her until the modeling session regrettably ends. In his rapturous descriptions of the young woman's anatomy, Hearn skillfully avoids getting objectionably graphic. He manages to cloak his lust with lofty, poetic language, imbuing his story with a veneer of respectability. Comparing her to a Greek goddess, he idealizes his subject and tries to make his interest in her appear more aesthetic than sexual.

But Hearn didn't confine his appreciation of feminine pulchritude to artists' models. He praises the pretty faces and comely figures of several women in a September 13, 1874, story about—of all things—a religious revival camp.[17] Modern journalism generally discourages descriptions of people's sexual appeal, especially women's. But it was permitted in Hearn's day. Hearn's *Enquirer* editors must have had a hard time suppressing their laughter when they assigned him to cover the Methodist Revival Camp Meeting on a hilltop in a wooded area near Loveland, just northeast of Cincinnati. An agnostic who generally viewed Christianity with scorn, Hearn couldn't have been

---

[17]Hearn, "Camp Santo. Sights and Sounds of Rustic Religion," *Cincinnati Enquirer*, September 23, 1874, 1.

a more implausible choice to cover such an event. But he didn't allow the solemnity of the revival camp to prevent him from having fun with the assignment. Maybe that's what his editors were counting on. Early in his front-page Sunday story, Hearn himself acknowledges the incongruity of his situation. "…an *Enquirer* reporter who went out last Thursday to the grounds of the Methodist Revival Camp-meeting at Loveland, not to pray, but to watch better people than himself pray…"

Just as he couldn't resist staging pranks when he was a schoolboy, Hearn couldn't refrain from making inappropriate observations in this story. Fifty small tents surrounded a mammoth Tabernacle tent where the religious services were held. On his first night there, Hearn crept close to some of the tents to watch the shadows of the people inside. As a Peeping Tom, he breathlessly describes the interaction of two shadows in one tent: "There were two strongly-defined silhouettes there; one of an old lady with spectacles and a very long nose; the other of a very shapely little woman, swan-throated and full-bosomed, with long eyelashes and long hair. The shadow had beautiful little bare arms, nice and round; and it put them around the neck of the motherly looking shadow, and it pursed up its plump little lips. Then the thin, wrinkled lips of the motherly shadow responded; the heads of the two shadows mingled into one big, black blot on the canvas, and the reporter's mouth began to water."

The next day, Hearn notices a young woman at one of the services, "the very prettiest girl on the grounds…with glorious masses of glossy black hair brushed back from either temple and falling over the prettiest little shoulders imaginable…" Then he sees twin sisters, "blondes, dressed in white, with dovelike eyes and peachy cheeks and lips ripe for kisses; but they were accompanied by a terrible…mother, a tall, thin, gorgon-eyed woman, who looked at you so wickedly if you looked at her daughters that you immediately turned your face the other way." He also observes that during one of the services a "charming little brunette" peeked through her fingers during prayer time at some good-looking boys. Near the end of his long story, he notes that only he and the little brunette failed to march to the preacher's stand with the rest of the congregation to be converted. Hallelujah!

Another ill-suited assignment given to Hearn involved interviewing Cincinnati's religious leaders and writing mini-profiles of each. This may have been more odious to Hearn than going to the religious revival, which at least provided him with a pleasant outdoor setting and a little adventure. He makes his displeasure with this assignment evident at the beginning of his story ("Cincinnati Saints") published on October 11, 1874.[18] He opens the story by listing nine questions he was supposed to ask each person to obtain the following information: age, birthplace, name of father, occupation before entering the ministry, place and length of study, previous churches where employed, most interesting episodes in religious career, marital status and salary. Then he writes, "An *Enquirer* reporter was sent forth a few days since, with orders to interview the Chief Priests and the Ancients of the Synagogues, by propounding to them these modest catechetical queries. He did not, however, do altogether as well as had been expected of him; partly because many of the Evangelical gentlemen objected to the nature of the questions in themselves; partly because those who might not have objected were mostly absent from the city, and partly because the reporter, not being a member of any church in good standing, found considerable difficulty in obtaining the requisite information from church members."

Hearn writes respectfully about each subject and packs the mini-profiles with many interesting details. But with schoolboy mischievousness, he casts the story in the form of a contest report. Each mini-profile has a different heading: "THE HANDSOMEST MINISTER," "MOST LATITUDINARIAN AND SCHOLARLY," "MOST AGGRESSIVELY DOGMATIC," "THE MOST SUAVE AND AFFABLE," "OUR MOST VENERABLE RABBI" and "THE MOST POPULAR COLORED PASTOR."

Although he relished stories that rattled his readers, Hearn also earnestly applied his reporting skills to conventional news topics. He wrote a well-researched straight-forward story ("Hold Your Noses!") about how the completion of a sewer project could have prevented the outbreak of a horrible stench that spread over the West End neighborhood.[19]

"Original, deep, pungent and all-pervading is the awful odor that broods from Eighth street to Harrison avenue and from Central avenue to the western hills," he writes May 14, 1874, story. "McLean-av-

---

[18]Hearn, "Cincinnati Saints," *Cincinnati Enquirer,* October 11, 1874, 9.
[19]Hearn, "Hold Your Noses!," *Cincinnati Enquirer,* May 14, 1874, 8.

enue sewer has been built in part. Had it been completed, as it should ere this, to the river, and tapped by sewers running west, our city would have escaped this present direful baptism in an atmosphere of unbearable stench…The effect is terrible. People are growing sick. The stink goes everywhere. One cannot get used to it. No shutting of doors or airing of rooms avails. It is too strong for disinfectants. People who can are preparing to get out of its way and that of the pestilence with which it threatens the city."

Despite Hearn's limited eyesight, he often noted visual details in his stories that other reporters missed. Aided by a small eyeglass he often carried with him, he made a special effort to observe and take notes about the site of whatever story he was writing. *Cincinnati Gazette* reporter Joseph S. Tunison, who became a close friend of Hearn's, noticed Hearn's special powers of observation. "…Hearn never missed anything that could be seen, heard or touched," he recalls in a Dayton, Ohio, newspaper column he wrote in 1908. "There was a running revolver fight between a squad of police and a band of house-breakers far out in the West End of Cincinnati. Several men were either wounded or killed…It goes without saying that Hearn wrote the best story. He had the pen with which to do it. In important particulars which comprised the entire area of the battlefield, Hearn's narrative was the most accurate. It must be remembered that the telephone had not then been invented. If a reporter wanted a thing he had to go after it. Hearn did not depend on hearsay. He saw, heard and touched what he described. Of course no newspaper man could get to the scene in time to see the fight. That part of the tale was taken as given by the police; but all the rest was a matter of immediate, independent observation on the part of each reporter."[20]

Other reporters at the *Enquirer* resented Hearn's special status as Cockerill's protege and the prominent play many of his stories received in the Sunday paper, which had the highest readership of the week. But Hearn developed some strong friendships with reporters at rival newspapers, both English- and German-language publications.

In addition to Tunison, *Cincinnati Gazette* reporters Henry Krehbiel and Henry Feldwisch and *Cincinnati Volksblatt* reporter Charlie Johnson respected Hearn's writing ability and intellect and enjoyed his

---

[20]Joseph S. Tunison, "Concerning Lafcadio Hearn," *Dayton Journal*, May 11, 1908.

biting wit. For a time, Krehbiel was a night police reporter, like Hearn. The two men often made their nightly rounds together, stopping at police stations to get information about the latest arrests and covering riots, bar fights and other criminal activities. They had sharply contrasting physical features and personalities. Krehbiel, the son of a Methodist minister, was tall, blond-haired, fair-skinned, serious and even-tempered, while Hearn was short, dark-haired, swarthy, puckish and high-strung. Yet they shared a deep love of the arts, especially folk music, and their career ambitions extended far beyond newspapers and Cincinnati. Krehbiel, a violinist, wanted to make a career of music criticism, and Hearn wanted to write books and to translate his beloved modern French romanticist authors. While Hearn was still in Cincinnati, Krehbiel became a music critic for the *Gazette*. He and Hearn went to concerts together, and when walking along the riverfront, they often would stop to listen to the African-American dockworkers sing. Later, Krehbiel moved to New York City and became a nationally renowned music writer.

Tunison later served as literary editor at the *New York Tribune* and then as the editor of the *Dayton Journal* in Ohio. A Latin scholar, Tunison also wrote books about the classical and medieval eras. Johnson later was appointed U.S. Consul in Hamburg, Germany, by President Benjamin Harrison's administration. In the mid-1870s, Feldwisch went to Florida to recuperate from tuberculosis and then moved to Denver, where he became owner and editor of a weekly newspaper called the *Denver Inter-Ocean* and later became the Colorado Dairy Commissioner. He died of a hemorrhage in 1887, one day before his 34th birthday.

But in Cincinnati, they all were young reporters who often ate together at Jake Aug's tavern, where they enjoyed laughs and banter as well as more serious conversations about their work, their aspirations and more personal matters. Hearn seldom drank alcoholic beverages, but he enjoyed cigars, often smoking five a day.

One of the few non-newspaper members of their informal social group was the artist Henry Farny. Farny's French immigrant family had moved from Pennsylvania to Cincinnati in 1859 when Farny was 12. After studying art in Germany, Farny returned to Cincinnati and supported himself by such commercial art as book and magazine illustrations, posters and pamphlets. In 1879, he redesigned and illustrated the popular *McGuffey Readers*. He later earned international renown for his paintings of Native Americans and American Western landscapes.

Not long after Hearn's May 22, 1874, story about him, Farny persuaded E. H. Austerlitz, manager of the Western German Advertising Agency, and C.A. Hunthum, foreign and amusement editor of the *Cincinnati Daily Courier*, to publish a weekly German-language literary and satirical periodical called *Kladderadatch*, the same name as a well-established periodical published in Berlin. The name was supposed to represent the sound of something crashing. Farny would draw the illustrations for Cincinnati's periodical. When the first few issues of *Kladderadatch* failed to generate much interest or income, Farny proposed that Austerlitz fund an English-language, illustrated, highbrow satirical weekly similar to *Punch* in England. Hoping to recoup some of his losses from *Kladderadatch*, Austerlitz agreed. Farny, who would be the illustrator and do some writing, enlisted Hearn to be editor and chief writer. After rejecting several names for the new weekly, they decided on *Ye Giglampz*, a reference to Hearn's large, thick glasses. Hearn thought the weekly would be a nice outlet for his more creative writing. He decided to keep his full-time job with the *Enquirer* until he was sure *Ye Giglampz* would provide him with sufficient income. His initial weekly salary was $2.

The first issue of *Ye Giglampz*, "an illustrated weekly devoted to art, literature and satire," appeared on June 21, 1874. Farny's cover illustration shows one man, "Herr Kladderadatch," introducing another man, "Mr. Giglampz," to a cheering audience. Farny drew Mr. Giglampz, wearing thick glasses and a goatee, to resemble Hearn.[21] Hearn wrote 14 of the 19 articles in the inaugural issue, although his name didn't appear in the issue. In this era, it was customary for daily and weekly newspapers not to print writers' by-lines. Farny signed only the two-page centerfold illustration he drew for this issue.

Despite all the work Hearn and Farny put into this first issue, it barely created a ripple with the reading public. The nickel-a-copy publication had cost $60 to produce and generated only $1.77 in

---

[21] *Ye Giglampz, a Weekly Illustrated Journal Devoted to Art, Literature and Satire Edited by Lafcadio Hearn and Henry Farny*, ed. Jon Christopher Hughes (Cincinnati: Crossroads Books with the Public Library of Cincinnati and Hamilton County, 1983) contains reproductions of all nine issues of the short-lived weekly publication.

sales. Alarmed, Austerlitz called Farny and Hearn to an emergency staff meeting. Austerlitz and Farny criticized Hearn's content for being too serious and not funny enough. Actually, some of his work is quite humorous. In his introductory essay to this inaugural issue of *Ye Giglampz*, Hearn employs flowery language and a mood of mock horror as he concocts a lengthy fantasy about the birth of the periodical. He also wrote amusing short pieces, including one that pokes fun at a board member of Spring Grove Cemetery for traveling to England to buy $1,000 worth of shrubs that Hearn says could have been obtained from "the verdant banks of an American creek." Hearn did write several blistering commentaries about Spanish brutality, the evils of European colonialism and England's disregard for her poor. He intended these pieces to stir moral outrage, not to provoke laughter.

At the staff meeting, Hearn at first defended himself from the criticism, but finally agreed that changes had to be made in the content for the second issue. He felt so badly about the commercial failure of the first issue that he told Austerlitz to withhold his $2 salary for that week.

The enterprise received a boost during the next two weeks when bar owners and other anti-temperance people agreed to buy 500 copies of *Ye Giglampz* per week. The newspaper had won their loyalty by printing several articles ridiculing the temperance advocates. Hearn didn't approve of drunkenness, but he also didn't believe alcohol should be banned. At Hearn's request, two writers were added to the staff. Despite this infusion of money and labor, the newspaper's financial status continued to be precarious.

Part of the problem was that neither Farny nor Hearn had a speck of business sense and both tended to be very impractical and stubborn. The two men clashed constantly over the content of *Ye Giglampz*. Farny insisted on toning down some of Hearn's articles that he felt were too off-color. In reaction to Farny's attempts to edit or censor his stories, Hearn resigned four different times during the newspaper's first eight weeks. Each time, he reconsidered and returned.

In a comical story he later wrote for the *Enquirer* about the life and death of *Ye Giglampz*, he refers to himself as the Ghoul and to Farny as O'Pharney.[22] He writes: "O'Pharney, seeing the proof sheets,

---

[22] Hearn, "Giglampz!," *Cincinnati Enquirer*, October 4, 1874, 9.

declared that the Ghoul was pandering to depraved tastes, and ordered the Ghoul's articles to be in part distributed. The remainder he
'corrected,' with what he styled "emendations and embellishments' of
his own. The Ghoul thought both the literary tastes and the English
of the critical O'Pharney susceptible of vast improvement…"

At one point, Farny and Hearn talked Austerlitz into scrapping
Kladderadatch to improve *Ye Giglampz*' chances of survival. But it
didn't seem to help, and Austerlitz decided to end his investment in
the money-losing newspaper. Farney put up his own money to fund
half of the operation and persuaded Hearn to step in and put up the
other half. Believing the weekly would demand even more of his time
and would give him a chance to cash in on his investment, Hearn quit
the *Enquirer*, much to the surprise of his editors and fellow reporters.

"Our City Editor sat down and laughed until his ribs threatened
to burst asunder, and the tears rolled down his cheeks in torrents,"
Hearn writes. "The idea of an *Enquirer* man resigning his position in
order to accept an interest in The *Giglampz* was too much for him.
When he recovered the use of articulate speech, however, he iron-
ically congratulated the Ghoul on his extraordinary good fortune.
Then all the *Enquirer* boys went down to Jake Aug's, and gave the
Ghoul an ovation."

But Hearn soon realized he couldn't live without his *Enquirer*
salary. "He wended his way to the *Enquirer* office, expressing deep
repentance, and acknowledging his sin, like the Prodigal Son," Hearn
writes. "They killed the fatted calf for him, and kindly reinstated him
in his old post."

After resuming his *Enquirer* duties, Hearn continued to write
for *Ye Giglampz*. But in the newspaper's eighth issue, Farny committed a major public relations gaffe. On Thursday, August 4, 1874, the
day before *Ye Giglampz*'s deadline, the steamer Pat Rogers, full of
passengers, caught fire on the Ohio River near the Cincinnati levee
and quickly became engulfed in flames and smoke. Forty-five people died. It was a major disaster. The next day, Farny decided to try
to scoop the daily newspapers and be the first to run illustrations of
the catastrophe. He sent an artist, Alfred Brennan, to the scene of the
wreck to draw sketches for *Ye Giglampz*'s next issue, which would be
published Sunday.

Farny achieved his scoop. His newspaper contained the first illustrations of the tragedy.[23] Three illustrations were spread over two pages. A large headline beneath the illustrations says, "Burning of the Steamer Pat Rogers. Scenes on the day after the catastrophe." One, with the caption "Fishing for bodies," shows two men in a rowboat pulling a body from the river. Another, captioned "Waiting for identification," depicts two men standing near the river bank looking at the bodies of two passengers that had been pulled ashore. The third illustration shows the Pat Rogers, a smoking half-sunk wreck.

But Farny's scoop badly backfired on him. Because *Ye Giglampz* was a satirical publication, readers presumed it was mocking the horrifying event. Farny had provided no explanation for the paper's abrupt shift from satire to serious breaking news. Readers were outraged. The bar owners and other anti-temperance readers—who formed the bulk of the paper's readership and advertising base—cancelled their subscriptions. Hearn, embarrassed, quit for a fifth time and the other two editorial employees also resigned. But Farny was determined not to shut down his paper yet. The following Sunday, he published a ninth issue that included two Hearn articles that he had written before he quit. Farny wrote an apology and explained that there had been no intention to make light of the Pat Rogers disaster. But it was too late. *Ye Giglampz*, which had been on life-support for almost all of its short existence, was laid mercifully to rest for good.

On the positive side, this ill-fated journalism venture gave Hearn the opportunity to stretch his literary skills by writing some poetic prose fantasies, a genre he more fully developed at a later stage of his career. On the negative side, it wiped out his savings. Hearn hid his chagrin over the demise of *Ye Giglampz* when he later wrote his farcical story for the *Enquirer* about the nine-week fiasco. He ends the story with a final jab at the ill-fated enterprise: "A complete file of *The Giglampz*—nine numbers—is for sale cheap at this office."[24]

Hearn's own set of those issues are preserved at the Public Library of Cincinnati and Hamilton County. In the 1880s, Farny came across that set while browsing a rack in front of a Cincinnati book store. Eight issues of Ye Giglampz, were bound in black pebble cloth. Farney recognized Hearn's handwriting on the front flyleaf. Hearn had writ-

---

[23] Jon Christopher Hughes, ed., *Ye Giglampz*, 1983, 17.
[24] Hearn, "Giglampz!," *Cincinnati Enquirer,* October 4, 1874, 9.

ten, "Reminiscences of an Editorship under difficulties," and signed his name with the date, 1877. Hearn also had written "L. Hearn" or "LF" above some of the stories he had written. Farny bought the set and kept it. In 1944, 28 years after Farny's death, the public library acquired the set from Farny's son, Daniel, for $1,500. He told library officials he had been offered $8,000 by two different out-of-town collectors and that a few years before the Pearl Harbor bombing, the Japanese government expressed an interest in buying the set. But Daniel Farny wanted to work out a deal with the public library to keep the set in Cincinnati. The library bought the set with a private donation.

At the time, library officials thought there had been eight issues of *Ye Giglampz*. But in 1952, they learned that a bookseller was offering to sell issues 3, 4, 6, 7, 8 and 9. The library bought those issues and added the ninth issue to its set. It recovered its expenditure by selling the other duplicate issues.[25] Alas, *Ye Giglampz* didn't became a money-making venture until neither Hearn nor Henry Farny were around to enjoy the benefits.

---

[25] *Ye Giglampz* Archive, Cincinnati Room, Cincinnati & Hamilton County Public Library.

CHAPTER 4

The Ghastly and the Grim

*D*URING HIS CINCINNATI YEARS, Lafcadio Hearn lived primarily as a nocturnal creature. The evening and early morning hours, when the city's seamier side became more active and visible, yielded some of his most sensational stories. Early in his stint with the *Enquirer*, Hearn's editors realized that the night police beat best suited the talents and temperament of their young, eccentric reporter. The horrific crimes and macabre incidents that often occurred after dusk would enable him to exercise his flair for writing about the ghastly and the ghoulish.

Hearn understood the importance of developing good sources on his beat. In his night reporting duties, he got to know not just the captains and the lieutenants in Cincinnati's four police station-houses, but also the patrol officers. For his own protection, he sometimes asked to tag along with the officers who patrolled the most dangerous parts of town, such as Rat Row and Sausage Row along the riverfront and nearby Bucktown, where many African-American levee hands lived and where the Black steamboat workers, longshoremen and stevedores stayed during layovers in Cincinnati. Sometimes Hearn mentioned the patrol officers by name in his stories.

After he had been on the night police beat for more than a year, he profiled 17 police captains and lieutenants in two stories that ran a week apart. In the first story ("Blue and Brass; The Faithful Guardians of Our Treasures and Thresholds"), Hearn acknowledges his debt to them.[1] He calls them "those genial and great-hearted Guardians of the Peace who have done so much during the past year to comfort

---

[1] Lafcadio Hearn, "The Faithful Guardians of Our Treasures and Threshholds! Personal Peculiarities of Some Popular Police Officers," *Cincinnati Enquirer*, April 11, 1875, 9.

the reporter on his nightly round, to furnish him with items of public interest, and to warm his half-frozen toes on cold winter nights by the roaring station-house fires." The two stories are largely "puff pieces" meant to flatter his subjects. But they also illustrate Hearn's growing ability to write insightful personality profiles. He describes their faces and physiques with acute preciseness and humanizes them with details about their personalities and working habits.

In his sketch of Captain Welsh, he writes about how the captain's manner of walking reveals his military background. Welsh "is easily to be distinguished among his comrades by a certain military bearing, which tells of years spent in the cavalry saddle. He walks with that peculiar swinging, ringing step of a soldier accustomed to make his spurs jingle on the pavement. In looking forward, he bends his neck rather than his chest, with the air of one long in the habit of stooping a little over the saddle, in order to get a better look over his horse's ears at the foe; and he involuntarily strides along the street with this bridle-hand up to his chest, while the other muscular limb droops downward as though seeking a saber-hilt to grasp."

Hearn reveled in creating pictures with words. He wanted readers to be able to visualize what he saw. Descriptive writing, which included a person's appearance and manner of speech, he believed, had its place in news stories as well as in feature stories. That's why he worked so hard to gather as much information as he could when covering a news story. Covering sensational crimes proved to be Hearn's forte. The drama, emotion and mystery connected with crimes—especially violent ones—stirred his curiosity and imagination. He wasn't satisfied with simply learning what and how a crime had been committed. He wanted to know the motivation behind the actions of those who committed the crimes and the impact on the crime victims and the community. With the zeal of a police investigator, he questioned suspects, witnesses and anyone else he thought might give him pertinent information.

On the morning of September 30, 1874, a murder-attempted suicide occurred that involved the death of a 2-year-old girl and marital infidelity by both her mother and her father. The tragedy provided Hearn with all the drama and pathos of an Edgar Allen Poe horror story and he took full advantage of it.

Julia Perkins had sliced the throat of her 2-year-old daughter,

Clara, with a jagged piece of glass in the bathroom of their home, carried the little girl's bloody, fully-dressed body into a bedroom and laid
it on the bed. She laid down beside the body, slit her own throat and
waited to die. The night before, her husband, Charles, had spied on
her and confirmed his suspicions that she was having an affair with
his business partner who lived outside Cincinnati and occasionally
stayed at their house when he had to come into the city. Charles, who
had kept a mistress with Julia's knowledge for more than a year, confronted her and his partner. After an all-night argument, he told her
she had to leave the house the next morning. After both men left that
morning, Julia was supposed to wait for a carriage to pick up her and
Clara and take them to her father's house in Medina, Ohio. Her father
would take them to a train station, where they would catch a train to a
friend's house. But after her husband and his partner left their house,
Julia dismissed the maid, shut all the windows and turned on the gas
without lighting it. She killed Clara and then tried to kill herself. But
to her chagrin, she was rescued before she died.

Hamilton County Coroner Dr. Patrick F. Maley, a prime news
source for Hearn throughout his Cincinnati years, held the inquest at
the Perkins' home. Maley, the inquest jury and Hearn went upstairs
to see little Clara's body and to listen to Maley gently interrogate
Julia. Hearn used telling details to stir his readers' emotions. Julia
said she killed her daughter because she planned to kill herself and
didn't want to leave her behind. Hearn describes Clara's body still in
her blood-stained clothing: "She was clad in a dress that had been
white Marseilles, exquisitely embroidered, and with lace at the hem.
But only a small portion of the front of the skirt revealed what color
it had been. It was crimson down each sleeve to the very cuff. It was
crimson in the dainty waist. The delicate underclothing, the fancifully
worked pantalettes, and the neat stockings, the pretty pink garters and
close-fitting boots were deeply blood-dyed, as was also, as shown by
the Coroner's investigation, the silken under-vest. Despite the frightful, gaping wound in the throat, the little body was beautiful. The
golden ringlets were deeper tinted here and there than nature made
them, but still fell gracefully over the fine brow to the blood-stained
ribbon which bound them; the blue eyes were half open, the little lips
just parted enough to show pearly teeth, and the tiny hand half folded

and whiter than marble because of the exhausted veins."[2]

Based on the mother's testimony at the inquest, Hearn narrates Clara's murder in chilling detail: "(She) armed herself for the terrible work by breaking the glass that covered the little ivory clock, and grasping in her right hand one of the cruelly sharp fragments. She then knelt down near the washstand, and, calling little Clara to her in the dark, deliberately proceeded to cut the child's throat. She tells us the child prayed, and that amid the gurgling rush of the arterial blood, several times after came the appeal, 'Mamma! Oh, mamma!'"

Hearn wrote three stories about this tragedy in a week, each one delving further into the messy domestic strife that led to Clara's murder. He interviewed dozens of the Perkins' relatives, friends and neighbors. He even talked to Charles Perkins' mistress. As heartrending and exhaustive as his coverage of this case was, it served as a mere prelude to the stories he wrote a month later about an even grislier crime.

A raging fire destroyed the Werk candle factory near Findlay Street, west of Central Avenue, in an area just north of downtown, on Saturday, Nov 16, 1875. A story about the fire ran in the Enquirer the next day. On Sunday morning, police discovered a man's body at the Freiberg Tannery, on Livingston Street and Gamble Alley, across Findlay Street from the candle factory. Hearn was in the vicinity at the time, possibly to write a second-day story about the fire focusing on suspicions of arson. But when word spread about the discovery of the burnt remains of a body in the tannery furnace, Hearn latched onto the story. At first, some thought there might be a connection between the candle factory fire and the body. The more details Hearn learned about the murder in his first hour at the tannery site, the more excited he became about its news value. The hideous nature of the crime and the sordid circumstances that led to it might been too outlandish even for Poe.

Young German-born George Schilling, whose remains were found in the furnace, had been a watchman at the tannery, located in an area known as the Tallow District. Immense candle and soap factories, slaughterhouses and hog pens dominated the narrow streets and alleys, often filling the neighborhood with a sickening stench. Primarily German immigrants populated the area. For a time, Schil-

---

[2]Hearn, "A Motherly Murder," *Cincinnati Enquirer*, October 1, 1874, 4.

ling boarded with Andreas Egner, who owned a saloon and boarding house connected by a gate to the tannery. Egner had a buxom, pretty and flirtatious 15-year-old daughter, Julia, who worked at her father's saloon primarily to lure in male customers. Without her father's knowledge, Julia had flings with a few of the men, including the 25-year-old Schilling. One night, Egner caught Schilling with Julia in her bedroom and chased him out of the house. After that episode, Schilling ate his meals elsewhere and slept in a room in a shed at the tannery. When Julia became pregnant shortly afterward, her father beat her and banished her to the outhouse. She became ill with cancer, and died on August 6 in a hospital along with her unborn baby. The Egners believed Schilling had impregnated her. The day Julia died, Andreas and his son, Fred, tracked down Schilling and beat him with oak barrel staves. They might have killed him if bystanders hadn't intervened. Andreas Egner vowed he would kill Schilling at some later date.

Late on the evening of November 16, Egner fulfilled his promise with the help of his son, Fred, and his friend, George Rufer, who blamed Schilling for being fired from his job at the tannery earlier that day. As they talked that night in Egner's bar, Rufer suggested they go to the tanyard, where Schilling was on his job as watchman, and attack him. While Fred restrained the watchdogs, Rufer crept behind Schilling in the tannery's stable and slugged him with a club. After he hit him a second time, Andreas Egner thrust a five-pronged pitchfork into his thigh. He jabbed the pitchfork into his abdomen repeatedly while Rufer pounded his head with the club. "Oh God, you're killing me!," Schilling cried. Then he moaned and stopped struggling. Andreas and Rufer dragged Schilling's body about 100 feet and shoved it into a furnace in the boiler room and ran away.

Enquirer readers learned of the crime's nauseating details in Hearn's lengthy story on Monday, November 18, the day after Schilling's body was found.[3] The weekday front pages practically never carried local news stories. But on this day, Hearn's story, accompanied by five woodcut illustrations, dominated the front page. The first and largest of the nine headlines leading into the story read, "Violent Cremation." The technology to reproduce photographs in newspapers didn't exist yet.

---

[3] Hearn, "Violent Cremation," *Cincinnati Enquirer*, November 9, 1874, 1.

Woodcut illustrations usually accompanied ads and occasionally a local front page Sunday feature story, rarely news stories. The illustrations with Hearn's story included portraits of the three suspected killers, a sketch of the exterior of the tannery buildings along with a diagram of the interior rooms. These were drawn by Hearn's friends, Henry Farny and Frank Duveneck. Hearn himself sketched a fifth illustration showing Schilling's remains. Considering the *Enquirer's* small news staff on Sundays, Hearn himself may have asked them to illustrate the story and also might have lobbied for its placement on Page One.

Before the drawings could be printed in newspapers, they had to be engraved into wood. Farny and Duveneck likely created their own woodcuts, and Farny probably made the woodcut for Hearn's drawing. Hearn's name is misspelled as "Hearne" on the illustration. Much to Farny's annoyance, his name often was misspelled as "Farney." He may have purposely added the extra "e" to Hearn as a playful jab at his friend.

To gather information for his story, Hearn examined the stable and the furnace, went with Farny and Duveneck to the nearby Oliver Street police station house, where the three suspects were being held and where Schilling's remains had been taken. Hearn occasionally asked Duveneck to serve as his interpreter when he had to interview those whose first language was German. Coroner Dr. Patrick F. Maley empaneled a jury and conducted an inquest there. Some hours later, Hearn went with Maley to the undertaker's establishment on Sixth Street, where the corpse had been transported. Maley opened the coffin and allowed Hearn to view the burnt remains.

Hearn's story created a sensation locally and nationally. *Enquirer* newsboys sold thousands of copies on the streets. Newspapers across the country ran excerpts of the story. Hearn wrote the story as a dramatic narrative, sparing readers of none of the crime's horrifying details. At this time, American journalism had no established code of ethics. As a result, reporters sometimes took great liberties in their stories and would speculate about a crime suspect's guilt or innocence and include all kinds of conjecture about what had happened and the character of the people involved.

In his story, Hearn surmised that Schilling may have been alive when he was thrust into the furnace. "There is a horrible probability," he writes, "that the wretched victim was forced into the furnace alive, and suffered all the agonies of the bitterest death which man can die, while wedged in the flaming fire. His teeth were so terribly clenched that more than one spectator of the hideous skull declared that only the most frightful agony could have set those jaws together." Further investigation proved later that Schilling had died before being put into the furnace.

No detail was too gruesome for Hearn's story. He describes Schilling's corpse with excruciating precision: "On lifting the coffin-lid a powerful and penetrating odor, strongly resembling the smell of burnt beef, yet heavier and fouler, filled the room and almost sickened the spectators. But the sight of the black remains was far more sickening. Laid upon the clean white lining of the coffin they resembled great shapeless lumps of half-burnt bituminous coal than aught else at the first hurried glance; and only a closer investigation could enable a strong-stomached observer to detect their ghastly character—masses of crumbling human bones, strung together by half-burnt sinews, or glued one upon another by a hideous adhesion of half-molten flesh, boiled brains and jellied blood mingled with coal. The skull had burst like a shell in the fierce furnace-heat; and the whole upper portion seemed as though it has been blown out by the steam from the boiling and bubbling brains...The brain had all boiled away, save a small wasted lump at the base of the skull about the size of a lemon. It was crisped and still warm to the touch. On pushing the finger through the crisp, the interior felt about the consistency of banana fruit, and the yellow fibers seemed to writhe like worms in the Coroner's hands. The eyes were cooked to bubbled crisps in the blackened sockets, and the bones of the nose were gone, leaving a hideous hole."

With assistance from at least one other reporter, Hearn covered the tanning yard murder case relentlessly, writing seven stories in the next seven days. No other Cincinnati newspaper approached the breadth and depth of Hearn's coverage. At the beginning of his second story about the case ("Killed and Cremated," November 10), Hearn reports that the previous day's *Enquirer*, "containing the fullest details of the terrible tragedy, with illustrations, was in tremendous demand. It sold even after the afternoon papers came out with reports of the inquest, and thousands of extra copies went off day and evening, and yet there is no cessation of the call for it. Around the scene of the murder hundreds of morbid people hung all day, many of them with

Enquirers in their hands, comparing, with a universally satisfactory result, the picture with the reality."[4]

After this self-congratulatory opening, Hearn relates the testimony at the coroner's inquest from tannery owner Henry Freiberg, who talked about Schilling and Rufer's disdain for each other, and from John Hollerbach, who, while walking by the tannery, heard the scuffle and the desperate shouts of Schilling for help. Hearn and possibly another *Enquirer* reporter interviewed George Rufer in his jail cell. While maintaining his innocence, Rufer implicated the Egners and said they tried to draw him into their murder plot so they could pin the blame on him.

The next day, the *Enquirer* ran 14 stacked headlines above Hearn's story ("It Is Out!/The Terrible Tannery Tragedy/Confessions of Fred Egner/How the Horrible Deed Was Done…").[5] The story includes young Egner's testimony at the inquest implicating only Rufer and then his confession later in the day admitting his and his father's involvement in the crime. The story climaxes with Egner repeating his confession for Hearn and other *Enquirer* reporters and then confessing again after his father was brought in to sit next to him and hear what he had to say. "The painful and dramatic interview ended," Hearn writes, "by Andreas Egner springing to his feet, wildly declaring that the boy was crazy, and that further talk was useless. When the door closed on him Fred quietly remarked: 'No, I am not crazy. Nor is he.'" This story also contains a moving profile of Julia Egner, the 15-year-old whose death precipitated Schilling's murder. From information gathered from Egners' neighbors and others who knew the family, Hearn wrote about Andreas Egner's gross mistreatment of his daughter before and after her pregnancy. He shows her to be as much a victim of her father as Schilling was.

Hearn continued his blanket coverage of the case over the next five days. Highlights included:

> The revelation that Rufer had served three years in the state penitentiary for horse-stealing, had beaten his current wife and had another wife and child in Louisville.

---

[4]Hearn, "Killed and Created," *Cincinnati Enquirer*, November 10, 1874, 8.
[5]Hearn, "It is Out. The Terrible Tannery Tragedy," *Cincinnati Enquirer*, November 11, 1874, 4.

Rufer's emotional encounter with his 15-month-old daughter in jail. "Then the icy man, who had remained cynically calm through all the investigation, all the cross-questioning, all the shame of being exhibited to the curious crowd a human monster—who had never changed the color or moved a muscle when all but he trembled with excitement, fairly broke down. He reached out his hands to his little one through the grating and kissed it over and over again with a passionate tenderness which few could have believed him to possess. then he sat down and cried like a woman."[6]

Mrs. Rufer's mental breakdown and her attempt to kill her daughter shortly after returning home from her heart-wrenching visit with her husband at the jail. She slammed her daughter face-first against a large trunk and was about to do it again when someone stopped her. A short time later after she quieted down, she threw the girl between a door jamb and a closet. The girl, with cuts and bruises on her face, was taken to a hospital and treated and then at least temporarily removed from her mother's custody.

The inquest jury's finding that Rufer and Andreas Egner caused Schilling's death and that Fred Egner had been an accomplice.

A story capturing the repulsive atmosphere of the Tallow District, where Schilling's murder had occurred, a neighborhood of German immigrants, soap and candle factories, tanneries, hog pens and slaughterhouses Hearn refers to the area as "a quarter of shambles." A butcher's table was called a shamble. Hearn's phrase means a place of slaughter or carnage, referring not only to the animal slaughterhouses but also, of course, to Schilling's murder. In just a few sentences, Hearn encapsulates the gritty character and difficult lives of the Tallow District workers. "Amid these scenes and smells lives and labors a large and strangely healthy population of brawny butchers, sinewy coopers, muscular tanners—a foreign population speaking a foreign tongue, and living the life of the Fatherland—broad-shouldered men from Pomerania;

---

[6] Hearn, "The Furnace Fiends," *Cincinnati Enquirer*, November 14, 1874, 8.

tall, fair-haired emigrants from Bohemia; dark, brawny people from Bavaria; rough-featured fellows from the region of the Hartz Mountains; men speaking the strange dialects of strange provinces. They are mostly rough of aspect, rude of manner and ruddy of feature. The greater part of them labor in tanneries, slaughter-houses and soap factories, receiving small salaries upon which an American workman could not support his family, and doing work which Americans instinctively shrink from—slaughtering, quartering, flaying—handling bloody entrails and bloody hides—making slaughter their daily labor, familiarizing themselves with death and agony, and diurnally drenching themselves in blood."[7]

Five months later, Hearn wrote a short story about rumors that the Freiberg tannery was haunted.[8] Charges against Fred Egner were dropped, but his father and Rufer were convicted of murder and were sentenced to life in prison. After the elder Egner became deathly ill in prison, the governor pardoned him to allow him to die at home. But he recovered and lived several more years as a free man before dying in 1889.[9]

The Tanyard murder stories catapulted Hearn to star status in journalism circles, although the general public didn't know him because newspaper stories contained no bylines then. The *Enquirer* raised his salary from $20 to $25 a week and granted him more freedom in choosing his stories.

Shortly after he wrapped up the series of stories about Schilling's murder, Hearn wrote a memorable story about grave-robbers or resurrectionists, as they were sometimes called. Hearn persuaded Maley to go with him to question the sexton of Potter's Field, a pauper's cemetery, about the large number of grave robberies that had been occurring there. The robbers would sell the stolen bodies to a medical college.

---

[7] Hearn, "Quarter of Shambles," *Cincinnati Enquirer*, November 15, 1874, 1. September 18, 2010.

[8] Hearn, "A Goblin Tale. The Scene of the Tan-Yard Horror Haunted," *Cincinnati Enquirer*, April 10, 1875, 8.

[9] *Murders by Gaslight*, a blog concerning notable 19th Century American murders, http://www.murderbygaslight.com/.

In this story, Hearn skillfully fuses investigative reporting with captivating story-telling.[10] Sexton Shafer was suspected of allowing graves to be robbed in exchange for money. Hearn relates the dialogue between Maley and Shafer that reveals serious flaws in the cemetery's operation. The interrogation induces Shafer to admit that he gives no receipts for bodies received and doesn't alert authorities when bodies are stolen. He also confesses that he buries empty coffins after the bodies that were in them are stolen.

"But don't you bury all the bodies sent there," Maley asked.

"I buries all the coffins!," Shafer replied.

"Not all the bodies?"

"No; because they steals 'em afore I can bury 'em."

"How's that?"

"Why, often more bodies comes here'n I can dig graves for in one day. So I have to leave 'em lie over till the next day; and, in the meantime, they steals 'em."

"But where do you leave them?"

"I leaves 'em, coffins and all, right by the grave."

"And if you find the coffin empty in the morning, what do you do?"

"Bury the box, of course. I gets a dollar and a quarter for every one I buries; and it's just as much trouble to bury a full coffin as an empty one."

While Hearn's journalism career was progressing smoothly, his personal life was in turmoil. Before he began working for the *Enquirer*, Hearn moved into a boarding house at the northeast corner of McFarland and Plum streets where a beautiful light-skinned African-American, Alethea "Mattie" Foley, worked as a cook. During the evenings, she and Hearn would talk, and before long, he fell in love with her. Foley had been born a slave in 1854 on a farm near Augusta, Ky., about 45 miles upriver from Cincinnati. When she was freed after the Civil War, she worked for several families in the vicinity of Maysville, Ky. In 1868, she had a son out of wedlock by a Scotsman named Louis Anderson. Between 1869 and 1872, she moved to Cincinnati with her son, William L. Anderson.[11]

---

[10]Hearn, "Golgotha. A Pilgrimage to Potter's Field. The Sexton-Guardian of Nameless Graves. His Secret Alliance With the Ghouls," *Cincinnati Enquirer*, November 29, 1874, 1.

[11]O. W. Frost, *Young Hearn* (Tokyo: Hokuseido Press, 1958), 120-121.

The romance between Foley and Hearn blossomed and developed into a long-term relationship, risking the wrath of a society that condemned interracial unions. Out of a sense of chivalry and rebellion, Hearn wanted to marry Foley even though Ohio forbade interracial marriages. Foley hesitated about agreeing to marry him because of the potential social backlash and her feeling that he was motivated more by a sense of duty than love. Foley finally gave in to his dogged persistence and consented to marriage. Hearn asked a newspaper colleague, George Mortimer Roe, to help secure a marriage license, but knowing Foley was Black, Roe refused to do it. Without a marriage license, Hearn and Foley were married on June 14, 1874, by the Rev. John King, an Episcopal minister, in the home of Lottie Cleneay, a Black woman who lived on the north side of Longworth Street, two doors east of Plum Street. Another Black minister had refused to marry them because he worried he might get into trouble. Although the law didn't recognize the marriage, Lafcadio and Mattie considered themselves husband and wife. They lived for a while at 114 Longworth St., next door to the old Adams express stables.

By entering into a marriage that violated the social norms, Hearn was unwittingly imitating his father, who had breached the cultural norms of Rosa Cassimati's birthplace and family by wooing and marrying her. Just as his father's marriage ended unhappily, so did Hearn's.

Seven months after they wed, Lafcadio and Mattie decided to live separately. The psychological strain caused by being in a marriage that society scorned and outlawed took a heavy toll on both of them. In addition, their personalities and lifestyles clashed. Hearn could be temperamental, taciturn and irritable, while Foley could be capricious and irresponsible. Because of Hearn's long working hours, they saw very little of each other. After their separation, Hearn gave her $5 a week and tried to help her as much as he could. Her behavior became more erratic. She lost some of her clothes and other belongings, mishandled money and got into violent arguments. In one of her fights, she threatened to slash a woman with a razor. Hearn had encouraged her to move to the country with her son. She did move away briefly, but returned to live in Bucktown. Hearn feared for her safety and worried that she might resort to prostitution.

During this troubled period, Hearn expressed his sadness and pain in a letter to his trusted friend, Henry Watkin. He explained to

Watkin that he felt more comfortable telling him of his distress in writing than in conversation.

"I have been much more troubled about Mattie than you have any idea of," he wrote, "and the prospect of leaving her to ruin herself is something I can scarcely bear. Whatever I may have said or done, I love her,—more I fancy than I will ever love any woman; and somehow the lower she falls, the fonder I feel of her. I think I have been unjust to her—unjust in marrying her at all—lifting her up only to let her fall lower than ever. Had I never taken her, she would suffer far less in going to the devil…She is so utterly helpless, and yet so proud and willful; that I don't know what to do, except to cry about her."[12]

For some months, John R. McLean, *Enquirer* publisher, had been receiving pressure from a group of politicians to get rid of Hearn. They had been offended by Hearn's critical attitude toward Christianity and what he regarded as its tepid efforts at social reform. They also were disturbed by his exposes of religious hypocrites, spiritualists, and various charlatans; his anti-temperance writings in *Ye Giglampz*; and his sympathy for Cincinnati's social outcasts, especially African-Americans. The *Enquirer* was a Democratic paper and Hearn's racial and social views aligned more with the Republicans of his day. Before the Civil War, the Democratic Party was pro-slavery, while the Republican Party was anti-slavery. After the war, the Democratic Party opposed equal rights for African-Americans, and the Republican Party supported them.

Cincinnati played an important role in the Underground Railroad in the pre-Civil War era and helped free thousands of slaves. But, at the same time, the city as well as its state contained powerful pro-slavery and anti-Black forces. In the early 19th century, the state enacted a series of so-called "Black Laws" designed to make it difficult for Black people to permanently settle in the state, to deprive them of the right to attend public schools and to relegate them to second-class citizenship.

Cincinnati's economy depended significantly upon selling manufacturing goods and other products to the Southern states. As a result, many city residents wanted to cooperate with the South by tolerating slavery and returning fugitive slaves to their owners.

During the first half of the 19th century, there were many out-

---

[12]Elizabeth Stevenson, *Lafcadio Hearn*, 68-69.

breaks of violence against Cincinnati's Black residents. One of the worst occurred in 1829, when a horde of whites, alarmed by the rapid rise in the number of African-Americans in Cincinnati, rampaged for three days, attacking and sometimes killing Black people in their homes. Fearing for their lives, about 1,000 Black people moved out of Cincinnati. In the racial violence during 1836, white rioters attacked African-Americans and abolitionists and destroyed the printing press of James Birney, who was using it to publish his abolitionist newspaper, *The Philanthropist*.

Following the Civil War, the Northern Democrats sympathized with the South and opposed equal rights for African-Americans. The Republican Party opposed racial segregation and supported equal rights. In the post-Civil War years before and during Hearn's tenure with The *Enquirer*, the newspaper's editorials clearly reflected the Democrats' opposition to any form of racial integration and civil rights for Black people.

The *Enquirer* opposed Congressional ratification of the Fifteenth Amendment giving African-American men the right to vote. It also castigated Cincinnati's people of color who were planning a public celebration of the ratification. Stated a February 9, 1870, editorial: "Nothing can permanently be done without the assent of a majority of the people, and by people we mean white people. They (the negroes) may rejoice in their new-fledged liberty and disport themselves like butterflies, but erelong a killing frost will overtake them and cast them down from their lofty and extravagant flights."

In a February 22, 1872, editorial, the *Enquirer* tried to justify the formation of the Ku Klux Klan and other white vigilante groups in the South by claiming they were needed to protect the whites from the former slaves. It acknowledged that these groups were illegal and violent, but said they "had a restraining and purifying effect upon the body politic." The *Enquirer* opposed a federal law prohibiting hotel-owners, restaurants and entertainment establishments from refusing to admit Black people. A March 3, 1875, editorial commented: "The law apparently affords opportunities to low, ignorant and vicious negroes to annoy white persons by thrusting their companionship upon them undesired at public gatherings…"

The *Enquirer* wasn't a vigilante rag. It was a popular, respected, mainstream newspaper, and a large segment of Cincinnatians agreed with these views and didn't want a racially integrated society. Hearn's stories humanizing Black people forced white readers to meet and learn about people they didn't want in their schools, churches or taverns. Hearn knew he risked upsetting some Cincinnatians by writing these stories, but he felt a moral and journalistic obligation to do it. But nothing he wrote was nearly as controversial as his marriage to Mattie Foley.

As word of this marriage slowly spread through the city, it provided more fodder for his critics. Using the marriage to Mattie as a pretext, McLean finally fired him in early August, 1875. Crestfallen, Hearn walked from the *Enquirer* offices to Vine Street bridge over the Miami Canal with the apparent intention of leaping into the canal and drowning himself. Concerned about him, his friend, Charley Johnson, followed him to the canal and stopped him from jumping.[13] Whether Hearn really intended to commit suicide is uncertain. He was a good swimmer, and the canal wasn't very deep, although the bacteria in the water might have made him very ill.

After an angst-filled week or two, the *Enquirer's* chief rival, the *Cincinnati Commercial*, hired Hearn for $20 a week, $5 less than he earned at the *Enquirer*. The *Commercial's* city editor Edwin Henderson had admired Hearn's work and, unfazed by the gossip about Hearn's marriage, recommended that *Commercial* owner and editor Murat Halstead add him to the staff.

Halstead, who had been born in 1829 on a farm in southern Butler County, north of Cincinnati. He graduated from college, became a lawyer and began writing for Cincinnati area newspapers. The *Commercial* hired him as a reporter in 1853. Within a year, he became news editor and part-owner of the newspaper. Over the next 15 years, he played a vital role in improving the quality of the *Commercial*, broadening its influence and doubling its monetary value. Halstead personally covered the political party presidential conventions in 1860 and reported on several Civil War battles. In 1867, he acquired a controlling interest in the newspaper and became its editor. Like Cockerill, his *Enquirer* counterpart, Halstead was bright and ambitious. He appreciated good writing and knew Hearn had a special talent that would enhance his newspaper.

---

[13] Ibid., 126-127.

CHAPTER 5

Race and Rancor

*A*BOUT TWO MONTHS AFTER HEARN began working for the *Commercial*, the *Enquirer* offered to reinstate him. But having vowed never to work for the *Enquirer* again, he immediately declined. He had been deeply hurt and humiliated by the firing and felt no inclination to return, even though his salary would be $5 a week higher than at the *Commercial*.

Oddly, Hearn decided to include Mattie Foley in one of his early stories for the *Commercial*. Without revealing her name or her connection to him, Hearn wrote a narrative purportedly in her words about her experiences with haunted houses and ghosts.[1] The story, which strongly reflects Hearn's prose style, is one of his earliest stories about ghosts, a topic he frequently wrote about throughout his career. In this story, Hearn describes her as a "healthy, well built country girl."

She says, "People call me a medium, sometimes, and ask me to sit in dark circles and help to call up spirits. I have always refused—do you wonder at it? I tell you the truth, sir, when I say that far from refusing to leave the dead alone, I would be only too happy if they would leave me alone." Maybe Hearn wrote this story as a gibe at the *Enquirer*, knowing that some of his former colleagues would realize he was writing about Mattie. He might have written it just because he thought her ghost stories were interesting in themselves. Even so, given his anger at the *Enquirer*, it's hard not to believe part of his motive was to taunt his former employer.

During his two years with the *Commercial*, Hearn's finest Cin-

---

[1]Lafcadio Hearn, "Some Strange Experience. The Reminiscences of a Ghost-seer, Being the Result of a Chat on the Kitchen Stairs," *Cincinnati Commercial,* September 26, 1875, 3.

cinnati writing appeared in his stories about the African-Americans living in Bucktown, an area east of Broadway in between Sixth and Seventh streets. Bucktown contained a mixture of dilapidated brick and frame residential buildings, along with bars, dance-houses, and brothels or "ranches," as they were called. Black levee and steamboat laborers, known then as roustabouts, and their Black and white mistresses comprised the greater part of Bucktown's population and clientele. Many of the Black people were former slaves who had escaped from their owners or moved to Cincinnati after being freed at the conclusion of the Civil War. Before 1865, Bucktown had been notorious for its violent crimes. In the years since, police had gained the upper hand and had sent many of Bucktown's worst criminals to penitentiaries or to the Cincinnati Workhouse. By the time Hearn explored Bucktown in the mid-1879s, it had been somewhat tamed, although it was still full of vices, thievery and other crimes. One police officer told Hearn that virtually all the women who lived in Bucktown carried knives.[2] During his expeditions in Bucktown, Hearn partook of some its vices, including the brothels.

He once went to a Bucktown brothel with Jere Cochran, a fellow reporter at the *Commercial*. Before going to separate upstairs rooms with prostitutes, they agreed to meet downstairs at a certain time. When Cochran later went downstairs, Hearn wasn't there. After waiting for a while, he got impatient and went back upstairs. To his surprise, he found Hearn in a room with the African-American woman Cochran had been with. The woman was standing in the middle of the room naked as Hearn admiringly walked slowly around her, his good eye inches from her body, as if he were admiring a Greek statue.[3]

Some of Hearn's friends and a few of his early biographers considered his attraction to Black and Asian women either a moral failing or an indication that he felt unworthy of white women. "The fancy for mulattos, Creoles and Orientals, which he displayed all his life," writes Ida H. Kennard, "is most likely to be counted for as an inheritance from his Arabian and Oriental ancestors on his mother's side. He but took up the dropped threads of his barbaric ancestry."[4] Besides being

[2]Hearn, "Levee Life," *Cincinnati Commercial*, March 17, 1876, 2.

[3]Edward Larocque Tinker, *Lafcadio Hearn's American Days* (New York: Dodd, Mead and Company, 1924), 23-24.

[4]Ida H. Kennard, *Lafcadio Hearn* (D. Appleton and Company, 1912), 84.

inaccurate about the ancestry of Hearn's mother, Kennard displays a racism common among people who couldn't conceive that a white man could be find a Black or an Asian woman more attractive than a white woman.

In his August 22, 1875, story, Hearn recounts a night wandering through Bucktown with two police officers who were searching for a female thief.[5] He writes: "Bucktown is nothing if not seen by gaslight. Then it presents a most striking effect of fantastic chiar'oscuro; its frames seem to own doresque facades—a mass of many-angled shadows in the background, relieved in front by long gleams of light on some obtruding post or porch or wooden stairway; its doorways yawn in blackness, like entrances to some interminable labyrinth; the jagged outline of its dwellings against the sky seems the part of some mighty wreck; its tortuous ways are filled with long shadows of the weirdest goblin form. The houses with lighted windows appear to possess an animate individuality, a character, a sentient consciousness, a face; and to stare with pale-yellow eyes and hungry door—mouth all agape at the lonely passer-by, as though desiring to devour him."

Hearn had been in Bucktown many times before this, sometimes with police officers, sometimes accompanied by his friend, Henry Watkin, and others. In this story, he relates fascinating stories about the people and places they encounter on this nighttime trek. They visit the house of Mary William, "notorious as a panel den, a hive of thieves, a resort for criminals and roughs of the lowest grade…Mary Williams and a Black girl, with a red bandana turban, receive the patrolmen with a smile and a note of recognition. Mary is on her best behavior, having escaped a long sentence but the week before through the failure of a prosecuting witness to appear…Mary swore 'to her just God' that no one was concealed about the premises; but the policemen lighted their candles and proceeded to examine every nook and corner of the building, under beds and tables, behind doors, and in shadowy places where giant spiders had spun gray webs of appalling size and remarkable tenacity."

One Saturday morning just before sunrise, two police officers pulled a drunken Black man from the Ohio River at the foot of Broadway. They brought him, dripping wet but emerging from his alcoholic

---

[5]Hearn, "Pariah People," *Cincinnati Commercial*, August 22, 1875, 3.

stupor, to the Hammond Street station. When the man said his name was Albert Jones, the police sergeant said, "Albert Jones! That man can imitate the whistle of any boat on the Ohio or Mississippi River."

Delighted to be recognized for his singular talent, Jones cupped his hands around his mouth and proceeded to imitate the whistles of seven steamboats, which he named, and countless towboats. Hearn witnessed this on one of his nightly rounds. It inspired him to write a story ("A Child of the Levee") of great charm and lyrical beauty about Cincinnati riverfront life.[6]

He writes: "All along the Rows there indeed dwell many who know by heart the whistle of every boat on the Ohio; dusky women, whose ears have been trained by rough but strong affection, as well as old stevedores who have lived by the shore from infancy, and wonderingly watched in their slave childhood the great white vessels panting on the river's breast. But Albert Jones offers the typical exhibition of this peculiar faculty. The steamboats seem to his rudely poetic fancy vast sentient beings, as the bells of Notre Dame to the imagination of Quasimodo, and their voices come to his ear as mighty living cries, when they call to each other across the purple gloom of the summer night—shouting cheery welcomes in sweetly-deep thunder-tines, or shrieking long, wild warning. Other melody he seems to have little conception of—neither the songs of the stevedore nor the vibrant music of banjo-thrumming. The long echoes of the steam calls and the signal whistles of the night patrolmen—sounds most familiar of all others, indeed, to those who live on the levee-slope—form the only chords of melody in this little musical world. Possibly to him the Song of Steam is the sweetest of all musical sounds, only as a great tone-record of roustabout memories—each boat whistle, deep or shrill or mellow, recalling some past pleasure or pain in the history of a life spent along the broad highway of brown water flowing to the Crescent City of the South. Each prolonged tone awakes to fresh life some little half-forgotten chapter in the simple history of this Child of the Levee—some noisy but harmless night revel, some broil, some old love story, some dark story of steamboat disaster, a vessel in flames, a swim for life. Probably the first sound which startled his ears in babyhood was the voice of a steamboat passing by his birth place; and

---

[6]Hearn, "A Child of the Levee," *Cincinnati Commercial*, June 27, 1876, 4.

possibly the same voice may serve for his requiem some night when patrolmen do not happen to hear a sudden splash in the dark river. We left him slumbering in his wet and muddy rags, dreaming, perchance, fantastic dreams of a strange craft that never whistles, and is without name—a vessel gliding noiselessly by unfamiliar banks to a weird port where objects cast no shadows, and even dreams are dead."

Hearn wrote many other memorable personality portraits of the Black denizens of Bucktown and the nearby Sausage and Rat Rows. While his writing isn't completely free of racial stereotyping, Hearn's portrayal of Black people generally transcends the racist attitudes of that era. He neither romanticized nor denigrated them. On the whole, he depicted his African-American subjects as full-blooded individuals with virtues and flaws, trying to survive in oppressive living conditions by legitimate and illegitimate means.

There was Dolly,[7] an illiterate but proud woman who resorted to prostitution to raise bail for her jailed boyfriend and doted on a little boy who had been adopted by a neighbor; Henry "Ol' Man" Pickett,[8] a strong-willed but kindly tavern-keeper who often fed and sheltered people who might otherwise have starved or died from exposure to the harsh winter weather; Auntie Porter,[9] who, throughout her long life, cared for and raised babies abandoned by their mothers; and Jot,[10] a voodoo man who lived in a dark basement apartment where his clients came to buy spells for snaring lovers or for avenging enemies and to pay for charms to guard them against danger and for talismans to ward off evil spirits.

As Hearn delved deeply into Cincinnati's African-American subculture, he discovered its jubilant and tender aspects as well as its sordid and sorrowful ones. The riverfront's Black stevedores and longshoremen and their wives and mistresses sought relief from the tensions and miseries of their impoverished lives through the nightly music-making and dancing in the dingy Bucktown and riverfront bars and ballrooms. To the accompaniment of banjos, fiddles and tambourines, the patrons sang songs they learned during their bondage south of the Ohio River, rhythmically slapped their thighs (known

---

[7]Hearn, "Dolly/An Idyl of the Levee," *Cincinnati Commercial*, August 27, 1876, 6.

[8]Hearn, "Ole Man Pickett," *Cincinnati Enquirer*, February 21, 1875, 1.

[9]Hearn, "Mrs. Lucy Porter," *Cincinnati Commercial*, July 14, 1876, 8.

[10]Hearn, "Jot/The Haunt of the Obi-Man," *Cincinnati Commercial*, October 22, 1876, 2.

as "patting juba"), and pounded their feet on the wooden or earthen floors as they swayed, shimmied, whirled and jigged until the early morning hours.

Hearn appreciated the artistry of this music and wrote down the lyrics of many of the roustabouts' songs. With pen and notebook in hand, he would approach certain roustabouts and ask them to sing several river songs so that he could record the words. Occasionally, he would induce their cooperation by giving them cigars or drinks. When his friend, Henry Krehbiel, then the music critic for the *Cincinnati Gazette*, was with him, he sometimes would notate the music for a particular song. Hearn fervently believed this music was as worthy of preservation as the classical and popular music being heard at the fancier venues uptown.

Writing down these songs' lyrics in Black dialect and publishing them in some of his newspaper stories, Hearn served the valuable role of folklorist. One of the most popular songs among the roustabouts was called "Limber Jim" or "Shiloh." It had so many lyrics that it took 20 minutes to sing the whole song. The only person in Cincinnati who knew all the lyrics was a Black laborer who lived in Bucktown and whose mastery of the song earned him the nickname Limber Jim. At Hearn's request, Limber Jim sang all the verses for him one night. Hearn jotted down the verses and included some of the less risqué ones in an October 1, 1876, *Cincinnati Commercial* newspaper story.

Hearn discovered that many of the Black singers who performed in the dance halls and bars along the Ohio River levee and in Bucktown could sing Irish songs in a convincing Irish brogue. In that same story, Hearn described how one Cincinnati police officer of Irish descent listened appreciatively as a Black man named Jim Delaney sang an Irish ditty known as "The Hat Me Father Wore." Although Delaney "had little or no Irish blood in his veins," Hearn writes, he would "certainly make a reputation for Irish specialties in a minstrel troupe; his mimicry of the Irish character is absolutely perfect, and he possesses a voice of great flexibility, depth and volume."

In a story published in the *Cincinnati Commercial*, Hearn delineates the raw power and beauty of the roustabouts' songs and dances.[11] He includes portions of lyrics for several songs that aren't too risqué

---

[11] Hearn, "Levee Life," *Cincinnati Commercial*, March 17, 1876, 2.

for a daily newspaper. Bucktown's most popular dance-house occupied two stories of Kirk's building on the southeast corner of Culvert and Sixth streets. In concrete, precise prose, Hearn presents the raucous, high-spirited atmosphere of the ballroom: "With its unplastered and windowless limestone walls; sanded floor; ruined ceiling; half plank, half cracked plaster; a dingy black counter in one corner, and rude benches ranged along the walls, this dancing-room presented rather an outlandish aspect when we visited it. At the corner of the room opposite 'the bar,' a long bench was placed, with its face to the wall; and upon the back this bench, with their feet inwardly reclining upon the seat, sat the musicians. A well-dressed, neatly-built mulatto picked the banjo, and a somewhat lighter colored musician led the music with a fiddle, which he played remarkably well and with great spirit. A short, stout negress, illy dressed, with a rather good-natured face and a bed shawl tied about her head, played the bass viol, and that with no inexperienced hand. This woman is known to the police as Anna Dunn.

"The dancers were in sooth a motley crew; the neat dresses of the girls strongly contrasting with the rags of the poorer roustabouts, some of whom were clad only in shirt, pants and shocking hats. Several wickedly handsome women were smoking stogies…The best performer on the floor was a stumpy little roustabout named Jem Scott, who is a marvelous jig-dancer, and can waltz with a tumbler full of water on his head without spilling a drop…The musicians struck up that weird, wild, lively air, known perhaps to many of our readers as the "Devil's Dream," and in which "the musical ghost of a cat chasing the spectral ghost of a rat" is represented by a succession of 'miauls' and 'squeaks' on the fiddle. The dancers danced a double quadrille, at first, silently and rapidly; but warming with the wild spirit of the music, leaped and shouted, swinging each other off the floor, and keeping time with a precision which shoot the building in time to the music. The women, we noticed, almost invariably embraced the men about the neck in swinging, the men clasping them about the waist. Sometimes the men advancing leaped and crossed legs with a double shuffle, and with almost sightless rapidity. Then the music changed to an old Virginia reel, and the dancing changing likewise, presented the most grotesque spectacle imaginable. The dancing became wild; men patted juba and shouted, the negro women danced with the most fantastic grace, their bodies describing almost incredible curves forward and backward; limbs intertwined rapidly in a wrestle with each other and the music; the room presented a tide of swaying bodies and tossing arms, and flying hair."

In these stories, Hearn provides a penetrating depiction of Black people facing the challenges of surviving in American society soon after the Civil War and of trying to acclimate from rural life to urban life. Some of his friends and newspaper colleagues were puzzled by his fascination with African-Americans and considered it a sign of moral weakness. But others admired his desire to study with empathy and insight people of a different race and background. In an unpublished essay written in 1907 about Hearn, his friend Joseph S. Tunison tried to explain Hearn's attraction to Black people who lived in Cincinnati's riverfront area:

"The men and women of the Levee were strong and Hearn worshipped strength; they were as laughter-loving as Aphrodite, and Hearn loved laughter though he indulged so little in it himself; they were nature-folk, too, or at least they continually suggested in word and manner and mood and life of those African ancestors from whom they were removed by an interval of only two or three generations, and Hearn was looking for something as different as possible from the ways of English, French, and Americans which gave no stimulus to his imagination. He wrote many attractive essays on the traits of his dark friends. People read them and were entranced by them without understanding them or the author."[12]

Hearn had felt like an outsider his whole life—as a child growing up without his parents in his great-aunt's home in Dublin; as a rebellious teenager in strict Catholic schools in France and England; and as a foreigner entering a country where he had no family or friends. This sense of alienation helped him identify with the uneducated, struggling Black people on the levee. He understood to some extent the anger, fear and sorrow they often felt as a result of their status as second-class citizens.

---

[12]From the personal research archives of Jon Christopher Hughes, ed., *Period of the Gruesome* (Lanham, New York, London: University Press of American, 1990), who obtained a copy of this manuscript from the Library of Congress. A note by Tunison on the first page says it is a rough draft of an article that he sent to *The Atlantic Monthly* in the 1890s, but was never published and never returned to him. Tunison says he was told that Hearn persuaded the magazine not to publish it.

During his two years with the *Commercial*, Hearn wrote many other notable stories besides his portraits of African-American life. He continued developing stories in which he himself played a central role. One of his most famous and comical involved his treacherous climb to the top of St. Peter-in-Chains Cathedral, the highest building in Cincinnati.[13]

One day in May 1876, steeple-jacks Joseph Rodriguez Weston and John Klein walked into the offices of the *Cincinnati Commercial*. They told city editor Edwin Henderson they were going to climb to the top of the cathedral spire later in the week to remove decorations that had been placed there to celebrate the archbishop's Golden Jubilee. They wondered if a reporter might be interested in accompanying them and writing about the climb and the view from the cross at the top of the spire. Henderson asked Hearn to do it, and he readily agreed.

At 4 p.m., on Thursday, May 25, Weston and Klein arrived with a buggy at the *Commercial* offices to pick up Hearn. Henderson handed Hearn an expensive field glass to enable him to see more of the city from the steeple. But Hearn handed the field glass back to Henderson and said, "Perhaps I better not take these. Something might happen."

Hearn's anxiety increased as he, Weston, Klein and steeple-jack Peter Depretz climbed the long, narrow stairs inside the cathedral to reach the tower's clock. They crawled between the clock's bells to a window where they had to climb out to get to the top of the steeple. As Hearn looked out the window and saw "nothing but a sheer precipice of smooth stone," he was seized with fear. Weston gave him a drink from a whiskey flask to quell his nerves. Weston buckled a thick leather strap around Hearn's waist, and fastened a harness strap under and over his right thigh. He tied one end of a rope to the straps and passed the other end up the ladder outside the window. That end was pulled inside a window 25 feet above and tied to a beam. Sensing Hearn was about to back down, Depretz grabbed his thigh and pulled him out through the window. Hearn had no choice but to climb the ladder. After yet more ladder-climbing, he reached the cross. Tied to the lightning rod by a rope, Hearn sat on top of the cross, rested his feet on its northern arm and enjoyed the panoramic view. With his bad eyesight, he couldn't see distant objects in detail. But by looking

---

[13]Hearn, "Steeple Climbers," May 26, 1876, 8.

through his own eyeglass, he saw enough to be able to give readers a feeling for what the city looked from his high perch.

"Fear gradually passed off while thus seated," he writes, "and it was possible to turn and look in any direction over the city. From the great height, two hundred and twenty-five feet, every portion of the city encircled by the hills was distinctly visible. The City Buildings and the surrounding edifices seemed dwarfed to toy-houses; the circular fountain-basin of the City Park seemed like a ring of muddy water at the foot of the Cathedral; the summits of the Synagogue's minarets were visible below; in every direction the city lay out in regular squares like an elaborate map. For three or four blocks, north, south, east and west, the centers of thoroughfares were distinctly visible, with wagon-teams, buggies and carriages straggling along, apparently no larger than flies. The crowds below, with faces upturned to the cross, were lilliputians; even with a small opera-glass it was difficult to distinguish faces. All the Plum street canal bridges from the elbow eastward, were plainly visible; Mill Creek shimmered with a golden gleam in the west, and the Ohio curved in blue serpentine on the south. We seemed to stand above the city smoke and the evening mists; sounds from below came faintly to the ear, like echoes of another world; the tone of the giant clock below striking the chimes and the hour of five, were weird and thin; the least whisper was audible; the sky seemed nearer, and the ripple of fleecy clouds, coming up from the west, in white breaker lines against the sea of azure, seemed purer and clearer than ordinary."

Weston told Hearn to stand up on top of the cross. He detached the cords that tied Hearn to the lightning rod.

"His indifference to danger," Hearn writes, "inspired the visitor with sufficient confidence to perform the feat, and extend his arms for an instant 225 feet above *terra firma*. Suddenly the reporter caught sight of something that caused him to clutch the lightning-rod convulsively and sit down. Weston's braces were adorned with great brazen buckles, which bore in ghastly bas-relief the outlines of a skull and crossbones.

'What on earth do you wear such ill-omened things for?' we asked.

'Oh,' replied he, laughing and dancing on the northern arm of the cross, 'I thought I'd get smashed up some day, and took a fancy to these suspenders, as they serve to remind me of my probable fate. You seem to believe in omens. Well, I tell you I never like to do climbing on Friday, although I know it's all foolishness.'

"After inspecting the initials of the climbers out into the summit of the cross, we performed a descent which seemed far easier than the ascent. As we re-entered the belfry the clock boomed out six times, and the 'Angelus' chimed in measured strokes of deeply vibrating music from the big bell. The mists climbed higher as the sun commenced to sink in a glory of mingled gold and purple, and a long streamer of ruby light flamed over the western hills. 'That is a lovely view,' Weston exclaimed, 'but I think it is not so fine as the bird's eye view of the city by night, sparkling with ten thousand lights. You must come up on the cross some fine night with me.'

"The reporter shivered and departed."

In a later letter to Krehbiel, Hearn told him jokingly that he had omitted from his *Commercial* story the "Mephistophelian delight" he felt when, atop the cathedral's steeple, he "piddled on the universe."[14] He may have thought of doing it, but, considering his climb occurred during the day in public view in the presence of others, even he wouldn't have dared perform such an act.

Another of Hearn's participatory journalism stories for the *Commercial* involved a different kind of danger. He took a tour of some animal slaughterhouses in the Tallow District with the purpose of highlighting the cruel methods used to kill the animals. He witnessed and described in gory detail the process by which sheep, cows, hogs and other animals are slaughtered. Near the end of his story ("Haceldama," which means field of blood), Hearn writes about some people who stopped at the slaughterhouses regularly to drink the fresh blood of the animals.[15] They believed the blood would cure many ailments and make them stronger. While visiting a Jewish slaughterhouse, Hearn decided to find out for himself how the animal's blood tasted. Jewish law requires animals to be slaughtered in a particular way that's more humane than other methods. The man known as a shochet—someone who had been trained and authorized to slaughter animals

---

[14]Elizabeth Stevenson, *Lafcadio Hearn* (New York: Macmillan, 1961), 67.

[15]Hearn, "Halcedama. Humanity and Inhumanity in the Shambles. Hebrew Slaughterers, Gentle Butchers, and Consumptive Blood-Drinkers," *Cincinnati Commercial*, September 5, 1875, 3.

according to Jewish law—asked Hearn if he would like to try some blood. Here's Hearn's account:

"The Shochet passed by with his long knife. 'I am going to cut a bullock now,' he observed, 'if you want a glass of blood.'

"It once occurred to the writer to try the experiment for curiosity's sake, and give the public the benefit of his experience. A large tumbler was rinsed and brought forward, the throat of the bullock severed, and the glass held to the severed veins. It was filled in an instant and handed to us, brimming over with the clear, ruddy life stream which warmed the vessel through and through. There was no odor, no thickening, no consequent feeling of nausea; and the first mouthful swallowed, the glass was easily drained.

"And how did it taste: Fancy the richest cream, warm, with a tart sweetness, and the healthy strength of the pure wine 'that gladdeneth the heart of man!' It was a draught simply delicious, sweeter than any concoction of the chemist, the confectioner, the winemaker—it was the very elixir of life itself."

Despite his effusive praise for the taste of bullock's blood, there's no evidence to suggest that he made a habit of blood-drinking or even that he imbibed a second time. But the slaughterhouse visits served a more serious purpose for Hearn. It enabled Hearn to use his vivid prose not just to help readers sense what an animal's blood would taste like, but also to make them face the inhumane ways animals were killed in some of the slaughterhouses.

Hearn didn't flinch from covering killings of any kind, including public hangings. Hearn was sent to Dayton, Ohio, on August 26, 1876, to write about the execution of a 19-year-old man who had been convicted of murdering one of the city's most popular and prominent citizens. On August 31, 1875, Colonel William Dawson, superintendent of the Champion Plow Works in Dayton, refused to allow a drunken James Murphy to crash a private wedding party for one of Dawson's employees. The police said that a short time later, Murphy told one of his friends to induce Dawson to come outside on the pretext of getting a drink. When Dawson came out, Murphy punched him. As the two men fought, Murphy pulled out a knife and thrust it into Dawson's side. Dawson died a few moments later without identifying his killer. But Murphy was arrested later, convicted and sentenced to die.

It turned out to be anything but a routine execution. After confessing to the murder he previously had denied committing and expressing regret for his actions, Murphy stood on the scaffold platform, a rope around his neck, a black cap covering his face. When the sheriff pressed a lever with his foot, the trap door sprung open and Murphy began dropping. But the rope snapped and Murphy fell through the trapdoor to the floor below. After he became conscious, he was carried back to the scaffold and hanged successfully.

Hearn wrote about the botched hanging in graphic, horrifying detail.[16] He even felt the pulse of the young man as he lay on the ground, alive but unconscious from his fall after the rope around his neck broke. But his purpose in describing the hanging wasn't merely to titillate readers, although that certainly was part of it. Hearn, who opposed capital punishment and believed hanging to be an unusually cruel means of execution, also wanted to convey on an emotional level what a hanging was like, especially one that required two attempts.

"The poor young criminal had fallen on his back, apparently unconscious, with the broken rope around his neck, and the black cap veiling his eyes. The reporter (Hearn) knelt beside him and felt his pulse. It was beating slowly and regularly. Probably the miserable boy thought then, if he could think at all, that he was really dead—dead in darkness, for his eyes were veiled—dead and blind to this world, but about to open his eyes upon another. The awful hush immediately following his fall might have strengthened this dim idea. But then came gasps, and choked sobs from the spectators; the hurrying of feet, and the horrified voice of Deputy Freeeman calling, 'For God's sake, get me that other rope, quick!' Then a pitiful groan came from beneath the black cap.

'My God! Oh, my God!'

'Why, I ain't dead—I ain't dead!'

'Are you hurt, my child?' inquired Father Murphy.

'No, father, I'm not dead; I'm not hurt. What are they going to do with me?'

"No one had the heart to tell him lying there blind and helpless and ignorant even of what had occurred. The reporter, who still kept

---

[16]Hearn, "Gibbeted. Execution of a Youthful Murderer. Shocking Tragedy in Dayton. A Broken Rope and a Double Hanging. Sickening Scenes Behind the Scaffold-Screen," *Cincinnati Commercial*, August 26, 1876, 8.

his hand on the boy's wrist, suddenly felt the pulsation quicken horribly, the rapid beating of intense fear; the youth's whole body trembled violently.

'His pulse is one hundred and twenty,' whispered a physician.

'What's the good of leaving me here in this misery?' cried the lad. 'Take me out of this, I tell you.'

"In the meantime they had procured the other rope—a double thin rope with two nooses—and fastened it snugly over the crossbeam. The prisoner had fallen through the drop precisely at 1:44 1/2 p.m.; the second noose was ready within four minutes later. Then the deputies descended from the platform and lifted the prostrate body up.

'Don't carry me,' groaned the poor fellow, 'I can walk—let me walk.'

"But they carried him up again, Father Murphy supporting his head. The unfortunate wanted to see the light once more, to get one little glimpse at the sun, the narrow world within the corridor, and the faces before the scaffold. They took off his ghastly mask while the noose was being readjusted. His face was livid, his limbs shook with terror, and he suddenly seized Deputy Freeman desperately by the coat, saying in a husky whisper, 'What are you going to do with me?' They tried to unfasten his hand, but it was the clutch of death-fear. Then the little Irish priest whispered firmly in his ear, 'Let go, my son; let go, like a man—be a man; die like a man.' And he let go. But they had to support him at arm's length while the Sheriff pressed the trap-ever—six and one-half minutes after the first fall. It was humanely rapid work then."

H.S. Fuller, editor of the *Dayton Journal* who had encountered Hearn a couple of times when he had worked in Cincinnati, watched in amazement as Hearn, ever the diligent and thorough reporter, carefully examined Murphy's body after the second hanging even after Murphy had been declared dead.

"I shall not forget," Fuller wrote in a 1908 review of two biographies about Hearn, "that after the doctors had pronounced life extinct that Hearn still lingered over the pale body under the scaffold, lifting the pulse to his ear, listening to the heart, and going over the body, inch by inch, eyes and nose in close contact, like a veritable gad-fly, his eyes alight with interest to detect a flicker of life that had been overlooked."[17]

Hearn applied this intense scrutiny, his aptitude for exhaustive research and his knowledge of arcane subjects to whatever topic he covered—teeth, spirit photography, card games, phlebotomy, cigars, barber shops and suicides. In his last two years in Cincinnati, he continued to write about violent crimes and various scams. One of his most entertaining exposes involved the Black Hills Gold Rush, which began in 1874 with an expedition led by George Armstrong Custer. The initial modest gold discoveries caused thousands of fortune-seekers to head to the Dakota Territory. As in most American gold rushes, a scant few struck it rich. Some unscrupulous people tried to take advantage of this Black Hills mania by going to various large cities to organize mining expeditions. For a certain fee, they would provide supplies, transportation and a guide for those wanting to join Black Hills expedition parties. Most of these expeditions never materialized, and the expedition organizers would flee town with their clients' money.

In 1876, two Black Hills expedition companies set up "offices" in a couple of Cincinnati saloons. The *Commercial* unleashed Hearn to expose the dubious enterprises. He visited both offices and bombarded the expedition organizers with penetrating questions and skeptical comments.

With persistent questioning and droll wit, Hearn unmasks the charade created by the expedition organizers in a story entitled "Black Hills Bamboozle. How the 'Fever' Afflicts Cincinnati. Expeditions in Embryo and Their Prospective Development—Some Wholesome Facts for Greenhorns."[18] In a newspaper ad, the Cincinnati Black Hills Expedition encouraged prospective customers to come to its headquarters at 56 W. Third St."

Hearn notes that this respectable-sounding business address isn't what it seems to be. "'No. 56 West Third street' sounds very finely," he writes, "but the office of the Cincinnati Black Hills Expedition is in a saloon in the basement; and the office furniture consists of a beer hall table and a chair. 'Captain Mahoney,' the guide that is to be,

[17] H.S. Fuller, "Some Interesting Recollections of his Cincinnati Associations," *Cincinnati Enquirer*, June 17, 1908, 6.

[18] Hearn, "Black Hills Bamboozle," *Cincinnati Commercial*, April 13, 1876, 8.

and really the concocter of the whole scheme, is a tall, long-haired individual, who wears a natural sneer upon his upper lip, and an unnatural sombrero upon his flowing locks. Mahoney has neither the address of a lightning-rod agent, nor the argumentative readiness of an auctioneer, and has, therefore, delegated all necessary talking on the subject to an assistant, 'Doctor' R. R. Lynd, who possesses to an eminent degree those desirable qualities which Mahoney lacks. None of the so-called 'officers' of the expeditions seem to have attained any creditable notoriety in this city." Mahoney and Lynd couldn't even answer Hearn's questions about what route they planned to take from Cincinnati to the Black Hills.

During his Cincinnati years, Hearn developed into a very astute critic of the arts, especially theater. He loved going to plays, and Cincinnati had many theater venues. On his own initiative, Hearn wrote reviews for the *Enquirer*. In the winter of 1876–77, Hearn regularly reviewed plays and operas, most often at Wood's Theatre, but also at the Grand Opera House, the National Theatre and Robinson's Opera House. He would pinpoint the merits and flaws of a play and wouldn't hesitate to pan a performance he believed had completely failed to achieve its aesthetic goals. It didn't matter to him whether it was a locally written production or a touring national production. He wouldn't pander to local or business interests of any kind.

He writes in a review of a burlesque musical: "The announcement that the Lisa Weber variety performers would, last evening, open the week with an extravaganza of extraordinary merit, magnificent scenery, new wardrobes and a much-needed reinforcement of tolerable actors, was, as might have been expected, an impertinent fraud. The "Field of the Cloth of Gold" is an imposition of the brassiest description. It is not even good enough to be bad, or bad enough to be good; there is no new scenery, no 'famous historical extravaganza,' no good acting or tolerable singing, or endurable dancing…It is true that people laughed themselves hoarse last evening, during the performance, but is sincerely to be hoped that Lisa Weber et *cetera* did not interpret that laughter in a manner complimentary to themselves. The audience did not laugh because they fancied that they perceived or heard anything intrinsically funny on the stage, for no person in a rational frame of mind could have detected any comedy in that direction. What people were laughing at was the 'cheek' of Lisa Weber et *cetera.* There was no burlesque excepting the burlesque of advertising the performance as a burlesque, no joke in the thing except the joke of deluding the public. This was a good joke in its way, and caused a considerable amusement. but it is one of those entirely novel jokes which are at first grinned at and patiently borne only because they are novel, but which soon become stale, and will not bear much repetition. People laughed on Monday night, although the laughter was really upon themselves."[19]

Hearn deplored attempts to water down racy French operas to satisfy the more strait-laced tastes of American audiences. Hearn said doing that was as absurd and as offensive as producing a "revised and carefully corrected for family use" edition of Shakespeare. In a January 23, 1877, review, he unfavorably compares a current production of three French operas with a production that had recently played in Cincinnati. "From an artistic point of view," he writes, "the performances of the Soldene troupe were highly meritorious, and superior to those of Mrs. Oates' company, chiefly for the very obvious reason that there was no effort to anglicize French opera. They simply translated it faithfully…preserving the free display of limb, the extravagance of gesture, the impropriety of action and the *double-entendres* characteristic of the original. They presented French opera as it is—an exotic product, interesting as a small reflection of the social atmosphere which gave it birth."[20] To be fair, Hearn did praise the music of the Oakes production.

His review in the *Commercial* on September 20, 1875, of a play written by a retired Cincinnati African-American teacher, Francis A. Boyd, reveals Hearn's perceptiveness and even-handedness as a critic as well as his sensitivity to racial prejudice.[21] The play, "The Borgne," which is set in the ancient city of Babylon, had never been performed. Hearn was given a manuscript to review. In "A Drama in Five Acts by a Colored Man," Hearn summarizes the action of each act in the play. Then he critiques the manuscript, praising the "ingenuity" of the plot, its detailed directions for staging and costuming. "the drama is capable of magnificent spectacle," Hearn writes. "But it can never be

---

[19]Hearn, "Wood's Theatre," *Cincinnati Commercial*, March 6, 1877, 8.

[20]Hearn, "Grand Opera-House," *Cincinnati Commercial*, January 23, 1877, 4.

[21]Hearn, "A Drama in Five Acts by a Colored Man," *Cincinnati Commercial*, September 20, 1875, 2.

played in its present shape." He says the characters' speeches are too long and dull. Then he notes the difficulties Boyd has faced in his life. Born in 1842, he grew up as a free Black person in Lexington, where there were no schools for Black children. His mother taught him and he read on his own, learning Greek, Latin, French and other languages. During the Civil War, he served in the Union army under Gen. Benjamin F. Butler. After the war, he opened a school for Black children in Westchester, Ky., before moving to Mount Sterling, Ky. A white mob attacked his school in Mount Sterling, and Boyd barely escaped with his life. He later returned to teach there and was viciously assaulted by a white man. Boyd taught in other places in Ohio and in the South before sickness caused him to give up teaching. He wrote a book, "Columbiana: or, The North Star," (Steam Job and Book Printing House of G. Hand, Chicago, 1870). After two years of working on the railroad, he settled in Cincinnati.

Hearn writes that given the racism Boyd faced throughout his life, it's remarkable that he wrote a play like "The Borgne." But Hearn doesn't patronize him. He encourages Boyd to revise the play so it's more suitable for the stage. "...it is not too late for Mr. Boyd to rewrite it, stripping it of several anachronisms, and avoiding that cramp of rhyme which the octo-syllabic verse forces upon him, even to the verge of doggerel in many places. Certainly we see nothing in this attempt to discourage the hope of becoming a successful playwright." But Boyd died shortly after this story was published. He was only 32. The play was never performed.

Hearn had the talent and the artistic insights to become a full-time theater critic, but he didn't want to because it would have placed too much strain on his good eye. Besides, his private life provided him with far more drama than any of the plays he reviewed.

In the spring of 1876, he met a 41-year-old married woman who became a good friend. But, to his dismay, she soon tried to escalate their relationship into a romance. Eight Cincinnati residents planned to lend parts of their private collections of American Indian artifacts and human skeletal remains to a special exhibit of antiquities in Philadelphia. In preparing a story about this for the *Commercial*, Hearn visited several of the collectors' homes to interview them and to see the artifacts. In one of these visits, he met Ellen Freeman, whose family was lending its artifacts to the exhibit. After Hearn's story appeared on April 24,[22] Freeman, the wife of a prominent Cincinnati surgeon, wrote a note to Hearn complimenting his writing style.

She soon invited him to her home for dinner. Within days, she took him to a special butterfly exhibit at a museum in Avondale. His story about this exhibit appeared on May 9.[23] Emboldened, Freeman gave him books and they began exchanging letters that suggested a warm friendship but not a romance. Hearn, who was still involved with Mattie, though no longer living with her, felt gratified by Freeman's deep appreciation of his work and accepted her initial gifts as tokens of their friendship. Freeman invited him to parties, but Hearn, uncomfortable in high society, usually made excuses and politely declined. Before long, Freeman became totally infatuated with Hearn and began hinting in her letters that she viewed him as a potential lover. When Hearn realized this, he became more reticent in his letters and finally stopped writing to her. Freeman reacted by sending him more letters and unwanted gifts. She even appealed to his friend, Henry Watkin, to intercede. She asked Watkin to give Hearn a sedative so that she could go to his bed, wrap him in a silk quilt, hold his head in her arms and leave before he woke up. Alarmed at the request, Watkin refused to cooperate.[24]

Hearn tried as delicately as he could to discourage Freeman's romantic overtures. But her obsession with him grew. She inundated him with letters, books and flowers. He feared she would come into the *Commercial* newsroom to see him. Freeman finally pushed him too far. She sent him a photo of herself in a low-cut dress. He realized he had to take extreme measures to end this relationship.

He wrote her a scathing letter telling her in the harshest possible terms what he thought of her photo and her amorous intentions:

"I do not like the picture at all—in fact I cannot find words to express how much I dislike it.

"You were never physically attractive to me; you are neither graceful nor beautiful, and you evidently know nothing of the laws or properties of beauty. Otherwise you could not have sent me such a picture, as it could only disgust me.

---

[22]Hearn, "Cincinnati Archaeologists," *Cincinnati Commercial*, April 24, 1876, 3.

[23]Hearn, "Butterfly Fantasies," *Cincinnati Commercial*, May 9, 1876, 8.

[24]Paul Murray, *A Fantastic Journey: The Life and Literature of Lafcadio Hearn* (Sandgate, Folkestone, Kent: Japan Library, 1993), 44-46.

"Whatever liking I have had for you, it has never been of such a character that I could be otherwise than disgusted by such a picture as that. It is unutterably coarse and gross and beefy. It is simply unendurable.

"Not that I object to low dresses—or even to an utter absence of dress, when the unveiling reveals attractions which the eye of the artist loves as something shapely and beautiful. I have an instinctive and cultivated knowledge of what physical beauty is, and anything in direct violation of my taste and knowledge—like your picture,—simply sickens me. I have studied every limb and line in the bodies of fifty young women, and more; and know what form is and beauty is. You must not think me a fool. You are a fine woman in regard to health and strength; you are not a handsome or even a tolerably good looking woman physically, and your picture is simply horrible, horrible, horrible.

"This is plain speaking; but I think it is necessary for you. You cannot make yourself physically attractive to me. Don't try. I am an artist, a connoisseur, a student of beauty, and it is very hard to please me. Don't disgust me, please —"

He signed it, "Yours truly, L. Hearn."[25]

Freeman began hounding Watkin to intercede for her. Her letters became increasingly irrational. In one letter, she even threatened to commit suicide. When she found out that her attempted affair with Hearn had become known to a widening circle of people, she panicked. Fearful that her husband would discover her romantic interest in Hearn, she begged Watkin to get her letters back from Hearn. She returned Hearn's letters to him, but he kept hers. Before he left Cincinnati, he gave all the letters to Watkin. After Hearn's death, some of his letters to Freeman were published without naming her in a book, *Letters from the Raven* (Bretano's, 1907). The book, edited by Milton Broner, consists mostly of Hearn's letters to Watkin.

Hearn's problems with his wife and Freeman by themselves could have been enough to drive Hearn out of Cincinnati. But a combination of other factors made Hearn anxious to leave Cincinnati for a fresh environment. He felt that staying any longer in Cincinnati

[25]Hearn to Freeman, undated, quoted in *Wandering Ghost, The Odyssey of Lafcadio Hearn*, Jonathan Cott (New York: Alfred A Knopf, 1991), 184.

would limit his development as a writer. He had tired of covering crimes and believed he had nearly exhausted the subjects in the city he was interested in writing about. He also had been translating Theophile Gautier's lengthy short story, "One of Cleopatra's Nights." After he finished his newspaper stories in the wee hours of the morning, Hearn would sit at his newsroom desk in the dim light cast by a jet of gas and work on his Gautier translation. This was one of the new literary avenues Hearn wanted to explore. From the standpoint of physical comfort, he also wanted to escape Cincinnati's cold winters and abrupt changes in climate.

One winter night in 1877 in the *Commercial* newsroom, Hearn listened intently as city editor Edwin Henderson described a scene in a Southern state along the Gulf Coast.

"It was something about a grand old mansion of an ante-bellum cotton prince," Henderson writes under the pen name, Conteur, in an April 17, 1921, newspaper story, "with its great white columns, its beautiful private drive down to the public road, whitewashed negro quarters stretching away in the background, in the distance some cypress and live oaks and Spanish moss, and close by a grove of magnolias with their delightful odors and the melody of mocking birds in the early sunlight. Hearn took in every word of this, though he had little to say at the time, with great keenness of interest as shown by the dilation of his nostrils. It was as though he could see and hear and smell the delights of the scene."[26]

In October of that year, Hearn told Henderson he was moving to New Orleans. "I had lost my loyalty to this paper, and change was inevitable," Hearn said to him. "Perhaps it isn't so much the lack of opportunity here or the lack of appreciation of associations as this beastly climate. I seem to shrivel up in this alternation of dampness, heat and cold. I had to go sooner or later, but it was your description of the sunlight and melodies and fragrance and all the delights with which the South appeals to the senses that determined me. I shall feel better in the South and I believe I shall do better."[27]

The *Commercial* agreed to pay Hearn for free-lance dispatches

---

[26]Edwin Henderson (under the pseudonym, Conteur, "Origin of Hearn's Literary Career," *Cincinnati Enquirer*, April 17, 1921, F3.

[27]Henderson, "Origin of Hearn's Literary Career," *Cincinnati Enquirer*, April 17, 1921.

about Louisiana politics and culture, although no contract was signed. One morning not long after his conversation with Henderson, Hearn walked to the train station with plans of going to Memphis, where he would stay until he could catch a riverboat to New Orleans. Henderson, who carried Hearn's suitcase, *Commercial* publisher Murat Halstead, and his friend Henry Watkin, accompanied him to the train platform. Eight years after coming to Cincinnati as a confused, shy, unskilled 19-year-old, Hearn left the city as its best writer and one of its most eccentric personalities.

CHAPTER 6

Going Down South

*H*EARN EXPECTED to get off the train in Memphis and immediately board the *Thompson Dean* steamboat to New Orleans. The *Thompson Dean* had been built in Cincinnati in 1872 and was considered one of the finest steamboats of the day.[1] But when Hearn arrived in Memphis, he learned the steamboat hadn't even left New Orleans yet for its journey to Memphis and back. Lacking enough money to pay for alternate transportation, Hearn had no choice but to stay in Memphis and wait for the *Thompson Dean* to arrive.

This formerly thriving Mississippi River city that had been one of the South's bellwether state capitals still languished in the throes of its post-Civil War economic depression. The heart of its downtown contained boarded-up shops, rows of dilapidated buildings and dingy hotels. Before the war, large cotton-bearing boats lined up along the riverbank to unload their cargo in this city where about 400,000 bales were sold each year. Without the support of slave labor, the South's cotton business dropped precipitously and many of the cotton warehouses along Memphis' riverfront stood empty.

Hearn found himself trapped in this grim setting. As his money dwindled, he had to move to cheaper boarding houses, first paying $2 a night, then a dollar a night and finally 25 cents a night. Lonely and depressed in a strange city, Hearn turned to his old friend Henry Watkin for comfort. "I suppose you will not laugh," he wrote, "if I tell you that I have been crying a good deal of nights,—just like I used to when a college boy returned from vacation."[2]

---

[1]Ohio Memory Collection blog, https://ohiomemory.org/digital/collection/p267401 coll36/id/21960/.

[2]Hearn to Henry Watkin, October 31, 1877, in *Letters to the Raven*, ed. Milton Bronner, New York: Bretano's, 1907, 36-38.

Hearn, having been dubbed "The Raven" by Watkin, signed post cards to his Cincinnati friend with an illustration of a raven, the bird sometimes drawn to express Hearn's mood at the time. In his first post card Memphis in which he told Watkin about being temporarily stuck there, he drew a confused raven scratching his head. In one particularly clever sketch on a post card, he drew an angry-eyed raven sitting on a riverbank marked "Memphis" while far downriver, a snail labeled "Thompson Dean" sits on a riverbank marked "New Orleans." "I am terribly tired of this dirty, dusty, ugly town," Hearn wrote of Memphis, "a city only forty years old, but looking old as the ragged, fissured bluffs on which it stands." Serious eye trouble added to his stress. His eyes bothered him to the point that reading was painful for him and caused him to worry that he was going blind. Thoughts of Mattie also tormented him. "I feel all the time as if I saw Mattie, looking at me, or following me," he wrote, "and the thought comes to me of the little presents she made for me, and the little lock of black hair she sent me, and her despairing efforts just to speak to me once more, and my only answer being to have her locked up all night in the police station."[3]

Despite his unhappiness in Memphis, he didn't regret leaving Cincinnati. "It is time," he wrote to Watkin," for a fellow to get out of Cincinnati when they begin to call it the Paris of America."[4] But his prolonged stopover in Memphis did give him the opportunity to write the first of his dispatches or "letters," as he called them, to the *Cincinnati Commercial*. Memphis resident Nathan Bedford Forrest, former lieutenant general in the Confederate Army, died from diabetes on October 29, 1877, at the age of 56. Forrest was one of the Confederate's most effective and controversial military leaders. A millionaire businessman who had been a slave owner and trader before the Civil War, he was accused of ordering the massacre of Black and white Union soldiers at Fort Pillow, near Memphis, after they had surrendered. Forrest denied the allegations, and after investigating the incident, Union Major Gen. William T. Sherman did not charge Forrest with war crimes. Forrest's notoriety during and after the war made his death big news throughout the country, not just in the South.[5]

---

[3] Elizabeth Stevenson, *Lafcadio Hearn* (New York: Macmillan, 1961), 68-72.

[4] Hearn to Watkin, 1878, *Letters from the Raven*, 46.

[5] John Cimprich, *Fort Pillow, a Civil War Massacre, and Public Memory* (Baton Rouge: Louisiana State University Press), 2011.

Hearn wrote about Forrest's funeral on October 31, and it appeared in the *Commercial* on November 6 ("Notes on Forrest's Funeral.")[6] As a kind of private joke, Hearn used the pseudonym Oziah Midwinter as the byline for this story and the 13 subsequent stories he wrote for the *Commercial* from New Orleans. Midwinter was a character in Wilkie Collins' 1866 novel, *Armadale*, whose physical appearance and life's circumstances bore a striking resemblance to Hearn's. But there was nothing frivolous about Hearn's story about Forrest.

He packs the first-person story, written as a date-lined letter, with details and anecdotes about Forrest's life as the child growing up in a Bedford County, Tennessee pioneer family, as a businessman and slave trader, as a Confederate officer and as a struggling post-war cotton planter. Instead of casting him as a one-dimensional villain or hero, he portrays Forrest as a human being with deep flaws and some virtues. Before the funeral procession, which Hearn observed from a window of his boarding house room on Main Street, he interviewed many people in Memphis who had known Forrest as a Confederate officer and as a private citizen. It's a masterful profile of a complex man researched and written in just a few days.

"Old citizens of Memphis," Hearn writes, "mildly described him to me as 'a terror.' He would knock a man down upon the least provocation, and, whether with or without weapons, there were few people in the city whom he could not worst in a fight. Imagine a man about six feet three inches in height, very sinewy and active, with a vigorous, rugged face, bright gray eyes that always look fierce, eyebrows that seem always on the verge of a frown, and dark brown hair and chin beard with strong inclination to curl, and you have some idea of Forrest's appearance before his last illness."

Hearn talked to a former member of Forrest's military staff who saw Forrest stab one of his own soldiers with a penknife as the man shot him at point-blank range. Forrest had sent word to Andrew Wills Gould, a young artillery lieutenant, that he wanted him to resign because of cowardice and failure to obey orders. Gould walked into a hotel where Forrest, unarmed, sat by a window twirling a penknife in his fingers. In his account of this June 13, 1863, incident, Hearn

---

[6]Hearn under alias of Ozias Midwinter, "Notes on Forrest's Funeral," *Cincinnati Commercial*, November 6, 1877, 3.

demonstrated that his unhappiness with being stuck in Memphis hadn't harmed his knack for vividly describing an act of violence:

"...Gould entered in a desperate frame of mind. He had on one of those Kentucky coats with pleated tail, and belt attached, and in the right-hand side pocket he had a loaded pistol.

"'General,' he said rapidly and desperately, 'you said I was a coward, and it is a lie!'

"His hand was resting on the trigger of the cocked pistol in his pocket at the time, and he knew Forrest would hit him. So he pointed the pistol, still in his pocket, at Forrest and pulled the trigger.

"The pistol did not go off, the hammer had caught in the lining of Gould's coat pocket.

"With his left hand Forest seized the young man by his coat, collar and pulled him towards him; with his right hand he raised the white-handled penknife to his mouth, and opened the blade with his teeth. Gould got his pistol out of his pocket and Forrest opened the knife-blade with his teeth about the same time. Gould placed the muzzle of his pistol against Forrest's gown and fired, and almost simultaneously Forrest plunged the blade of the penknife into the artillery officer's abdomen, and with a single ripping cut nearly disemboweled him." Forrest survived, but Gould died two weeks later.

Finally, in the second week of November, the *Thompson* Dean arrived from New Orleans and rescued Hearn from his Memphis purgatory. His spirits lifted as he sailed down the vast Mississippi. He marveled at the beauty of the sunrise over Louisiana's sugar cane fields, observing that "an aural flush of pale gold and pale green bloomed over the long fringe of cottonwood and cypress trees, and broadened and lengthened half way round the brightening world."[7] As the large steamboat plied further south, Hearn also noted signs of Louisiana's economic decline—crumbling plantation mansions, vast acres of untilled farmland and clusters of empty cabins.

Despite plenty of visual evidence of its post-Civil War decay, New Orleans retained enough of its vitality and exotic charm to capture the hearts of visitors. With its French and Spanish architecture, wrought-iron balconies, colorful buildings and picturesque courtyards, it was

---

[7] Hearn, "Memphis to New Orleans, A Glimpse of the Mississippi Down Below," *Cincinnati Commercial*, November 23, 1877, 3.

the most European of American cities. Hearn immediately became enamored with the Crescent City. In his first article to the *Commercial* from New Orleans, he raves about broad, grand Canal Street, the Renaissance-style houses and plush gardens on St. Charles Street and the succulent fruits and pleasant aromas of the French Market.

"It is not easy to describe one's first impressions of New Orleans," he writes, "for while it actually resembles no other city upon the face of the earth, yet it recalls vague memories of a hundred cities. It owns suggestions of towns in Italy, and in Spain, of cities in England and in Germany, of seaports in the Mediterranean, and of seaports in the tropics…Whencesoever the traveler may have come, he may find in the Crescent City some memory of his home—some recollection of his Fatherland—some remembrance of something he loves."[8]

But within a few weeks, Hearn's money woes dimmed his infatuation with his new home. The *Cincinnati Commercial*, which was experiencing its own financial problems, delayed publishing Hearn's stories and paying for them. He had come to New Orleans with about $20 in his pocket and as of December 9, had received nothing for the four stories he had sent to the newspaper. He barely had enough money for postage stamps. Hearn also fretted that word of his ill-fated marriage to a Black woman might reach New Orleans, a city as rampantly racist as any in the South. "You cannot imagine how utterly the news of that time would ruin me here," Hearn wrote to Watkin. "It were better that I had committed incest or forgery. The prejudice here is unutterably bitter, and bottomlessly deep."[9]

Hearn wanted desperately to avoid becoming the kind of social misfit in New Orleans that he had been in Cincinnati. Soon after arriving in the city, he made special efforts to introduce himself to the class of highly educated and professionally accomplished aristocrats who could provide him with valuable insights about New Orleans and help him develop good story topics.

"I think I can redeem myself socially here," he wrote to Krehbiel, "I have got into good society; and as everybody is poor in the South, my poverty is no drawback."[10]

---

[8] Hearn, "At the Gates of the Tropics," *Cincinnati Commercial*, November 26, 1877, 2.
[9] Hearn to Watkin, 1877, quoted in Paul Murray, *A Fantastic Journey: The Life and Literature of Lafcadio Hearn* (Sandgate, Folkestone, Kent: Japan Library, 1993), 54.
[10] Hearn to Henry Krehbiel, 1877, in *The Life and Letters of Lafcadio Hearn*, vol. 1, ed.

With his proficiency in French, his mixed ethnic heritage and his enchantment with the macabre and the colorful, Hearn had a natural affinity for New Orleans. He felt more at home there than he ever did in Cincinnati.

With the 1880 Democratic National Convention scheduled to be held in Cincinnati, *Commercial* publisher Murray Halstead expected Hearn to write primarily about the political and economic landscape of the South. Instead, Hearn, who had never shown much interest in politics, chose mostly topics that fascinated him. He moved into the French Quarter, where he wasted no time in delving into New Orleans' Creole culture. With the aid of new friends like Greek-American professor Alexander Dimitry, and author George Washington Cable, Hearn quickly absorbed the nuances of Creole traditions, culture and language.

The Creoles, primarily people of French and Spanish descent who were born in New Orleans, were a proud, aristocratic group who felt superior to Americans. The Creoles of European lineage looked down upon African-Americans and the Creoles of color—that is, those of partly African-American descent. The Creole world flourished within the borders of the French Quarter. Hearn immersed himself in the Creole milieu with the same passion he had explored the African-American culture in Cincinnati. His obsessive curiosity drove him to explore every aspect of this strange new world he could. In his "letters" to the *Commercial*, Hearn wrote colorful accounts of Creole life, praising the beauty and grace of Creole women and describing the charm and alluring melodiousness of the Creole language.

He recalled first hearing the Creole of the Antilles spoken when he lived in London. He had listened with pleasure to the speech of the children of an English family from Trinidad who were visiting relatives in London. "You cannot help falling in love with it after having once heard it spoken by young lips," he writes, "unless indeed you have no poetry in your composition, no music in your soul. It is the most liquid, mellow, languid language in the world. It is especially a language for love-making. It sounds like pretty baby-talk; it woos like the cooing of a dove. It seems to be a mixture of French, a little Spanish, and West African dialects—those negro tongues that are vo-

Elizabeth Bisland (Boston: Houghton Mifflin Co., 1906), 167.

luminous with vowels."[11] Hearn even translated into English the lyrics of some Creole songs for his Cincinnati readers.

Only two of Hearn's 14 stories for the *Commercial* dealt with Louisiana politics. One of those stories, concerns a published article by Charles Gayarre, a Louisiana author, historian and politician who had lost his slaves and his fortune in the Civil War.[12] In the article quoted by Hearn, Gayarre asserts the inferiority of the Black race and the impossibility of the two races living together in a society that grants equal rights to Black people. Only as slaves can Black people survive in a white society, he says.

Hearn presents Gayarre's racist drivel without criticism. Although Hearn certainly opposed slavery and felt sympathetic to Black people, he was afraid to voice publicly his true feelings about racial segregation in a virulently racist city like New Orleans. He knew if he did, he would be driven out of his new home. He had suffered for his writings and actions regarding race in Cincinnati, and he didn't want a repeat occurrence.

His other political story concerned Louisiana's view of President Rutherford B. Hayes, who had been Cincinnati solicitor before becoming an Ohio legislator and then governor.[13] A proponent of racial equality, he won the Republican presidential nomination and was elected in 1876, losing the popular vote but wining the electoral vote. Hearn's story contends Hayes lacks political support in the South despite the end of Reconstruction and it adeptly explains the reasons. This story shows Hearn had the acumen, if not the desire, for political journalism.

Hearn had counted on the earnings from his *Commercial* stories to sustain him until he found other sources of income. But the *Commercial* delayed paying him, forcing him into a state of desperate poverty. Living in squalid living quarters and having hardly any money for food, Hearn wrote to Henry Watkin. He knew Watkin was in no position to send him money, but he asked him to see if a couple of his old newspaper friends might help him. When his Cincinnati friend Charley Johnson learned of Hearn's plight, he immediately sent him

---

[11] Hearn, "The City of the South," *Cincinnati Commercial*, November 29, 1877, 3.

[12] Hearn, "A Southern Prophet," *Cincinnati Commercial*, November 26, 1877, 3.

[13] Hearn, "The Political Condition of Louisiana. Can a Hayes Party Be Created?," *Cincinnati Commercial*, April 5, 1878, 5.

$20, a gift that Hearn later said kept him from starving.[14]

After he wrote letters to Edwin Henderson explaining his dire situation, the *Commercial* sent him small sums on an irregular basis. After another long delay in payments, Hearn erupted. Unaware of the *Commercial's* financial struggles, Hearn wrote an angry letter to the *Commercial* demanding the money owed him. He received a biting reply lecturing him about "charity" and "newspaper value" and castigating him for "impertinence." Incensed, Hearn fired off an even nastier letter than the first. The *Commercial* sent him the money it owed and told him to send no more stories. In a letter to Watkin, Hearn described himself as "happily, discharged."[15]

Besides money problems, Hearn also had serious health issues. His right eye, overstrained from Hearn's long hours of reading and writing, gave him so much pain sometimes that he had to rest it for a few days before resuming his scholarly activities. During the first few months of 1878, Hearn contracted dengue, an infectious fever common in warm climates. Although it sapped his strength and laid him up for a week or two, Hearn considered himself fortunate. An outbreak of yellow fever that had begun in late 1877 grew to frightening proportions by the first couple of months of the next year. "Yellow fever deaths occur every day close by," he wrote to Krehbiel.[16]

During this period of ill health and dire financial circumstances, Hearn suffered what he later referred to as a nervous breakdown. He bought a pistol and kept it with his money under his pillow at night. He used the gun only once. As he was walking around one day, he saw a drunken man kick a kitten that was in his way, gouge out its eyes and throw it aside. Shaking with anger, Hearn fired his pistol at the man several times, but missed. He later stated that his only regret about the incident was that one of his shots hadn't hit the man.[17]

Despite his economic hardships, Hearn remained determined to avoid taking a full-time non-writing job, although he did do some odd jobs to pay rent and eat modestly. He wanted time to read, study and write. His subjects of study were vast, including Creole culture

---

[14]Stevenson, *Lafcadio Hearn*, 180-181.

[15]Hearn to Watkin, July 10, 1878, *Letters to the Raven*, 61.

[16]Hearn to Krehbiel, 1878, in *Life and Letters*, vol. 1, 186.

[17]Milton Bronner, ed., *Letters from the Raven: Being the Correspondence of Lafcadio Hearn to Henry Watkin* (New York: Bretano's, 1907), 55.

and lore, Voodoo, the ancient literature of Egypt and China and the Spanish language. One of his new friends, Major William M. Robinson, editor of the *New Orleans Republican*, permitted Hearn unlimited access to his large personal library. Hearn initially approached him about working at his newspaper. Robinson told him there were no openings, and the paper had recently experienced layoffs. But Robinson enjoyed talking with Hearn about literary matters and continued inviting him to his house for dinner.

During Hearn's frequent visits, Robinson, a great admirer of French author Theophile Gautier, enthusiastically read the unpublished manuscript of Hearn's translation of the some of the French author's works. The two men would sit for hours discussing Gautier and other literary interests. Robinson's wife, however, didn't look forward to Hearn's frequent visits. She disapproved of his unkempt appearance and resented him for taking up so much of her husband's time.

Robinson introduced Hearn to Mark Bigney, the sole editor of a four-page daily called the *Daily City Item*. The publication had been started by a group of printers in June, 1877. After floundering financially, the printers sold it to Colonial John Fairfax. Bigney was impressed with Hearn's journalism background and intellectual pursuits and took him to be interviewed by Fairfax for a job. Although Fairfax had reservations about Hearn's racial views and his slovenly appearance, he hired him on June 15, 1878, to help Bigney produce the *Item*. The job paid only $10 a week, half of what his salary had been at the *Commercial*. But living expenses were far lower in New Orleans than they had been in Cincinnati. He could subsist on that amount if he budgeted his money carefully. More importantly, the job allowed him to fall into a comfortable daily routine for the first time since he arrived in New Orleans. After eating a 25-cent breakfast of figs, corn muffins, one egg, a dish of cream cheese and a cup of black coffee at a restaurant, he worked at the *Item* for a half-day clipping items to use from the rural Louisiana newspapers and scouring the New York City dailies for editorial material. He had the afternoons free to study and read. On Sunday afternoons, he swam in Lake Pontchartrain, a pleasure that recalled his boyhood summers at Tramore in Ireland.[18]

But Hearn spent most of his free time at serious intellectual

---

[18]Stevenson, *Lafcadio Hearn*, 84-85.

pursuits. He believed that knowing Spanish along with French and English would allow him to travel around the world "without fear of starving to death after each migration."[19] Escaping the kind of arduous daily journalism he had toiled at while living in Cincinnati, he writes to Krehbiel, "has afforded me opportunities for self-improvement which I could not otherwise have acquired. I should like, indeed, to make more money; but one must sacrifice something in order to study, and I must not grumble, as long as I can live while learning."

As soon as Hearn began working for the *Item*, Bigney realized he had hired a very talented and resourceful writer. He gave his new employee great latitude in subject matter and writing style. The main restriction was the limited space in the four-page paper. Besides re-writing and reprinting news stories from out-of-town newspapers, Hearn wrote editorials, book reviews, sketches of local life, including short impressionistic part-fictional pieces that he called "fantastics." The *Item* also gave him an outlet for his artistic talent, which had been confined to drawing amusing little caricatures on his private letters. With Bigney's encouragement, Hearn made 200 wood cuts between May 1880 and December 1880 to illustrate some of his writings in the *Item*. Besides making this modest little publication the first daily newspaper in the South to publish illustrations, Hearn's illustrations—along with his writing—attracted more readers and helped signifi-cantly boost The *Item's* financial fortunes. Hearn enjoyed carving the woodcuts for his illustrations, but he had to stop doing it after seven months because it strained his eyes too much.[20]

Through Hearn's editorials, the *Item* became an enthusiastic ad-vocate for government reform in a city marked by corruption and ineptitude. Despite his Republican political leanings, Hearn avoided writing about racial injustices in New Orleans. Instead, he directed his reform efforts to crime, police brutality, public health issues and polit-ical graft. He employed satiric verse to decry the laxness of the police:

> "Murder and Robbery walk the street,
> Armed with the weapons of deadly strife;

---

[19]Hearn to Krehbiel, 1878, in *Life and Letters,* vol. 1, 194.

[20]Delia LaBarre, ed., "Introduction" in *The New Orleans of Lafcadio Hearn* (Baton Rouge: Louisiana State University, 2007).

While the mild policeman sleeps on his beat,
Caring for naught save his precious life."[21]

To accompany this piece, Hearn drew a line of ghastly-looking skeletons walking in between two sleeping policemen.

He also wrote hard-hitting conventional editorials about public problems. He targeted opium dens in one of these editorials (May 28, 1880), criticizing public officials for ignoring the issue. "The subtle and pernicious influence of the Chinese opium vice is spreading rapidly through the city. We spoke yesterday of a den on Dauphine street; but the public must not suppose that this is the only one. There are also public smoking dens on St. Peter street and on Royal street, and on other streets where the vice is less publicly indulged in, the clientele being chiefly composed of Mongolians. At these public dens numbers of degraded women and men assemble nightly to drown thought and stifle memory with the fumes of opium. For those who once acquire this fatal vice, all hope is dead. The motto which Dante inscribes above the gates of hell should be inscribed above the doors of opium dens. It is curious that the authorities, who are well aware of the prevalence of his vice, have not yet taken measures against its further extension. We recommend the matter to the attention of the State Board of Health, the Sanitary Association, and the City Council. The latter can crush these infamous places out of existence by passage of a much needed law upon the subject."[22]

But his most entertaining editorials contain a sharp sardonic edge. In "A Visit to New Orleans," one of his best political satires written for the *Item*, Hearn imagines the Devil coming to New Orleans to corrode the moral values of the government's elected leaders and employees. But as the Devil observes the police, the board of health and other public institutions in operation, he realizes New Orleans doesn't need him. "'I was a fool to come down here at all,' he said, 'this Board of Health can do my work better than I can do it myself, and the people seem to be just fools enough to let them do it. Instead of honest poverty, I find vicious poverty; instead of reform, demoral-

[21] Hearn, "Police Board," June 1, 1880, *The Item, in The New Orleans of Lafcadio Hearn*, ed. Delia LaBarre (Baton Rouge: Louisiana State University Press, 2007), 7.

[22] Hearn, "The Opium Vice," May 18, 1880, *The Item*, in *The New Orleans of Lafcadio Hearn*, 4.

ization; instead of law, I find lawyers; instead of justice, oppression.'" After a visit to the State House, the Devil decides state officials don't need his help to act unethically. "What is the use of staying in a city that is going just where I am going?," he says.[23]

Some of Hearn's strongest pieces for the *Item* were his sketches of daily New Orleans life, Creole culture and customs and ordinary people. He brought an outsider's curiosity and perspective to his sketches and captured the essence of New Orleans life more successfully than hardly any other writer had up to that time. One of the quirks he noticed was that many of the city residents would talk to themselves as they walked through the streets or sat in public places. Hearn discreetly watched some of these people and tried to hear what they were saying. The topic often appeared to be money, understandable in a city mired in an economic depression.

But in the midst of one of the yellow fever epidemics, he writes, there seemed to be more people talking to themselves and the topic often was death.[24] Hearn skillfully connects the residents' private behavior to a public tragedy. In doing so, he imbues the sketch with an emotional gravity that lifts it to a higher literary plane. A light, amusing sketch about an eccentricity becomes a solemn meditation on death.

"They spoke of the dead," Hearn writes, "and muttered remembered words uttered by other tongues—and asked information from waving shadows and white walls regarding people that God only knows anything about.

"Perhaps they remembered that the only witnesses of some last interview were the same white walls and waving shadows. And the shadows lay there at just the same angle—well, perhaps, the angle was a little sharper—and they were waving as dreamily as then. And perhaps a time might come in which all Shadows that have been must answer all questions put to them.

"Seeing and hearing these things, we somehow ceased to marvel that some people dwelling in the city of New Orleans should speak

---

[23] Hearn, "A Visit to New Orleans," May 10, 1879, *The Item*, in *The Writings of Lafcadio Hearn*, vol. 1 (Boston and New York: Houghtin Mifflin Company/Cambridge: The Riverside Press, 1923), 126.

[24] Hearn, "The City of Dreams," March 9, 1879, in *The Writings of Lafcadio Hearn*, vol. 1, 113.

mysteriously and hold audible converse with their own thoughts; forasmuch as we, also, dreaming among the shadows, spoke aloud to our own hearts, until awakened by an echo of unanswered words."

Hearn consistently demonstrated his ability to capture the nuances and textures of New Orleans' daily life. Through the use of telling details and of descriptions that appealed to the readers' senses, he created vivid snapshots of what it was like to live in New Orleans in the 1880s. In "Voices of Dawn" (July 22, 1881), Hearn describes the distinctive cries of the many vendors roaming the streets.[25] "The vendor of fowls pokes in his head at every open window with cries of 'chick-EN, Madamma, Chick-EN,' and the seller of 'Lem-ONS—fine Lem-ONS!' follows in his footsteps. The peddlers of 'Ap-PULLS,' of Straw-BARE-eries' and "Back-Breezes," all own sonorous voices. There is a handsome Italian with a somewhat ferocious pair of black eyes, who sells various oddities and has adopted the word 'lagniappe' for his war cry,—pronouncing it Italian wise. He advances noiselessly to open windows and doors, plunges his blazing black glance into the interior, and suddenly queries in a deep bass, like a clap of thunder, 'LAGNIAPPA-Madam-a!—lagniap-PA!' Then there is the Cantelope Man, whose cry is being imitated by all the children:

> "'Cantel-lope-ah!
> Fresh and fine,
> Jus from the vine,
> Only a dime!'"

Hearn's deft ear for dialect allowed him to write with authenticity in the Creole vernacular. He wrote some of his sketches completely in the Creole dialect, as if the story were being told by a fictional Creole. One of these, "Why Crabs Are Boiled Alive?" (October 5, 1879) is extremely short, but effective.[26]

"And for why you not have of crab? Because one must dem boil 'live? It is all vat is of most beast to tell so. How you make for dem kill so you not dem boil? You not can cut dem de head off, for dat day

---

[25]Hearn, "Voices of Dawn," July 22, 1881, *The Item*, in *The Writings of Lafcadio Hearn*, vol. 1, 206-208.

[26]Hearn, "Why Are Crabs Boiled Alive?," October 5, 1879, *The Item*, in *The Writings of Lafcadio Hearn*, 135.

have not of head. You not can break to dem de back, for dat dey not be only all back. You not can dem bleed until dey die, for dat dey not have blood. You not can stick to dem troo de brain, for dat dey be same like you—dey not have of brain."

Just as Hearn had tried to make Cincinnatians appreciate the culture of the African-Americans living among them, he also attempted to show New Orleanians the value of the Creole sub-culture of their city. Hearn, who had no knowledge of musical notation, helped Cable collect Creole song lyrics for a book Cable was working on. Hearn's insightful and entertaining sketches of Creole life earned him the affection and the trust of the Creole community. One day, a woman brought him the lyrics of a French Creole song. Hearn published the French lyrics in the *Item* ("A Creole Song," July 26, 1880) along with his own English translation.[27] At the end of the story, he encouraged his readers to bring him other Creole songs.

Hearn certainly earned the respect of the Creoles for his poignant tribute to Marie Laveau in the *Item* on July 17, 1881, the day after her death on at the age of 97.[28] Although she was known as "Queen of the Voodoos," Hearn downplayed any connection she might have had with voodoo and stressed her use of natural herbal medicines to treat sick people. In his brief sketch, he de-mythologizes and demystifies Laveau, portraying her as a kind-hearted woman who used her folk wisdom to help others.

"Whatever superstitious stories were whispered about her," he writes, "it is at least certain that she enjoyed the respect and affection of thousands who knew her, of numbers whom she befriended in times of dire distress, of sick folks snatched from the shadow of death and nursed by her to health and strength again with that old Creole skill and knowledge of natural medicines which is now almost a lost art."

The short, impressionistic and meditative pieces he called fantastics provided Hearn with the opportunity to tap into a more fanciful aspect of his literary talents, free from the shackles of straight-forward journalism. Many are part fiction and part non-fiction. In form, they

---

[27]Hearn, "A Creole Song," July 26, 1880, *The Item*, in *The Writings of Lafcadio Hearn*, vol. 1, 164-165.

[28]Hearn, "The Death of Marie Laveau," July 17, 1881, *The Item*, in *Lafcadio Hearn/American Writings* (New York: The Library of America, 2009), 717-719.

were modeled after the French *feuileton*, an essay often designed to depict brief slices of life, evoke moods or embark on imaginative ruminations. Hearn had experimented with this kind of writing in Cincinnati. In "Tantalus in a Street Car" (November 1, 1874) in the *Cincinnati Enquirer*, Hearn writes about a brief encounter with an attractive young woman on a crowded street car.[29] Nothing happens between them. They don't even speak to each other. But in this essay, Hearn writes about his observations of her and the impassioned thoughts racing through his mind as they sit next to each other, her shoulder touching his, her silky dress brushing against his pants and the fragrant scent of her perfume filling his nostrils. When the conductor comes around to ask the passengers for their tickets, she fumbles in her purse looking for hers. Seeing an opportunity to ingratiate himself with her, Hearn starts to tell her he'll pay for her ticket. But before he can finish his sentence, she finds her ticket, gives him a half-smile and gets off the street car. It ends on a light, humorous note, with Hearn seeking solace in a Vine Street bar.

"The Tale of a Fan," published in the *Item* on July 1, 1881, also revolves around a ride in a street car and Hearn's musings about the beauty of a certain woman.[30] Except in this sketch, he never sees the woman. He picks up a colorful Japanese fan a woman had accidentally left on her seat. The appearance and perfumed scent of the fan launches Hearn on a reverie speculating about her looks—he decides that she must be a brunette—and the nature of her charms. It's a winsome, well-written sketch that delightfully captures a man's ability to fantasize.

Hearn sent some of his New Orleans writings to Krehbiel, who told him he felt the fantastics didn't measure up to his talent. Hearn conceded to his friend that the fantastics were "trivial" by normal journalism standards. But he explained in a letter to Krehbiel that the nature of the fantastics were artistic, not journalistic. "They are my impressions of the strange life of New Orleans. They are dreams of a tropical city. There is one twin-idea running through them all—Love and Death. And these figures embody the story of life here, as

[29]Hearn, "Tantalus in a Street Car," Nov. 1, 1874, *Cincinnati Enquirer*, 1.

[30]Hearn, "The Tale of a Fan," July 1, 1881, in *The Writings of Lafcadio Hearn*, vol. 11, 327-329.

it impresses me."[31]

Hearn felt compelled to preserve in writing the alluring, unique aspects of New Orleans life that he feared commercialism would soon destroy. That's why he focused so much on the Creoles, whose culture he could see already had begun to fade. The fantastics offered him a strong literary form for sketching snippets of Creole life.

In his least successful fantastics, Hearn uses archaic English words and syntax and pseudo-poetic phrasing, substituting "thou" for you, ending verbs in "eth," and freighting his sentences with too many classical references. He too often allows Victorian cliches to creep into his writing. Later in his New Orleans years, though, he dropped this pretentious manner of writing. He also realized that his writing tended at times to be overly ornate. "What troubles my style especially is ornamentation," he wrote to Krehbiel.[32]

His book reviews that appeared in the *Item* were as candid and incisive as his theater reviews had been during his Cincinnati years. He despised the mawkish, saccharine Southern novels that idealized and stereotyped antebellum life. "In all we find the same kind of 'gush,' the same floriated English, the same adoration of 'titles' and 'noble blood' and other antiquated nonsense, and they all end in the discovery that some young American is the legitimate son or heir of some member of the English nobility.... Such wishy-washy trash ought to be severely handled by the press of this city and of other Southern cities, as libels upon the intelligence of the reading public."[33] He praised George Washington Cable's work, which he considered a true artistic representation of Creole life.

Translating the French romanticists became an increasingly important part of his aesthetic development. Their writing influenced Hearn's creation of the fantastics. In New Orleans, he had a sizable French-speaking audience providing him with an outlet for his translations that he wouldn't have had in any other American city. The modest little *Item* newspaper published some of the first English translations of certain prominent French writers available in the United States. While he was working for the *Item*, some of Hearn's

---

[31]Hearn to Krehbiel, 1880, *Life and Letters,* vol. I, 220-221.

[32]Hearn to Krehbiel, May, 1884, *Life and Letters,* vol. I, 324.

[33]Hearn, "Southern Novels," November 26, 1879, *The Item,* quoted in *Young Hearn,* O.W. Frost (Tokyo: Hokuseido Press, 1958), 191.

translations also appeared in the Sunday editions of the *New Orleans Democrat*. The French writers he translated included Gautier, Anatole France, Pierre Loti, Guy de Maupassant and Gustav Flaubert. Hearn viewed the work of a translator as an art and took it very seriously. "One who translates for the love of the original," he wrote, "will probably have no reward save the satisfaction of creating something beautiful, and perhaps of saving a masterpiece from desecration by less reverent bards. But this is worth working for."[34]

He had finished translating a collection of Gautier stories, *One of Cleopatra's Nights and Other Fantastic Romances*, which he had begun working on in Cincinnati. But he hadn't yet placed it with a publisher. Some of the stories were considered risqué for their time, and Hearn, mischievous as ever, relished shocking his readers. "It gives me malicious pleasure," he told Krehbiel, "to inform you that my vile and improper book will probably be published in a few months. Also that the wickedest story of the lot—"King Candaule"—is being published as a serial in one of the New Orleans papers, with delightful results of shocking people."[35]

Although his literary pursuits consumed a lot of his time and energy, he decided to try to bolster his meager income by opening a restaurant. His partner in this venture was a man from the North whom Hearn described to Watkin in a letter as "a large and ferocious man, who kills people that disagree with their coffee." Hearn, of course, was totally unsuited to manage any business. He may have agreed to this scheme because his primary role would involve little more than providing the initial capital. His partner apparently convinced him that he could handle the management and the operation of the restaurant. The decidedly low-end eatery, located at 160 Dryades Street, was called variously The 5 Cent Restaurant and The Hard Times Restaurant. Hearn wrote advertisements that he placed in the *Item* and printed a promotional handbill, which read, in part: "This is the cheapest eating-house in the South. It is neat, orderly, and respectable as any other in New Orleans. You can get a good meal for a couple of nickels. All dishes 5 cents. A large cup of pure Coffee, with Rolls, only 5 cents. Everything half the price of the

---

[34]Hearn to Jerome A. Hart, January, 1883, in *Life and Letters*, vol. I, 250.
[35]Hearn to Krehbiel, 1890, in *Life and Letters*, vol. I, 213.

markets."[36] In keeping with the social mores of the South, Hearn's restaurant was racially segregated, with the front room reserved for white customers and the back room for African-Americans. Hearn had little or no role in the actual operation of the restaurant. During some of his leisure time, he would come in, sit in a back corner of the restaurant and observe. But, like *Ye Giglampz* in Cincinnati, this commercial enterprise of Hearn's quickly ended in failure. After the eatery operated for a month with some success, his partner took the profits and left town. In the end, The 5 Cent Restaurant wasn't worth even a nickel to Hearn.

He complained to Krehbiel about his financial struggles in an economically depressed city: "Times are not good here. The city is crumbling into ashes. It has been buried under a lava-flood of taxes and frauds and maladministrations so that it has become only a study for archaeologists. Its condition is so bad that when I write about it, as I intend to do soon, nobody will believe I am telling the truth. But it is better to live here in sackcloth and ashes, than to own the whole State of Ohio."[37]

Yet his despondency about money didn't blind him to New Orleans' special charms and didn't deter him from his literary endeavors. No matter how discouraged he became, he seemed able to lift himself out of the doldrums. "I see beauty all around me,—a strange, tropical, intoxicating beauty," he wrote to Krehbiel. "I consider it my artistic duty to let myself be absorbed into this new life, and study its form and colour and passion. And my impressions I occasionally put into the form of the little fantastics…"[38]

Hearn's perseverance eventually paid off. In December 1881, the *New Orleans Democrat* merged with the *New Orleans Times*. The newly formed *Times-Democrat* hired Hearn as its literary editor and translator at a salary of $30 a week, three times his salary at the *Item*.[39]

---

[36] Edward Larocque Tinker, *Lafcadio Hearn's American Days* (New York: Dodd, Mead and Company, 1924), 102.

[37] Hearn to Krehbiel, 1880, in *Life and Letters*, vol. 1, 215.

[38] Hearn to Krehbiel, 1880, in *Life and Letters*, vol. 1. 217.

[39] Vera Seely McWilliams, *Lafcadio Hearn* (Boston: Houghton Mifflin Co., 1946), 136.

CHAPTER 7

Creole Chronicles

*T*HE *TIMES-DEMOCRAT* provided Hearn with a more prominent, visible venue for his work. Major E. A. Burke, who had
owned part of the *Democrat*, demonstrated his belief in New Orleans'
economic future by creating this new publication. He wanted it to
become the most influential Southern daily newspaper. He appointed as editor-in-chief Page Baker, a former Confederate officer and a
businessman who held literature in high regard. His brother, Marion
Baker, edited the paper's Sunday edition, where most of Hearn's stories would appear.

Hearn's new bosses gave him a great degree of freedom in story
topics and writing style. He was expected to write local sketches and
one or two editorials a week on any topic he desired and to translate articles and editorials from French and Spanish newspapers. Of
course, the *Times-Democrat* also published his translations of short
stories by prominent French writers of the day. Page Baker, a determined but kind man, took a special interest in Hearn. He quickly
learned Hearn's inner drive was so strong no one needed to prod
him. Baker not only encouraged him but befriended him, inviting
him to his home for meals with his family. During working hours,
he allowed Hearn to come into his office and read his stories and
translations before they were published. After work, he often would
accompany Hearn out of the office, and they would go somewhere
for a drink and conversation. Baker made sure Hearn wasn't saddled
with any of the more routine duties most newspaper reporters had
to perform, such as chasing breaking news and writing boilerplate
filler stories. Whenever Hearn complained to Baker about an editor
or a printer changing his idiosyncratic punctuation to conform with
the newspaper's style, Baker supported him and told the editors to

let Hearn's odd semicolon-dash combination alone. Old Semicolon definitely hadn't mellowed.

On the personal front, Hearn found a more comfortable and stable domestic arrangement. He began eating all his meals at Margaret Courtney's boarding house at 68 Gasquet Street, which later became Cleveland Street. She was a cheerful, sensible woman who treated Hearn like a member of her family and took pride in having a distinguished newspaper writer in her house. She sensed his loneliness and felt a deep sympathy for him. Knowing Hearn's desire for privacy, she would seat him by himself at a table in a room separated from the other boarders. Courtney often would take a break from her duties and stop at his table to talk with him. When she was too busy, her husband would sit down briefly at Hearn's table. The Courtney's little girl, Ella, also became friends with Hearn and often came to his table to chat with him. He grew especially fond of Ella and gave her many little gifts. Her favorite was an animal picture book with tabs that made the animals move. Hearn wrote his own translation of Victor Hugo's poem, "To Her," in Ella's album on May 19, 1887. Three days later, Hearn published this poem in *Times-Democrat*.[1]

With Margaret Courtney, Hearn could relax and talk easily about his work or his personal life. One of their bonds was a shared Irish heritage. She became so close to Hearn that she could chide him good-naturedly about his lapsed Catholicism. When he would talk about his attraction to Buddhism and other Eastern faiths, she would say, "Ah! and I pray God every night on my knees to make you a good Catholic, and you an Irishman, too!" Hearn would reply quietly, "I'm glad you pray to your God for me. Don't stop."[2]

He had all his mail delivered to Courtney's house even though he wasn't a boarder. Before long, he began living in a boarding house around the corner from her house. It was a clean, homey place operated by Kate Higgins. Whenever Hearn became ill, Higgins and Courtney looked after him. Courtney even took meals to Hearn at Higgins' house. Sometimes, Higgins herself would pick them up and take them to Hearn. He also developed an unlikely friendship with her nephew, Denny Corcoran, a tall, hulking man who usually carried

---

[1] Edward Larocque Tinker, *Lafcadio Hearn's American Days*, 201-203.
[2] Ibid., 200.

two guns with him and who could be violent when provoked. But he was at heart a gentle, simple-minded person who accompanied Hearn on night-time walks through some of the rough areas of the city. At Hearn's suggestion, they frequently stopped to admire statues in parks. As they sat on a park bench near a statue, Hearn would explain its artistry in great detail to Corcoran, who understood little of what Hearn was saying but nonetheless enjoyed his company. These sojourns sometimes included visits to bordellos.

Still smarting from his ill-fated marriage to Mattie Foley and from his distressing experiences with Ellen Freeman, Hearn carefully avoided romantic relationships with women in New Orleans. "I don't feel like getting tangled up with womens';—don't believe I could love a woman if I tried," he wrote to Henry Watkin, "and after all, so long as all women have to be bought, one might as well buy 'em when he wants 'em."[3] He admitted to Krehbiel that he visited brothels, just as he had in Cincinnati. "I eat and drink and sleep with members of the races you detest like the son of Odin that you are," he wrote to Krehbiel.[4] Foley no longer asked for money from Hearn after she married—legally—John Kleintank, a Black man, in Cincinnati in 1880, although there is no evidence that Hearn knew about this marriage. The longer he went without any contact from Foley, the less he worried about her.

Even though Hearn had no romantic relationships in New Orleans, he developed several strong friendships with admirers of his work. In addition to Page Baker and George Washington Cable, Hearn also became close friends with the wife of Marion Baker, Julia Wetherill. She was a poet who not only appreciated Hearn's talent, but also understood Hearn's personality quirks as well as anyone.

"His character presented strange contrasts," she writes. "He was warm-hearted and affectionate, though at the same time extremely prone to distrustfulness; often suspecting his best friends of a design to slight or injure him. He took offence inexplainably at times, and could easily be turned against his sincere well-wishers by the malicious words of some mischief maker…Hearn was not a good judge of

---

[3]Lafcadio Hearn to Henry Watkin, unpublished portion of letter.
[4]Elizabeth Bisland, *The Life and Letters of Lafcadio Hearn,* vol. 1 (Boston: Houghton Mifflin Co., 1906), 217.

character, and would often accuse quite simple and harmless persons of deep, dark subtlety."[5]

Hearn also became good friends with three others—a Creole physician devoted to racial equality, a Catholic missionary who worked among the local Native American population and an ambitious young woman who wrote poetry for the *Times-Democrat* and would go on to a successful journalism career of her own.

Rudolph Matas, a young doctor of Spanish Creole heritage who also served as editor of the *New Orleans Medical and Surgical Journal*, admired Hearn's anonymous stories and editorials in the *Times-Democrat*. He learned from a friend who worked at the newspaper that Hearn was the author of these colorful sketches and translations. Matas arranged for the man to bring Hearn to his offices, where he introduced himself. Matas spoke French and Spanish and, like Hearn, had an intense curiosity about many things. Soon after meeting him, Hearn asked Matas for information he needed for an anatomical dream-sketch. Matas provided him with the material. Their common interests and their compatible personalities quickly forged a close friendship. Hearn often met with him several times a week. With his personable nature and non-judgmental attitude, Matas filled the void created by the absence of Henry Watkin from Hearn's daily life. Hearn trusted him as he would a brother.

In later years—long after Hearn had left New Orleans—Matas invented many key surgical procedures that brought him international renown and taught for many years at his alma mater, Tulane University. In 1941, Matas, then 81 years old, participated in the dedication of the Lafcadio Hearn Room at Tulane's Howard-Tilton Memorial Library. Tulane later honored Matas by naming the library in its Health Sciences Center after him.[6]

Pere Adrien Emmanuel Rouquette, a missionary Catholic priest of Creole descent who was living among the Choctaw Indians in the pine woods on Lake Ponchartrain's north shore, liked Hearn's writings about Creole culture and French authors in the *Times-Democrat*. He concocted a clever way of introducing himself to Hearn. He published

[5]Tinker, *Lafcadio Hearn's American Days, 362, 364.*
[6]Tulane University Health Sciences Center Rudolph Matas Library's Web site, http://www.tulane.edu/~matas/historical/charity/charity5.htm.

a poem in Creole French in a French Catholic newspaper that he knew Hearn would read. This is the translation of the first four lines: "Your papa came from England/Your mama came from Greece/If you want to come to visit me, my friend Buckley/Will bring you here with courtesy."[7]

The poem had its intended effect. Despite Hearn's long-standing antipathy toward missionaries and Catholicism, he met with Rouquette in a small room at the Presbyter in New Orleans. Hearn became enthralled with Rouquette, who was in his mid-60s. Unlike the missionaries Hearn disliked, Rouquette loved the Indians' culture and their nature-centered vision of the world and didn't try to convert them to the white man's way of life. The Choctaws called him Blackrobe Father. As he helped them, he adapted to their customs and learned the Choctaw language. He wore Indian garb except when celebrating Mass. Hearn spent many nights talking with Rouquette about Creole traditions and songs, the French Romantic authors and Choctaw music and lore. Their conversations reawakened in Hearn the attraction to pantheism he first experienced as an adolescent in Dublin. In 1879, Hearn wrote a laudatory review of Rouquette's narrative poem, "La Nouvelle Atala" in the *Item*.[8] The Imprimerie du Propagateur Catholique published the poem later that year in a bound cover, with Hearn's review included. "Hearn's first appearance in book form," noted Elizabeth Stevenson, one of Hearn's biographers, "was thus ironically through the courtesy of a Catholic publishing firm."[9]

But Hearn's close relationship with the priest didn't last. Besides the obvious clash of their religious views, they argued over Rouquette's phonetical spelling of Creole words. More importantly, Rouquette publicly denounced Cable's novel, *The Grandissimes*, which Hearn had effusively praised in a review. Rouquette detested Cable because he felt his writings misrepresented the Creole people. To maintain his friendship with Cable, Hearn felt he had to distance himself from Rouquette.

Yet his friendship with Cable didn't last long either. Cable's conservative religious beliefs were a source of tension between him and

---

[7]Tinker, *Lafcadio Hearn's American Days*, 143-144.
[8]Hearn, "A Louisiana Idyll," *The Item*, February 25, 1879.
[9]Elizabeth Stevenson, *Lafcadio Hearn*, 97.

Charles Bush Hearn, Lafcadio Hearn's father, was a surgeon-major in the British army. He met Hearn's mother, Rosa Cassimati, in 1848 while stationed on the Greek island of Cerigo.

Hearn, age 8, and his great-aunt, Sarah Brenane. She assumed legal responsibility for Lafcadio after his parents divorced and raised him in Dublin.

Hearn, pictured at age 16, lived with his great-aunt until her health and finances declined. When Lafcadio was 19, her estate manager sent him to start a new life in America.

Hearn around 1873 when he was working as a reporter for the *Cincinnati Enquirer*. His duties included visiting the city's police stations at night hunting for news.

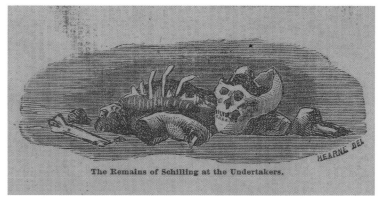

The Remains of Schilling at the Undertakers.

An illustration drawn by Hearn for an article in the *Cincinnati Enquirer* about the murder of Herman Schilling (1874). Hearn's lurid crime stories shocked readers and raised his stature as a reporter. *Photo: Cincinnati and Hamilton County Public Library.*

From 1882 to 1887, Hearn lived in two rooms in this house at 1565 Cleveland Street in New Orleans. Now called the Lafcadio Hearn House, it is registered as a national historic landmark.

St. Jean Street in St. Pierre, Martinique (1887–89). A volcanic eruption destroyed St. Pierre in 1902. Either Hearn himself or a photographer he hired took this photo. *Photo: Koizumi Family Archive.*

Matsue Castle in Shimane Prefecture. The castle, which was completed in 1611, rises above the old Samurai district where Hearn lived. It's the second largest remaining castle in Japan and one of the few still in its original wooden form.

The former Samurai house in Matsue where Hearn and his family lived from August 1890 to November 1891. The house is now open to the public. A museum devoted to memorializing his life and work is next to the house.

An interior view of Hearn's home in Matsue with his writing desk to the right. When writing, Hearn, blind in his left eye, would sit bent over his desk, his right eye a couple of inches from the paper. *Photo: Irisgazer @ flickr.*

A view of Hearn's garden in Matsue, which has been kept as it was during his time there. One of his finest essays concerns the beauty of the Japanese garden and its significance in the country's culture. *Photo: Koizumi Family Archive.*

Minnie Atkinson, Hearn's half-sister, with whom he exchanged a series of letters while he was in Japan. Minnie was one of Hearn's three half-sisters, none of whom he ever met in person.

Japanologist Basil Hall Chamberlain helped Hearn land teaching jobs in Matsue, Kumamoto and Tokyo. Hearn's contact with his students and their families taught him much about his adopted country.

Elizabeth Bisland worked with Hearn at the *New Orleans Times-Democrat* in the 1880s and became his life-long friend and confidant. Bisland, who became an editor at *Cosmopolitan* magazine, edited Hearn's collected letters after his death.

Hearn and Mitchell McDonald, who was Paymaster in the U.S. Navy in Yokohama. McDonald was close friends with Hearn and advised him about many practical issues. McDonald served as Hearn's literary executor after his death.

ABOVE: Hearn (front row, fifth from right) and his colleagues at the Imperial University of Tokyo, where Hearn taught English literature from 1895 to 1903. Hearn turns his head to hide his disfigured left eye from view. *Photo: Koizumi Family Archive.*

LEFT: Hearn at Kumamoto's Fifth High School, where he taught English literature from 1891 to 1894. In this photo, his left eye is partly visible, a rarity for photos of Hearn. *Photo: Koizumi Family Archive.*

The Peony Lantern, an illustration of the famous ghost story from the first edition of Hearn's book *In Ghostly Japan* (1899). In this tale, the ghosts of a young woman and her servant enter the life of a young man the woman had fallen in love with before she died.

Hearn and his wife, Setsu, the daughter of a former Samurai warrior. The marriage was arranged by a mutual friend not long after Hearn moved to Matsue. They had four children. *Photo: Koizumi Family Archive.*

Hearn and one of his former students shortly before embarking on their trek to the top of Mount Fuji in 1897. Adzukizawa, who now went by the adopted name of Fujisaki, visited Hearn in Yaidzu, where they planned their climb. *Photo: Koizumi Family Archive.*

Hearn's sons Kazuo and Iwao practicing Ju-Jitsu. Their younger siblings were Kiyoshi and Suzuko. Hearn, who took the Japanese name, Yakumo Koizumi, became a Japanese citizen so his family would inherit his estate.

Kazuo Koizumi, Lafcadio Hearn's oldest son, aged about 17 (c. 1910). Kazuo wrote a book about his relationship with his father entitled *Father and I: Memories of Lafcadio Hearn* (1935).

Hearn in Japanese garb. He much preferred the comfort of his Japanese robes and sandals to the Western clothes he had to wear in the schools where he taught. *Photo: Koizumi Family Archive.*

The exterior of the *Cincinnati Enquirer* building on Vine Street where Hearn worked in the second-floor newsroom. Hearn, who began writing for the *Enquirer* in 1872, quickly became known for his provocative stories and his distinctive literary style.
Photo: Cincinnati Enquirer.

Japanese stamp depicting Hearn on the 100th anniversary of his death in 2004. *Kwaidan*, a Japanese term meaning ghost stories, was the title of his most famous book, in which he retold ancient Japanese folk tales. *Photo: Shutterstock © rook76*

TOP: Lafcadio Hearn's grave in the Zōshigaya Cemetery, Tokyo, a place Hearn had enjoyed walking among the tall trees. He died of a heart attack on September 26, 1904, and was given a Buddhist funeral.

ABOVE: A float picturing Hearn is prepared for the 2008 Mardi Gras parade with his quote that was popularized after Hurricane Katrina: "Times are not good here....But it is better to be here in sackcloth and ashes than to own the whole state of Ohio."

Statue of Lafcadio Hearn in Matsue, Japan. Hearn lived in this city located on the Sea of Japan for a year and loved it for its beauty and its adherence to ancient traditions. He left Matsue only because of its nasty winters.

Hanamigata Cemetery in Kotoura along the shore of the Sea of Japan, about 45 miles east of Matsue. In "By the Japanese Sea" from *Glimpses of Unfamiliar Japan*, Hearn vividly describes this huge cemetery while on a honeymoon trip in 1891. *Photo: Author's collection.*

A first edition of *La Cuisine Creole* (1885), the first book of collected Creole recipes. Hearn gathered the recipes from the wives of his Creole friends. Its recipes are still followed by Creole chefs today.

"White Sepulchers," an illustration drawn by Hearn for the *New Orleans Daily Item* in 1880, to protest the horrible condition of many of the city's cemeteries. Hearn illustrated many of his stories for this newspaper.

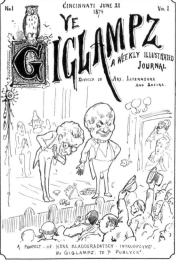

The first issue of *Ye Giglampz*, the satirical periodical created in Cincinnati by Hearn and artist Henry Farny from 1874. The man shown bowing in the illustration is Hearn. "Giglampz" is a reference to Hearn's thick glasses. *Photo: Cincinnati and Hamilton County Public Library.*

Lafcadio Hearn's personal seal. The bird pictured in the seal is a heron, obviously associated with the author's surname.

Hearn. But the main incident that caused Hearn to cool toward Cable occurred when Cable returned to New Orleans after a speaking tour with Mark Twain. Even though Cable introduced Hearn to Twain and helped Hearn professionally, Hearn felt the tour with Twain inflated Cable's sense of self-importance and that he snubbed him.[10] Hearn's excessive sensitivity and his ingrained mistrust of people often caused him to sever friendships because of minor offenses or imagined slights. This appears to be the case with his break with Cable, who was humble and warm-hearted. Cable was forced to leave New Orleans in 1885 because of two essays he wrote condemning the Jim Crow segregation laws and supporting racial equality. Cable had spoken out previously about the racial bigotry harbored by Creoles of French and Spanish descent. Unlike Hearn, who refrained from publicly expressing his racial views so that he could remain in New Orleans, Cable, a fervently religious man, felt compelled to speak out against social injustices, regardless of the criticism he might receive. His crusade against racism earned him enormous hostility. Fearing for his life, Cable moved with his family to Northampton, Mass., in 1885 and lived there for the next thirty years before moving to Florida.[11]

Elizabeth Bisland, a strikingly pretty and intelligent woman in her late teens, admired Hearn's writing when he worked for the *Item*. After he was hired by the *Times-Democrat*, she began contributing poetry to the newspaper's literary page—partly as a way of meeting him and asking him to critique her writing. With Hearn's assistance, Bisland soon became a staff writer. Still, it took Hearn a while to feel comfortable enough with her to befriend her, even though—or perhaps because—she openly idolized him. Her physical beauty and her confident, forthright manner intimidated Hearn, who tended to be shy around attractive women of social standing equal or superior to his. Initially, he was a bit standoffish and awkward around Bisland. She was not only talented, but also ambitious and assertive. He didn't like dealing with women he considered his intellectual equals.

A breakthrough in their relationship occurred when Bisland be-

---

[10]O. W. Frost, *Young Hearn* (Tokyo: Hokuseido Press, 1958), 207.

[11]Thomas J. Richardson, "George Washington Cable, 1844-1925)," *Encyclopedia of Southern Culture* (University of North Carolina Press, 1989), Charles Reagan Wilson and William Ferris, eds. Accessed through "Documenting the American South" Website, https://docsouth.unc.edu/southlit/cablecreole/bio.html.

came so seriously ill with a fever that doctors were afraid she might die. As she languished, Hearn regularly visited her at the hotel where she lived, nursing her and making sure she had enough to eat. She recovered, and they became close friends. In fact, Bisland was one of the few friends from his Cincinnati and New Orleans years he maintained until the end of his life. After he left New Orleans, Hearn began a warm, intimate correspondence with her that continued until the end of his life. Bisland, whom Hearn often addressed as "dear sister" in his letters, became a respected journalist in New York City, first writing for the *New York Sun*, and eventually becoming an editor at *Cosmopolitan* magazine. Her most famous journalism adventure occurred in 1889, when she engaged in a race around the world against famed reporter Nellie Bly, who worked for a rival publication. Bly won the race. But the highly publicized exploit enabled Bisland to write her first book, *In Seven Stages: A Flying Trip Around the World*. Fittingly, she later became Hearn's first biographer.

Hearn had been trying without success to interest a publisher in issuing a book of his translations of six of Theophile Gautier's stories when in 1882 he approached R. Worthington, a publisher in New York City. Worthington agreed to publish the book on the condition that Hearn contribute $150 to cover some of the printing costs. Desperate to crack the book publishing world, Hearn consented. *One of Cleopatra's Nights and Other Fantastic Stories* was issued later that year to a mixture of enthusiastic praise and shocked condemnation. One reviewer branded the book a collection of "stories of unbridled lust without the apology of natural passion" and declared that the translation "reeked with the miasma of the brothel."[12] Hearn believed that the criticism of the book on moral grounds caused R. Worthington and other publishers to reject his translation of Gustave Flaubert's *The Temptation of Saint Anthony*, which wouldn't be published until after Hearn's death.

By early 1883, the 32-year-old Hearn had gained enough confidence in his writing ability that he felt comfortable approaching national magazines with story proposals. With encouragement from Cable, Hearn began writing for *Harper's Weekly*, one of America's most prestigious magazines. His first story was "New Orleans in Car-

---

[12]Bisland, *Life and Letters*, vol. 1, 81-82.

nival Garb." Instead of writing the kind of glowing, sanguine account of New Orleans' Mardi Gras that was common even in Hearn's time, he told readers that the Carnival caused visitors to overlook some of the city's most appealing aspects.

"A very considerable number of those who visit New Orleans at Carnival-time," he writes, "do so quite as much for the sake of seeing the city itself as of witnessing the great pageant. But during Mardi Gras the place is disguised by its holiday garb—almost as much so indeed, as the King of the Carnival: the native picturesqueness of the quainter districts is overlaid and concealed by the artificial picturesqueness of the occasion. One finds the streets themselves masked, so much are their salient features concealed by those innumerable wooden frame-works temporarily erected to provide against the falling of galleries under an unaccustomed burden of spectators. The romantic charm of the old city is not readily obtained at such a time; the curious cosmopolitan characteristics that offer themselves to artistic eyes in other seasons are lost in the afflux of American visitors, and true local color is fairly drowned out by the colors of Rex."[13]

Hearn didn't confine his magazine topics to the borders of New Orleans. Accompanied by illustrator J. O. Davidson, Hearn sailed on a boat owned by the *Times-Democrat* to Saint Malo, a remote fishing village at the southeast corner of Lake Borgne, about 40 miles east of New Orleans. The village had been settled more than 100 ago by Fillipinos who deserted Spanish ships presumably because of the Spaniards' brutal treatment of them. The area was named after Jean Saint Malo, who in 1784 led a group of African slaves in their escape to the marshlands in the Lake Borgne area. The Spanish captured Saint Malo later in July of that year and hanged him in front of St. Louis Cathedral in New Orleans' Jackson Square.

The existence of this village had been secret for decades. The Fillipino fishermen who lived there were called Malays or Manilla-men. Because of St. Malo's harsh conditions, no women lived there. The Malays who were married housed their wives and children in New Orleans. Saint Malo, a little-known, self-enclosed sub-culture governed by its own laws and traditions, strongly appealed to Hearn's

[13]Hearn, "New Orleans in Carnival Garb," *Harper's Weekly*, in *Occidental Gleanings*, Albert Mordell, ed. (New York: Dodd, Mead and Company, 1925), 269-273.

desire for adventure and the exotic. *Harper's Weekly* sent Davidson with him to produce a story about St. Malo with illustrations.

To get to Saint Malo, their boat had to sail from Lake Ponchartrain through a waterway called the Rigolets leading to Lake Borgne. Then it had to travel the entire length of the lake before arriving at Saint Malo. Hearn's journey of about 100 miles brought him to a world unlike anything he had ever seen. The Saint Malo fishermen lived in small wooden houses on stilts above the swamp water. The window openings were covered with wire netting to keep out the mosquitoes and other insects. The houses had no furniture whatsoever. The men slept on mattresses filled with Spanish moss, and their diet consisted primarily of raw fish seasoned with vinegar and oil. Their chief entertainment was gambling. They didn't drink liquor, causing Hearn to observe that "these hardy fishers and alligator-hunters seem none the worse therefore. Their flesh is as hard as oarwood, and sickness rarely affects them…"[14] The fishermen allowed Hearn and his illustrator full access to their village in the swamps. When Hearn and Davidson entered the house where the men regularly gather to play gambling games such as monte and a Spanish version of keno, Hearn writes, "there was not a single person in the room who did not greet us with a hearty *buennoas noches*. The artist made his sketch of that grotesque scene upon the rude plank-work which served as a gambling table by the yellow flickering of lamps fed with fish-oil." Hearn's story in the March 31, 1883, issue of *Harper's Weekly* introduced Saint Malo to the rest of the nation. The settlement continued in its peculiar, harsh way of life until a hurricane wiped it out in 1915.

Just as Hearn had sensed the fragile nature of Saint Malo's existence during his visit, he also could see that New Orleans' Old World charm and Creole culture was fading. The influx of people from outside the region and the city's creeping commercialism threatened the qualities Hearn loved most about New Orleans. If many of his stories in the *Item* and the *Times-Democrat* reminded the city what made it unique, his articles in *Harper's* informed the rest of the nation about New Orleans' distinctive charms and culture.

---

[14]Hearn, "Saint Malo, a Lacustrine Village in Louisiana," *Harper's Weekly*, March 31, 1883, " in *Hearn: American Writings* (New York: The Library of America, 2009), 730-742.

In the summer of 1884, Baker insisted that Hearn take a paid vacation, a luxury he had never enjoyed in his newspaper career. Earlier in the year, he had taken a week off when Charley Johnson, one of his Cincinnati newspaper friends, came to town to visit. But that had been an unpaid vacation. Exhausted from his job and sporadic bouts of malarial fever, Hearn accepted Baker's offer and took a month's paid vacation on Grand Isle, located in the Gulf of Mexico southwest of New Orleans. Before the Civil War, a large sugar plantation manned by slaves operated on the island. When the plantation shut down some time after the war, a German named Krantz transformed the property into a traveler's resort. Guests stayed in the primitive whitewashed one-room cabins that had housed the slaves who worked on the plantation. The Krantz Hotel consisted of a complex of buildings that had functioned as a slave village. It included the cabins, a dining hall that had been the sugar house and a kitchen that had been the stables. Cattle now grazed in open fields where the cane had grown. The cows on the island were wild and hostile and would charge anyone who got too close. Island guests learned quickly to stay away from them.

Guests could walk the short distance to the beach or ride one of the mule-drawn outdated railway streetcars that Krantz had purchased in New Orleans. The brightly colored cars still had the names of New Orleans streets on them. Although the isle attracted vacationers, it also was home to several hundred permanent residents—mostly fishermen and their families. Much of the island's population descended from pirates.

On a typically sweltering August day, Hearn and Marion Baker boarded a white steamer at the city dock and sailed to Grand Isle. Later during their stay there, Elizabeth Bisland, who had become the Women's Page editor—joined them. Hearn's island sojourn proved to be just what he needed to relax and to rejuvenate himself. He hadn't swam in seawater since his summer vacations on the southeast Irish seacoast in his youth. Being at the beach delighted him so much he swam three or four times a day during his first week or so there. With his muscular shoulders and strong back, Hearn could out-swim the islanders as well as the guests. He would swim vigorously a long distance from shore, reveling in the coolness and beauty of the sea and returning to the beach tired but refreshed. Sunburn eventually forced him to reduce his swims to twice a day.

Hearn tried to avoid the other vacationers—except for Baker and Bisland—as much as possible. He enjoyed the solitude and the island's quiet, rural atmosphere and wanted as little contact as possible with people he found annoying. During this first stay at Grand Isle, he became irritated with a group of Jewish guests. He said nothing to them. But he lashed out at them in a letter to Margaret Courtney: "Mr. Baker came down last night and forty Jews went away,—so I am now able to take your mama's kind advice, and try to think there are no Jews in the world."[15] The remark was uncharacteristic of Hearn, who had written sympathetically and respectfully about Jews in Cincinnati and had argued fervently against anti-Semitism. When under extreme stress and in a state of physical exhaustion, he sometimes wrote offensive comments that contradicted his true sentiments. Perhaps that accounts for his spiteful outburst against the Jewish vacationers.

When Hearn wasn't swimming or writing in his cabin on Grand Isle, he wandered along the beaches, observed the trees, birds and insects and explored the fishing villages. He loved talking to the fishermen and their families, who spoke their own brand of Creole French. The islanders were so impressed by his sincere friendliness that they invited him into their small cottages or asked him to sit down on their porches and talk with them. In this way, Hearn shed the worries and tensions of his life in New Orleans and submerged himself into the simple, rustic world of Grand Isle. He became especially good friends with a Basque fisherman who captivated him with his tales about growing up in France and Algeria. The fisherman's beautiful daughter, who served them drinks and food as they talked, caught Hearn's fancy. She inspired him to write a story called "Torn Letters" after he returned to New Orleans. "I was very nearly in love—not quite sure whether I am not a little in love still," he confessed to Krehbiel, "but I never told her so. It is so strange to find one's self face to face with a beauty that existed in the Tertiary epoch,—300,000 years ago,—the beauty of the most ancient branch of humanity,—the oldest of the world's races!…I am so enamoured of those islands and tepid seas (the Gulf) that I would like to live there forever, and realize Tennyson's wish: —

---

[15]Tinker, *Lafcadio Hearn's American Days*, 218.

'I will wed some savage woman she shall rear my dusky race;
Iron-jointed, supple-sinewed, they shall dive and they shall
    run,—
Catch the wild goat by the hair, and hurl their lances in the
    sun,
Whistle back the parrot's call,—leap the rainbows of the
    brooks,—
Not with Blinded eyesight poring over miserable books.'"[16]

During his Grand Isle vacation, Hearn wrote Page Baker a long, playful letter filled with information and anecdotes about the resort, the activities and the people.[17] For Baker's amusement, Hearn drew sketches of some of the objects and people he mentioned in his letter. He drew Bisland in the water and, beneath that, drew his face, identifying himself as "Miss Bisland's A No. 1 Chaperone."

He dreaded the end of this pleasant respite on the island where he could swim every day. "Alas? the time flies too fast," he wrote to Baker. "Soon all this will be a dream:—the white cottages shadowed with leafy green,—the cows that look into one's window with the rising sun,—the dog and the mule trotting down the flower-edged road,—the goose of the ancient Margot,—the muttering surf upon the bar beyond bath-bell and the bathing belles,—the air that makes one feel like a boy,—the pleasure of sleeping with doors and windows open to the sea and its everlasting song,—the exhilaration of rising with the rim of the sun…. And then we must return to the dust and the roar of New Orleans to hear the rumble of wagons instead of the rumble of breakers, and to smell the smell of ancient gutters instead of the sharp sweet scent of pure sea wind…If I could live down here I should certainly live to be a hundred years old. One *lives* here. In New Orleans one only exists." To keep his star writer happy, Baker allowed Hearn to return to Grand Isle several more times. Besides swimming and talking to the residents, Hearn also took advantage of the placid, quiet atmosphere of the island to write articles for the *Times-Democrat* while staying there. He much preferred Grand Isle as a workplace to the newsroom.

---

[16]Hearn to Henry Krehbiel, October, 1884, in *Life and Letters*, vol. I, 333.
[17]Hearn to Page Baker, August, 1884, in *Life and Letters*, vol. I, 87-95.

In addition to allowing Hearn occasional trips to Grand Isle, Baker helped him attract a publisher for *Stray Leaves from Strange Literature*. A reader for James R. Osgood & Co. in Boston had rejected Hearn's manuscript by the time the publisher received Baker's letter of recommendation. The letter convinced Osgood to reconsider, and the book was accepted. One of the few extravagances Hearn allowed himself in New Orleans was the purchase of exotic books. By the time he wrote *Stray Leaves*, he had amassed a collection of more than 500 books, some imported from abroad. He boasted to Krehbiel that almost every one of his books would be unfamiliar to the average reader. He culled the stories for *Stray Leaves* from his personal library. He chose the ancient myths, legends and fables from French translations of ancient literature of Egypt, India, Buddhism, Finland and Moslem nations. Hearn took more liberties in translating these than he did with Gautier's. He retained the tales' basic narrative lines, but embellished and changed details to enhance the stories' appeal. In the book's introduction, Hearn states his purpose: "It is simply an attempt to share with the public some of those novel delights I experienced while trying to familiarize myself with some very strange and beautiful literatures…I hope my far less artistic contribution to the popularization of unfamiliar literature may stimulate others to produce something worthier than I can hope to do."[18] He dedicated the book to Page Baker.

These intriguing tales usually concern the relationships between human beings and the gods and goddesses who observe their many earthly foibles. Monsters and demons inhabit many of the stories, often intended to express spiritual truths about love, death, virtue and evil.

Although Hearn spent two years gathering and selecting the material for the book, he believed he hadn't spent enough time on the actual writing. "My poor little book will show some journalistic weaknesses—will contain some hasty phrases or redundancies or something which will mar it," he told Krehbiel. "What troubles my style especially is ornamentation. An ornamental style must be perfect or full of atrocious discords and incongruities; and perfect orna-

---

[18] Hearn, *The Writings of Lafcadio Hearn*, vol. II (Boston: Houghton Mifflin Company/ Cambridge: The Riverside Press, 1923), xx.

mentation requires slow artistic work—except in the case of men like Gautier, who never re-read a page, or worried himself about a proof. But I think I'll improve as I grow older."[19]

With *Strange Leaves* behind him, Hearn focused his attention on an upcoming event in New Orleans that would attract visitors from all parts of the country. The city would host the World's Industrial & Cotton Centennial Exposition from December 16, 1884 to June 2, 1885. To capitalize on the expected flood of tourists, Hearn prepared three small books that he felt would sell at this major public event. *Historical Sketch Book and Guide to New Orleans and Environs, La Cuisine Creole and Gombo Zhebes: A Little Dictionary of Creole Proverbs*. Hearn was one of several local writers contributing to the guide book, and he was the sole author of the other two. *La Cuisine Creole* contains recipes he collected from his friends' wives. He had compiled the book of Creole proverbs two years earlier. But when he couldn't get it published, he stashed it in a trunk. Hearn talked Will H. Coleman, a friend and a New York bookshop owner, into financing the publication of those three books. When Hearn first met Coleman, he operated machinery in New Orleans. Later he moved to New York and opened a book store.

Built on 249 acres on what is now the site of Audubon Park, the exposition ended deeply in debt and was marred by scandals and corruption. Yet it proved to be a huge commercial and public relations boost for New Orleans, attracting more than a million visitors. Unfortunately for Hearn, none of his three books sold very well because they weren't published until April 1885, less than two months before the exposition was scheduled to close. The book on Creole cuisine proved to be the most popular of the three, continuing to sell long after the end of the exposition. This was the first book on Creole cuisine ever published, and, even today, some New Orleans chefs refer to its recipes.

Although the exposition didn't generate the income Hearn had hoped it would, it did heighten his interest in Japanese culture. The simple but subtle beauty of the ancient bronzes and ceramics, vases, incense-burners, fans, ivory figurines, silks and the life-like lacquered insect creations completely entranced Hearn. In his article about the

---

[19]Hearn to Krehbiel, May 1884, *Life and Letters*, vol. I, 325.

exhibit for *Harper's Weekly*, he demonstrates his understanding and deep appreciation for Japanese art: "What Japanese art of the best era is unrivaled in—that characteristic in which, according even to the confession of the best French art connoisseurs, it excels all other art— is *movement*, the rhythm, the poetry, of visible motion. Great masters of the antique Japanese schools have been known to devote a whole lifetime to the depiction of one kind of bird, one variety of insect or reptile, alone. This specialization of art…produced results that no European master has ever been able to approach."[20]

Soon after Hearn's three little books were published in April, he went on a much-needed vacation with his gregarious, easy-going Cincinnati friend Charley Johnson. Johnson was the man who supposedly prevented Hearn from jumping into the canal in Cincinnati after the *Enquirer* fired him. They traveled by train from New Orleans to Florida's east coast. They stayed first in Jacksonville, where Hearn delighted in daily swims in the Atlantic. But the highlight of their adventures was a three-day steamboat trip from Jacksonville to the Silver Spring, traveling down the wide St. Johns River to the undulating Oklawaha River and then switching to a smaller boat to navigate the narrow Silver River. Even before the Civil War, the cold, crystal-clear waters of Silver Spring, now called Silver Springs, lured tourists. Hearn was overjoyed to be exploring a new environment.

In his written account of this trip which wasn't published until after his death, he displays his talent for describing nature. "Little frogs metallically bright as the lily-leaves on which they sit, chant in chorus; butterflies flutter on vermilion wing from bank to bank; sometimes the nose of an alligator furrows the river. The palmettoes, heretofore rare, begin to multiply; they assemble in troops, in ranks, in legions." He marveled at the palm trees, citing "the suppleness of their curves; the neck of the ostrich, the body of the serpent, seem less lithely beautiful." As they neared Silver Spring, the Silver River's water changed from green to translucent crystal, "a river of molten diamond, a current of liquid light."[21]

Although the vacation restored Hearn mentally, he returned to

---

[20] Hearn, "The New Orleans Exposition: The Japanese Exhibit," *Harper's Weekly*, January 31, 1885, in *Occidental Gleanings*, 211.

[21] Hearn, "To the Fountain of Youth," *The Writings of Lafcadio Hearn*, vol. I, 12.

New Orleans sick with a fever. After he recovered, he began reading the French translations of the novels of Fydor Dostoyevsky, Leo Tolstoy, Ivan Turgenev. Hearn became captivated by these authors and wrote essays about their work for the *Times-Democrat*. At the encouragement of a friend in New Orleans, Hearn reread the writings of the philosopher Herbert Spencer, whose work Henry Watkin had introduced him to in Cincinnati. The return to Spencer's writings reawakened his fervor for Spencer's notion of the gradual, inevitable and progressive evolution of all forms of life as well as human societies. It instilled some hope and tolerance in the skeptical Hearn. He tried to explain to Krehbiel the profound impact Spencer had on him. "I also learned what an absurd thing positive skepticism is. I also found unspeakable comfort in the sudden and, for me, eternal reopening of the Great Doubt, which renders pessimism ridiculous, and teaches a reverence for all forms of faith."[22] While it hardly qualifies as a religious epiphany, it represents a significant shift in thinking for someone who had long disdained Western religions.

Hearn's next literary project involved recasting and expanding six ancient Chinese folk tales. As he did in producing *Stray Leaves*, Hearn kept the basic narrative lines of these ancient legends and embroidered them in his own style. He relied on the French and English translations of these legends. Hearn selected the six tales for their "weird beauty," as he explained in preface of this slim book, *Some Chinese Ghosts*, published in 1887.[23] Although the book is slim, Hearn spent several months working on the stories. The extra time and effort paid off. On the whole, the prose is more polished and elegant than in *Stray Leaves*, and the stories flow more smoothly.

When trying to figure out in the spring of 1886 what he would write next, Hearn recalled an incident involving a small inhabited island in the Gulf of Mexico that Cable had told him about three years ago. On August 10, 1856, a hurricane smashed into Ile Derniere (Last Island), then a popular resort Gulf barrier reef island, southwest of New Orleans. Earlier that night, many guests on the island discounted the increasingly fierce storm and gathered in the hotel near the beach for a dance. The hurricane killed 200 people and destroyed all the veg-

---

[22]Hearn to Krehbiel, 1886, *Life and Letters*, vol. I, 374.
[23]Hearn, *Some Chinese Ghosts, in The Writings of Lafcadio Hearn*, vol. I, 213.

etation. Only one person survived—a little girl who had come to the island with her parents for a vacation. A fisherman found the girl and brought her to his house on another island. He and his wife, unhappily childless, lovingly raised the girl. Years later, a hunter recognized her from trinkets she wore. She was brought back to New Orleans to resume her life in the society she had been born in. But she hated living in the city, separated from her beloved adoptive parents and from the island she felt was her true home. Before long, she returned to the island and married a fisherman. The hurricane split Isle Derniere in half. Later storms divided it into five islands.[24]

Hearn decided to write a work of fiction based on that real-life catastrophe that occurred 30 years ago, five years after he was born. This kind of story appealed to Hearn for many reasons: It had heart-breaking tragedy, high drama, intense action and romance; it focused on the Creole culture and Louisiana Gulf life; and, most importantly, it revealed the devastating power of nature. Because of his familiarity with Grand Isle, which was very similar to what Isle Derniere had been, Hearn knew he could describe with authority the doomed island's landscape, sea shores, trees, plants, animals, human inhabitants and vacationers. During the year or so he worked on this novella called *Chita: A Memory of Last Island*, he enlisted the help of a few friends. Matas made sure the Spanish Hearn used in the book's dialogue was correct. Kreybiel looked up for Hearn what waltz the orchestra was playing at Isle Derniere's hotel when the hurricane struck. The piece was Weber's *l'Invitation* a la Valse, a detail Hearn used in his novella.

In the story, Julien La Brierre, a New Orleans Creole physician, and his wife, Adele, take their little girl, Zouzoune, to Isle Derniere for a summer vacation. The hurricane, like the real one in 1856, sweeps the hotel and the people in it out into the churning, tumultuous sea. The father is rescued, but the mother and the little girl are presumed to be dead. Zouzoune, found in the arms of her dead mother by a fisherman who is searching through debris, is barely alive. With her identity unknown, the fisherman and his wife raise the girl and name her Conchita or, for short, Chita. Years later, her birth father, Julien La Brierre, is called to the island to treat a man with yellow fever. He

---

[24]Stevenson, *Lafcadio Hearn*, 151.

strongly suspects this girl with long blond hair, a smile like his wife's and a telltale birthmark on her neck is his daughter. Before he can confirm it, he contracts yellow fever himself and dies on the island, without Chita ever knowing he was her father.

Though criticized by some for weak characterization and melodrama, *Chita* stands as a minor literary gem. The main character in this novella is the sea, not people. In poetic prose, Hearn portrays the sea in all its fury and capriciousness. The sea looms God-like over the human beings who live and vacation on Last Island and who travel on its waters. In willy-nilly fashion, it bestows pleasures and pain, bliss and misery.

Hearn observed and noted nature's nuances during his visits to Grand Isle so thoroughly that he was able to describe the island landcapes in *Chita* in a convincing, visual style. "On the Gulf side of these islands," the novella's narrator says, "you may observe that the trees—when there are any trees—all bend away from the sea; and, even of bright, hot days when the wind sleeps, there is something grotesquely pathetic in their look of agonized terror. A group of oaks at Grand Isle I remember as especially suggestive: five stooping silhouettes in line against the horizon, like fleeting women with streaming garments and wind-blown hair,—bowing grievously and thrusting out arms desperately northward as to save themselves from falling. And they are being pursued indeed;—for the sea is devouring the land. Many and many a mile of ground has yielded o the tireless charging of Ocean's cavalry: far out you can see, through a good glass, the porpoises at play where of old the sugar-cane shook out its million bannerets; and shark-fins now seam deep water above a site where pigeons used to coo. Men build dikes; but the besieging tides bring up their battering-rams—whole forests of drift—huge trunks of water-oak and weighty cypress. Forever the yellow Mississippi strives to build; forever the sea struggles to destroy;—and amid their eternal strife the islands and the promontories change shape, more slowly, but not less fantastically, than the clouds of heaven."[25]

Hearn vividly describes the violence of the sea. A steamboat, the *Star*, is struggling to get to Last Island in the midst of the horrific storm that was about to destroy the island. "...and now she was head-

---

[25]Hearn, *Chita: A Memory of L'ile Derniere*, in *Hearn: American Writings*, 81.

ing right for the island, with the wind aft, over the monstrous sea. On she came, swaying, rocking, plunging,—with a great whiteness wrapping her about like a cloud, and moving with her moving,—a tempest-whirl of spray;—ghost-white and like a ghost she came, for her smoke-stacks exhaled no visible smoke—the wind devoured it!"[26]

Hearn skillfully conveys the horror that suddenly seized the dancers in Last Island's hotel ballroom when they realized their lives were in danger: "Some one shrieked in the midst of the revels;—some girl who found her pretty slippers wet. What could it be? Thin streams of water were spreading over the level planking,—curling about the feet of the dancers…What could it be? All the land had begun to quake, even as, but a moment before, the polished floor was trembling to the pressure of circling steps;—all the building shook now; every beam uttered its groan. What could it be?…

"There was a clamor, a panic, a rush to the windy night. Infinite darkness above and beyond; but the lantern-beams danced far out over an unbroken circle of heaving and swirling black water. Stealthily, swiftly, the measureless sea-flood was rising."[27]

The characters and personalities of Chita, a little blonde girl from New Orleans high society, and her Spanish foster parents, Feliu and Carmen Viosca, are fully drawn. Hearn dramatizes brilliantly the deepening love between Chita and the Vioscas and Chita's gradual adaptation to island life. She learns to love nature—even the sea, which had taken her parents from her. *Chita* occasionally becomes a bit mawkish, but it doesn't occur often enough to become a major flaw. The novella's ending with the death of Chita's real father, Julien La Brierre, just after he discovers her on the island could have sunk to sheer bathos. But it didn't because of the realistic way Hearn portrays La Brierre in the throes of yellow fever. Hearn's rendering of the dying man's fever-induced thoughts foreshadows the stream-of-consciousness technique writers began experimenting with in the 1920s.

Even as Hearn waited to hear whether *Harper's Magazine* would publish his book, he decided he couldn't stay much longer in New Orleans. He had been restless for some time. He realized that to continue to develop as a writer he needed to leave New Orleans, just as

---

[26]Hearn, *Chita*, 89.
[27]Hearn, *Chita*, 93.

he had understood 10 years earlier that he needed to leave Cincinnati. His first preference was to explore the Creole culture on the Antilles islands in the Caribbean.

His chance meeting with a 26-year-old Creole woman in January 1887 helped him decide to make Martinique one of his prime Caribbean destinations. Hearn was poking around a secondhand bookshop in the French Quarter when Leona Queyrouze entered the store. The store owner introduced her to Hearn. The refined, pretty, dark-haired woman told him how much she admired his writing and asked him if he would critique some verses she had written. Noting her sincerity and enthusiasm, he reluctantly agreed to pay her a visit at her house and read some of her poetry. When he went to her house later, her maid, Marie, a brown-skinned woman from Martinique, let him in. He drank tea with Queyrouze and complimented her on her book collection. Just before he left, she gave him a few pages of her blank-verse poetry to take home and read. Wary of starting a romance with someone when he was planning to leave the city, Hearn said to her, "I would like to look upon you as a younger brother. Would you mind?" She told him she wouldn't mind, although she really did.[28]

A few days later, Hearn wrote her a letter telling her that her poems were too maudlin and overwrought. In advising her to strive for realism in her writing, he voiced some of his core aesthetic convictions. "What is wanted, what will succeed, what will endure," he wrote, "are reflections of real life, expressions of present existence, artistic and faithful records of what we hear, see and feel through the impressions made upon us by those social forces of which we form integers. Realism, if you please to call it such, but realism need not be dry, colorless and commonplace,—deftly utilized it never is. And it insures originality…But as no two lives are absolutely alike, no two minds alike, no two life-experiences alike, are who simply attempt to make a faithful picture of what is, or has been, a part of himself or herself,—without trying to ornament it or exaggerate it, or distort it—must become interesting if the true art-spirit is there."[29]

Queyrouze accepted his criticism well and invited him back to

[28]Leona Queyrouze Barel, *The Idyl: My Personal Remeniscences of Lafcadio Hearn* (Kanda, Tokyo, Japan: Hokusiedo Press, 1933), 24.

[29]Letter from Hearn to Leona Queyrouze, January, 1887, in *The Idyl*, 14, 16.

her house. Over the next few months, he came to her house many times, sometimes staying for dinner with her, her parents and other family members and friends. Hearn and Queyrouze, who knew seven languages and wrote for a couple of publications in New Orleans, talked endlessly about literature, languages and other cultural interests. Hearn was careful to keep their relationship on a tutor-student level, although Queyrouze secretly wanted to become romantically involved with him. During his visits, Hearn also questioned Marie about her native Martinique. Their conversations heightened his desire to go to this island of French-speaking Creoles.

In May 1887, *Harper's Magazine* accepted *Chita* with the plan of publishing it in three parts and then publishing it as a book. This good fortune boosted Hearn's confidence and made him believe he could support himself by traveling and writing on an independent basis. At the end of May, he resigned from the *Times-Democrat* and arranged to store his extensive book collection with Matas. Queyrouze was hurt and unhappy when he told her he was leaving New Orleans. She never forgot Hearn. For the rest of her life, she treasured her brief but intense friendship with him. She even wrote a short book in 1933 about their friendship. On his last visit to her house, they kissed goodbye, and he left. She immediately wrote down some of the things he had said during this final visit. One of his comments concerned the sources of writers' inspiration: "Do not seek inspiration merely around you in the exterior world and its powerful vibrations which fill our senses with the ecstasy of beauty. It is in the psychical depth of our own Self that we must look to find treasure which Aladdin's lamp never could have revealed."

Hearn knew that exploring more of the exterior world would help him delve deeper into himself and strengthen his writing ability. He would stop in Cincinnati to see his old friend, Henry Watkin, and continue to New York, where he would polish his Chita manuscript and confer with Harper's editors. If everything worked out, he would board a steamer for a long Caribbean Sea voyage. He planned to write stories from this trip that he hoped would appear in *Harper's Weekly* or another magazine. At long last, he would be free from the grind of daily journalism. He would seek the exotic locales in the world he had yearned to visit and write about them.

"I would give anything to be a literary Columbus," he had written to Krehbiel two years earlier, "to discover a Romantic America in some West Indian or North African or Oriental region,—to describe the life that is only fully treated of in universal geographies or ethnological researches."[30]

He was on the verge of fulfilling that dream.

---

[30]Hearn to Krehbiel, December, 1883, *Life and Letters*, 294-295.

CHAPTER 8

Mission in Martinique

*H*EARN KEPT HIS PLANNED stopover in Cincinnati on his way to New York City in early June 1887 as secret as possible. The only person he wanted to see in the city where he had launched his journalism career was his "Dear Old Dad," Henry Watkin. Most of his best reporter-friends had left Cincinnati. Given his acrimonious separations from the *Enquirer* and the *Commercial*, he had no desire to stop in those newsrooms and chat with his old co-workers. And he certainly didn't want Mattie Foley or Ellen Freeman to know he was in town. Mattie had remarried in 1880, but there is no indication he was aware of that. In a letter to Watkin shortly before he left New Orleans, he referred to his former home as "beastly Cincinnati."[1]

As soon as Hearn stepped into Watkin's printing shop at 26 Longworth St., he heard the familiar ticking of the old grandfather clock he had once said sounded like "the steps of a long-legged man walking on pavement."[2] Watkin, tears streaming down his face, embraced the man he loved as a son. They spent the entire afternoon in the shop talking about the past 10 years since they had seen each other. At some point during the day, Hearn stopped in the Mercantile Library, which wasn't far from Watkin's shop. In the early evening, Hearn caught the early evening train for New York City.

Henry Krehbiel, who now was music critic for the *New York Tribune*, met Hearn at the Jersey City train station. Krehbiel invited him to stay at the 57th Street Manhattan apartment he shared with his

---

[1]Hearn to Watkin, August 14, 1878, *Letters From the Raven: Being the Correspondence of Lafcadio Hearn to Henry Watkin*, ed. Milton Bronner (New York: Bretano's, 1907), 64.
[2]Hearn to Watkin, February 28, 1895, *Letters From the Raven*, 104.

wife and their young daughter. The two old friends talked well into the early morning hours. Within a few days, Hearn wrote Watkin a touching letter, telling him how much he had enjoyed seeing him again and how much his friendship meant to him. He said he appreciated Watkin more now than he had when he lived in Cincinnati. "I was too young, too foolish, too selfish to know you as you are, when we used to be together. Ten years made little exterior change in me, but a great deal of heart-change; and I saw you as you are,—noble and true and frank and generous, and felt I loved you more than I ever did before; felt also how much I owed you, and will always owe you,—and understood how much allowance you had made for all my horrid, foolish ways when I used to be with you."[3]

Krehbiel served as Hearn's guide around New York, introducing him to his colleagues at the *Tribune* and to others in the newspaper and publishing industry. Hearn also met with other friends who were living in New York: Joseph Tunison, a former *Cincinnati Gazette* reporter who was now the *New York Tribune's* literary editor, and Elizabeth Bisland, who moved to New York City in 1886 and was now an editor at *Cosmopolitan Magazine*. At Krehbiel's urging, Hearn, shy about meeting important people, introduced himself to *Harper's Magazine* editor Henry Alden. One of the most respected magazine editors in the country, Alden was glad to meet Hearn in person for the first time. Hearn greatly impressed him at this initial meeting, and he soon became one of Hearn's biggest advocates.

When Hearn told him about his tentative plans to take a trip to the Caribbean's Lesser Antilles, Alden said he would be interested in any articles he wrote during this adventure. He told Hearn to take a camera along for photos that could be used for drawing illustrations to accompany his stories. That provided Hearn with enough confidence to buy a $140 ticket for a month-long cruise that would stop at eight islands and at British Guiana on the northern coast of South America. More than three decades ago, his father had been stationed on two of the islands he would visit—Dominica and Grenada.

Hearn was anxious to leave New York. At first, he enjoyed the city's grandeur, but he soon became overwhelmed by its immense size and frenetic pace. He had been staying at the Krehbiels' apartment

---

[3]Hearn to Watkin, June, 1887, *Letters From the Raven*, 84.

for four weeks. The overlong visit strained the couple's hospitality and caused the friendship between Lafcadio and Henry to cool. Still, the Krehbiels accompanied Hearn in early July to the pier where he boarded the S.S. *Barracouta*, a small steamer he described as "long, narrow and graceful…with two masts, and an orange-yellow chimney."[4] Because this was the hottest part of the year in the Caribbean, there were only two other passengers on the *Barracouta*. "Nobody goes to such an outrageous part of the world at this most outrageous time, except physicians, and—fellows like me," he wrote in a letter to Page Baker.[5] The other two passengers were indeed physicians. They planned to disembark in Barbados, leaving Hearn as the lone passenger for the rest of the trip. "I shall then," he jokes, "have the smoking-room, the bathroom, the dining-room, and the blistering deck all to myself,—together with the pleasant spectacle of the sharks following tirelessly south, with their terrible patience and everlasting hope." He admitted to Baker that he felt nervous about going to a strange part of the world with no friends or a steady income.

As the steamer made its way to the Caribbean, the Atlantic waters were calm. Hearn marveled at the rich changing colors of the waters and the sky. On the second day at sea, Hearn remarked to a Frenchman from Guadalupe how blue the water looked. The man told him the water was more greenish than blue. He said he wouldn't see deep blue water until they reached the tropics. The next day, Hearn awoke from a nap in one of the deck chairs and was excited to see that the water looked much bluer than it had earlier in the day. But the man from Guadalupe laconically observed that the sea was "beginning to become blue."[6] On the fourth day of the voyage, the man allowed that the sea was "almost" the color of tropical waters.

The *Barracouta* arrived at its first port of call, St. Croix, on its seventh day at sea. Seen from the bay through gaps in a line of palm, mango, mahogany, bread-fruit and tamarind trees, Fredericksburg appeared to be a charming island town. But upon entering it, Hearn was disappointed in the dilapidated condition of the buildings. Much of the town had been heavily damaged by a fire during a revolt in 1878

---

[4]Hearn, *Two Years in the French West Indies* (New York: Harper & Brothers, 1890), 13.
[5]Hearn to Page Baker, June 1887, digital archive of Loyola University's Monroe Library.
[6]Hearn, *Two Years in the French West Indies*, 18.

by the Black residents against the Danish colonizers. The first stories, usually consisting of blocks of lava rock or brick, suffered little damage, but the second stories of many buildings had to be reconstructed. The Danish rebuilt second-story superstructures in a flimsy fashion and with cheap wood. While walking through the town, Hearn noticed that many of the Black women, carrying bundles on their heads, were smoking long cigars. In the marketplace, he sampled a delicious orange. He smoked Puerto Rican cigars and drank West Indian lemonade spiked with a generous amount of rum.

After another day at sea, the steamer stopped at St. Kitts, where a succession of green ribbed hills rose above the bay. Hearn found the town of Basse-Terre to be much less colorful than St. Croix. His favorite place on the island was the botanical garden, "with its banyans and its palms, its monstrous lilies and extraordinary fruit-trees, and its beautiful little fountains."[7]

After passing by Nevis and Monseurrat, the *Barracouta* landed at Dominica. The island's rugged natural beauty impressed Hearn. He writes; "A beautifully wrinkled mass of green and blue and gray;—a strangely abrupt peaking and heaping of the land. Behind the green heights loom the blues; behind these the grays—all pinnacled against the sky-glow—thrusting up through gaps or behind promontories. Indescribably exquisite the foldings and hollowings of the emerald coast."[8] But the steamer stopped there only long enough to drop off mail.

An hour after leaving Dominica, the *Barracouta* entered the bay at St. Pierre, Martinique, with a huge volcanic mountain, Mount Pelee, looming in the background, its top enshrouded in clouds. The mountain, whose name means bare or bald, was anything but that. Green trees and vegetations covered its sloping sides from the bottom to its veiled summit. Hearn calls it "one of the fairest sights a human eye can gaze upon."[9] After the steamer anchored in the bay, some distance from the shore, a small fleet of mostly flat-bottomed boats made from wooded shipping crates or lard boxes approached the steamer. Naked boys from 10 to 14 years old, rowing with pieces

---

[7] Ibid., 30.
[8] Ibid., 33.
[9] Ibid., 34.

of wood, formed a large circle near the steamer and yelled in high-pitched voices for passengers to toss coins into the water. As soon as the passengers began throwing British shillings and other coins, the boys dove head-first from their little jerry-rigged boats into the water to retrieve them.

St. Pierre, Martinique's capital, was a picturesque city known then as the "Little Paris of the West Indies." The inhabitants spoke French Creole, not too dissimilar to the Creole patois spoken in New Orleans. As soon as Hearn stepped ashore and began walking through its narrow, stone-flagged streets winding up into the hills, he became totally infatuated with the city and its people. The architecture reminded him of New Orleans' French Quarter. In presenting his first impressions of St. Pierre in a letter to Elizabeth Bisland, he wrote: "Imagine old New Orleans, the dear quaint part of it, young and idealized as a master-artist might idealize it,—made all tropical, with narrower and brighter streets, all climbing up the side of a volcanic peak to a tropical forest, or descending in terraces of steps to the sea;—fancy our Creole courts filled with giant mangoes and columnar palms (a hundred feet in height sometimes); and everybody in a costume of more than Oriental picturesqueness;—and astonishments of half-breed beauty;—and a grand tepid wind enveloping the city in one perpetual perfumed caress,—fancy all this, and you may have a faint idea of the sweetest, queerest, darlingest little city in the Antilles: *Saint-Pierre*, Martinique…I love it as if it were a human being."[10]

Hearn found the brown-yellow-skinned Creole women of Martinique irresistibly attractive. Matas had cautioned him before this trip about the dangers of syphilis and urged him to be prudent. Hearn promised him he would be careful. Right before Hearn arrived in Martinique, he wrote to Matas that so far he had been "strictly chaste. I think I shall be very temperate all the time."[11] But it wasn't to be. As he later told Matas: "My great and good resolves came to a furious termination at the delicious, dreamy little town of St. Pierre, Martinique…I'd like to see you live from one of these purple ports to another, in a condition of compulsory laziness and in view of all the

[10]Hearn to Elizabeth Bisland, July, 1887, *Life and Letters,* vol. I, 412.

[11]Stevenson, *Lafcadio Hearn*, 160. Quotes letter from Hearn to Dr. Rudolph Matas, *Newly Discovered Letters from Lafcadio Hearn to Dr. Rudoph Matas* (Tokyo, 1956), Ichiro Nishizaki, ed.

tantalizing things, and continue to neglect the Apples of Paradise."[12]

In Fort-de-France, Hearn was struck by the majestic beauty of the white marble statue of Josephine Tascher de La Pagerie, a white Creole who was born in Martinique and later became the wife of Napoleon Bonaparte and the empress of France. The statue of Empress Josephine stood on a high pedestal surrounded by tall palm trees in La Savane, an expansive, green public square. The statue gazed across the Bay of Fort-de-France toward Trois-Ilets, where Josephine lived as a girl. Hearn was intrigued by a story someone in Fort-de-France had told him about the statue, which was erected in 1859, 45 years after Josephine's death. He related the story in a letter to Bisland, whose face, he told her, resembled Josephine's.[13]

After France was defeated in the Franco-Prussian War and Napoleon III was deposed in 1870, some Martinique government officials wanted to remove the statue because they considered it a symbol of imperialism and slavery. France had abolished slavery in their colonies in 1789, but soon after Napoleon and Josephine, assumed their thrones in 1804, it was re-established. Josephine had a reputation for being kind-hearted. But some believed Josephine had urged Napoleon to reinstate slavery in its imperial lands to help bolster her family's failing plantation in Martinique. So one day in 1870, the island's officials ordered her statue to be taken out of La Savane. A rope was placed around the neck of Josephine's statue when the bell of a nearby church rang, calling people to come to La Savane and stop the statue's removal. An angry crowd, composed partly of former slaves, showed up and convinced the frightened officials to let the statue alone. But the statue's good fortune ended 121 years later.[14] In 1991, a group of unknown people decapitated the statue during the night in an evocation of the French guillotine. Later, someone splattered the area around her neck with blood-red paint. Her head has not been found or replaced.[15]

With regret, Hearn left Martinique on the *Barracouta* to continue

---

[12]Stevenson, *Lafcadio Hearn*, 160. Quotes letter from Hearn to Matas, *Newly Discovered Letters.*

[13]Hearn to Bisland, July, 1887, *Life and Letters,* vol. I, 417.

[14]Ibid., 417-419

[15]Andrew Milne, "In the Footsteps of Empress Josephine in Martinique," Explore France Web site. Accessed through https://us.france.fr/en/martinique/list/empress-josephine-martinique.

his excursion through the Caribbean. Hearn disliked the next port of call, Bridgetown, Barbados. He found the town to be too British in appearance, lacking color and originality in its architecture and in the clothing of its Black residents.

It took three days at sea to reach British Guiana on the northern coast of South America. The cruise then headed north to Trinidad, Grenada, and St. Lucia. While in Trinidad, Hearn visited an Indian coolie village outside Port-of-Spain. The coolies, with their exotic costumes, shiny jewelry and Hindu culture, fascinated Hearn. He took photographs of them so that an artist at Harper's could draw illustrations of them for the story he hoped to sell to the magazine. Although Martinique was clearly his favorite island, Hearn enjoyed the whole trip. The climate, the sea, the dazzling colors of the plants, flowers and fish, the volcanic landscapes and "the delightful displays of nakedness,"[16] as he phrases it in a letter to Matas, convinced him he had found a region of the world where he could live contentedly for many years. In the Caribbean he was far removed from the aspects of modern urban life he hated—the crowdedness, the furious pace, the commercialism and the absence of nature. "I have come to the startling conclusion that civilization is a cold and vapid humbug;—the tropics are the only living part of this dying planet…This is altogether divine."

Hearn decided he would delay his return to New York so that he could spend more time in Martinique and write his magazine story there. He had bought a round-trip ticket and could go back to New York on the *Barracouta* when it stopped on one of its future cruises. The cost of living was very cheap in St. Pierre, and he hoped his stash of money would allow him to stay there for as long as two months. As he set to work on the travel piece about his Caribbean voyage, he found it hard to concentrate. The brilliant tropical colors, the beauties of nature and the lithe, graceful Martinique women overwhelmed his senses. The island's indolent pace of life lulled him. "Strange as you may think it," he wrote to Krehbiel, "this trip knocks the poetry out of me! The imagination is not stimulated, but paralyzed by the satiation of all its aspirations and the realization of its wildest dreams."[17]

---

[16] Jonathan Cott, *Wandering Ghost: The Odyssey of Lafcadio Hearn* (New York: Alfred A. Knopf, 1991), 208. Quotes a letter from Hearn to Matas, in *Newly Discovered Letters*, 91-92.

[17] Hearn to Krehbiel, 1887, *Life and Letters*, 410.

But he conquered the distractions well enough to complete his long travel essay, "A Midsummer Trip to the Tropics." With his money running low, he boarded the S.S. *Barracouta* in September and returned to New York City. When he arrived at the Manhattan pier, there was no one to meet him. Krehbiel and Bisland were out of town. Hearn checked into a hotel near the waterfront and soon presented his manuscript to Henry Alden. To Hearn's great relief, Alden immediately bought it for $700 and said it would run in serialized form in *Harper's Magazine*. In order to get to know this talented new writer better, Alden invited him to stay for several days at his family home in Metuchen, N.J., a small town about 30 miles southwest of Manhattan. Hearn thoroughly enjoyed the company of Alden and his family in their country house as well as the break from frenzied, hectic New York City. As he usually did with children and teenagers, Hearn developed a rapport with Alden's young daughter, Annie.

Born in Vermont, Alden was a direct descendant of John Alden, one of the original settlers of Plymouth Colony who had come to the New World on the *Mayflower*, worked in a mill while attending Williams College in Williamstown, Mass. After teaching for a while and writing a few articles for periodicals, he was hired in 1863 by the Harper publishing firm. Six years later, he became the editor of *Harper's Magazine*. When Hearn met Alden, *Harper's* had surpassed the *Atlantic Monthly* as America's preeminent magazine.[18] In Alden, Hearn acquired a powerful and intelligent mentor and friend. Alden had a kind, even-handed disposition similar to Hearn's previous mentor, Page Baker. The introduction of Alden into Hearn's life occurred at a time when Hearn had begun to brood about the instances when Baker had censored his work. The more he thought about it, the angrier he became. As he did with George Washington Cable and other friends, the temperamental Hearn magnified minor grievances he had with Baker into major offenses and funneled his anger toward a man who genuinely cared about him and had immeasurably helped his career.

Hearn desperately wanted to go back to the tropics and perhaps spend the rest of his life there. "My venture has been more successful than I had hoped," he wrote to Matas, "and I find my self *[sic]* able

---

[18]"Henry Mills Alden," Prabook Web site. Accessed through https://prabook.com/web/henry.alden/3750327.

to abandon journalism, with all its pettiness, cowardice, selfishness, forever."[19] Alden told Hearn that if he decided to go back to Martinique, he would consider publishing whatever he wrote there. That assurance was enough to convince Hearn to return to the island that had won his heart. He bought some new clothes and spent $400 of his $700 payment he had received for "A Midsummer Trip to the Tropics" on a camera he had no idea how to use. Lacking the courage for a face-to-face goodbye meeting with Bisland, he left her a short note at her apartment. With his suitcase and camera, he boarded the S.S. *Barracouta* on October 2, 1887, and returned to Martinique.

He rented a room in St. Pierre and, in the sweltering heat, he carried his bulky camera around as he explored the city. He soon became a familiar figure to the canoe boys on the beaches and to the men who loitered on the bridges above the Roxelane River and eyed the young women standing in the cold river water washing their employers' clothes and linens. Occasionally the women would yell at them to go away. But the men paid no attention to their protests, and the women returned to their task.

Hearn planned to write long sketches of various aspects of Martinique life. Originally, he expected to stay in Martinique for about two months and then, with Martinique as his base, visit some other islands to gather more material for his sketches.

Hearn struggled to take acceptable photographs with his $400 camera. "As a photographer, I fear I am not a success;—moreover I believe my instrument is a fraud," he wrote to Henry Alden's daughter, Annie. "The focus-register is all wrong, and the lens cannot give a simultaneously sharp definition to background and foreground."[20] His photographic attempts sometimes led him into unexpected adventures. He once offered to pay 17 boys 10 cents each to pose for pictures with their canoes. After the pictures were taken, the boys lined up for their reward. Hearn began paying them. But other boys broke into the line and the ones who got paid went back to the end of the line in hopes of collecting a double fee for their efforts. Suddenly

[19]Stevenson, *Lafcadio Hearn*, 163. Quotes a letter from Hearn to Matas, in *Newly Discovered Letters*, 108.

[20]Hearn to Annie Alden, Winter, 1887, *New Hearn Letters from the French West Indies*, Ichiro Nishizaki (Reprinted from Ochanomizu University *Studies in Art and Culture* vol. 12, *Tokyo: June 1959*), 65.

engulfed by dozens of naked boys wanting to be paid, Hearn ran. The boys pursued him. Hearn headed to the tallest building in St. Pierre, the house of a photographer he knew, and scurried up to the fourth floor. The mob of boys gathered at the door and wouldn't leave. The police were called and dispersed the boys, allowing Hearn to walk safely out of the building. When he saw the boys later that day, they began to cry and Hearn felt sorry for them and paid them—even the ones who hadn't posed for him.[21]

On Martinique, foreigners often had live-in servants called *bonnes*. Hearn's *bonne* was a Creole woman named Cyrillia. On a typical day, Cyrillia would wake Hearn at 5 a.m. as the sun was beginning to light the sky. She would bring him coffee and a slice of "corossol," custard-apple. After this little snack, Hearn would take his towels, stroll down to the beach and swim in the tepid sea for a half-hour to an hour. Upon returning home, he would write until noon, when a breakfast usually consisting of fruits, vegetables and a wide array of fish would be served. The early afternoon heat was too oppressive to work. So Hearn, like the other island residents, would put on pajamas and lay down for a nap. He would work as much as possible in the late-afternoon heat and have supper at 7 p.m. He would go to bed at 9 p.m., the customary time for most of the islanders. "...the day is done," he wrote to Annie Alden. "No pleasant chats, walks, exchange of ideas; everybody has become too lazy and tired to talk."[22]

During his stint in Martinique, Cyrillia was the most important person in his daily life. She not only did the housework and the cooking, but she also diligently and devotedly guarded his well-being and provided an invaluable window into the culture and customs of the island's people of color. Hearn wrote a sensitive, tender portrait Cyrillia in a sketch called "Ma Bonne," that was included in his book, *Two Years in the French West Indies*. At his request, she prepared a wide array of Creole cuisine so that he could become familiar with the food the non-European islanders ate. He writes: "She always does her best to please me in this respect,—almost daily introduces me to some of the unfamiliar dishes, something odd in the way of fruit or fish."[23]

---

[21] Hearn to Annie Alden, Winter, 1887, *New Hearn Letters*, 66.
[22] Ibid., 65.
[23] Hearn, *Two Years in the French West Indies,* 350.

Hearn recognized the important place food holds in an ethnic culture because he describes these various dishes and the many varieties of fish, fruit and vegetables with the meticulousness of a gourmand.

Cyrillia often complained that Hearn didn't eat enough and made sure his diet included beefsteaks and roasts. She reprimanded him when he walked in the sun without an umbrella to shade himself. Like the other Creoles, she believed soap would "kill the light in the eyes," and she never stopped reminding him not to use soap to wash his face. Besides the sun and soap, Cyrillia also warned Hearn about zombies, witches or wizards. She fervently believed in the existence of zombies and told Hearn stories about ghosts and Creole superstitions.

Cyrillia had her own room with a bed, but she sometimes slept with Hearn. He naturally avoided mentioning this in "Ma Bonne," but it was customary for a *bonne* to have sexual relations with her unmarried male employer. There's no question Hearn had a strong emotional bond with Cyrilla as well as a sexual one. One day, she told him she would like to have a photograph taken of her adult daughter. He helped her arrange it. The photograph was delivered to the house when Cyrillia wasn't there. Hearn had it framed and put it in her room as a surprise. When she returned, she entered her room and closed the door. Hearn waited a few minutes, quietly opened the door and looked in. She was standing before the photo and talking to it as if her daughter's image could hear her.

"My child! My child!," she said in Creole as tears formed in her eyes. "Yes, thou art all beautiful; my child is beautiful." When she turned and saw Hearn, she laughed in embarrassment. "Why do they not make a portrait talk,—tell me?" she said to him. "For they draw it just like you!—it is yourself: they ought to make it talk."[24]

The touching incident caused Hearn to ruminate in "Ma Bonne" on the nature of love, humanity and the divine: "…And I, watching her beautiful childish emotion, thought:—Cursed be the cruelty that would persuade itself that one soul may be like another,—that one affection may be replaced by another,—that individual goodness is not a thing apart, original, untwinned on earth, but only the general characteristic of a class or type, to be sought and found and utilized at will!…Self-cursed he who denies the divinity of love! Each heart,

---

[24]Ibid., 378-379.

each brain in the billions of humanity,—even so surely as sorrow lives,—feels and thinks in some special way unlike any other; and goodness in each has its unlikeness to all other goodness,—and thus its own infinite preciousness; for however humble, however small, it is something all alone and God never repeats his work. No heart-beat is cheap, no gentleness is despicable, no kindness is common; and Death, in removing a life—the simplest life ignored,—removes what never will reappear through the eternity of eternities,—since every being is the sum of a chain of experiences infinitely varied form all others…To some Cyrillia's happy tears might bring a smile: to me that smile would seem the unforgivable sin against the Giver of Life!"[25]

Hearn's sense of the divine clearly had evolved since his years in Cincinnati, when he considered himself an agnostic, if not an atheist. Not long after arriving in Martinique, he confided in a letter to Page Baker that he came to the tropics hoping to experience some sort of spiritual awakening. "But I must make a confession. I hoped to find the Holy Ghost here: I am disappointed—feel further away from the infinite. The charm of the flesh here is too strong for deep mutual life: one is too much caressed by winds, tantalized by odor, dazzled by colors, dazed by light, intoxicated by grace of form in flora and in—human fauna."[26] But the above passage in his portrait of Cyrillia indicates he had made some progress toward his goal.

In his first couple of months back in Martinique, Hearn worked on a novella, *Lys*. Conceived as a sequel of sorts to *Chita*, *Lys* centered around a young Caribbean Creole woman's journey to the cold North. While writing this novella, Hearn also tried to develop ideas for sketches for *Harper's Magazine*.

In his exuberance for his new home, he tried to convince his New Orleans friend, Rudolf Matas, to come to Martinique, just as he had tried to lure his "Old Dad," Henry Watkin, to come to New Orleans. "Could I induce you to abandon the beastly civilization of the U.S., and live somewhere down here forever more where everybody is honest and good-natured and courteous, and where everything is divine? Man was not intended to work in this part of the world: while you are here, you cannot quite persuade yourself you are awake,—it is a dream

[25]Ibid., 379.
[26]Hearn to Page Baker, 1887, digital archive of Loyola University's Monroe Library.

of eternal beauty,—all the musky winds, all the flower-months of Paradise! New Orleans is the most infernal hole in the entire Cosmos."[27]

His "Paradise," however, soon developed some serious flaws. During the winter, scattered cases of smallpox broke out in St. Pierre. To escape the threat of a smallpox epidemic and the heat of St. Pierre, Hearn moved temporarily to Morne Rouge, a small mountain town a few miles from St. Pierre. But he found it to be too cold at times and a very lonely place, with almost no one speaking English. "I have to learn this Creole to get along," he wrote to Henry Alden, "and am managing very well with it. But occasionally one feels as if in exile, and you get tired of the eternal palms against the light, tired of the colors, tired of the shrieking tongue spoken around you, tired of hearing by night the mandibles of the great tropical insects furiously devouring the few English books upon the table."[28]

In January 1888, Hearn moved back to St. Pierre. The next month, he received a letter from Alden rejecting *Lys* with pointed criticism. The letter stung Hearn to the core. But he squelched any resentful feelings he had and meekly agreed with Alden's critique. "Your letter was not all harsh;—too kind, perhaps; and, as in most such cases, *opened my eyes.* I saw at once the faults, and judged them as severely—no, more severely than you."[29] Hearn felt so crushed that he threw away the manuscript of *Lys*. He later wrote a sketch entitled *Lys* that he included in his book, *Two Years in the French West Indies*. The rejection of *Lys* was not only a blow to his ego, but also to his pocketbook. He was counting on receiving an immediate payment for the novella, and now he would receive nothing.

Besides money woes, Hearn also had serious health concerns. A full-scale smallpox epidemic broke out first in Fort-de-France and then spread to St. Pierre. The entire island was under quarantine, with no ships being permitted to come in or leave. At the same time, an epidemic of typhoid fever gripped St. Pierre. Smallpox and typhoid claimed the lives of up to 400 St. Pierre residents each month. Many people—children and adults—Hearn knew by name or had become used to seeing in the streets or in the city's shops died during the

---

[27]Hearn to Matas, July 30, 1887. Quoted in George M. Gould, *Concerning Lafcadio Hearn* (Philadelphia: George W. Jacobs & Company, 1908), 91.

[28]Hearn to Henry Alden, January 5, 1888, *New Hearn Letters*, 68.

[29]Hearn to Henry Alden, February 8, 1888, *New Hearn Letters*, 70.

epidemic. Every day, caskets containing the bodies of the epidemic victims were carried out of homes as family members sobbed.

The extraordinary kindness St. Pierre's people of color displayed during these horrifying months made an indelible impression on Hearn, who called their selflessness "heroic." "There is never a moment's hesitation," he writes in his sketch, "La Verette," "in visiting a stricken individual: every relative, and even the most intimate friends of every relative, may be seen hurrying to the bedside. They take turns at nursing, sitting up all night, securing medical attendance and medicines, without ever a thought of the danger,—nay, of the almost absolute certainty of contagion. If the patient have no means, all contribute: what the sister or brother has not, the uncle or the aunt, the godfather or godmother, the cousin, brother-in-law or sister-in-law, may be able to give. No one dreams of refusing money or linen or wine or anything possible to give, lend, or procure on credit."[30]

The death that affected him the most was that of a Creole woman, Yzore, who lived across the narrow street from Hearn. She had three children by a white lover who had died before Hearn came to Martinique. As he sat on his balcony, Hearn sometimes would watch her children and others play in the street. He would hear them talk with their mother as they all sat next to each other on the front step of the building where they lived. Yzore became stricken with typhoid fever and died. Her body, covered in quick-lime, was carried out of the house. Her furniture was auctioned off to pay her debts. Her three orphaned children were left with nothing.

Hearn himself caught the fever and became dangerously ill. He collapsed while walking outside and had to be carried home. Some friends took him to Morne Rouge, where he was practically bed-ridden for six weeks. Since he couldn't afford to pay for a nurse, his neighbors looked after him and helped him recover. Despite his illness and the devastating of despair and grief that seized the island during the long epidemic, Hearn retained his affection for Martinique. "…I love this little island as much as ever," he wrote to Annie Alden. "It is not any the less beautiful to me because of the sinister period we have passed…"[31]

---

[30]Hearn, *Two Years in the French West Indies,* 228-229.
[31]Hearn to Annie Alden, April 27, 1888, *New Hearn Letters,* 73.

Once Hearn's health recovered, the quarantine ended, and he began receiving money for his work that was appearing in *Harper's Magazine*, he set out in a horse-drawn carriage with a friend and a professional photographer to a little town on the northeast coast of Martinique called Grand Anse. (It's now called Lorrain.) He hired photographer Leon Sully because he wanted to be sure to have good photographs for artists at Harper's Magazine to use for illustrations. His many struggles with his unwieldy camera had convinced him he couldn't rely on himself for acceptable photos. Hearn had become interested in Grand Anse through the porteuses, young female carriers who walked many miles each day transporting merchandise they balanced on their heads. He marveled at how swiftly and gracefully the lithe, barefoot women would carry their heavy burdens in the heat over long distances. The 35-mile journey from St. Pierre to Grand Anse was long and arduous—even in a carriage. The road rose sharply up to Morne Rouge and then mostly descended in winding curves through forests, through the hamlet of Ajoupa-Bouillon, up and down low mornes and into the valley where Grand Anse, a much smaller town than St. Pierre, nestled near the sea. Going from St. Pierre by horse or carriage took four to five hours. The return trip took longer because it was mostly uphill.

Hearn spent three days on this trip. In his sketch about this trip, "La Grand Anse," he shows how two towns on a small island can be extremely different from each other. Many inhabitants of St. Pierre and Grand Anse never ventured to the other one because of the mountain range that separated them and the difficult, winding route. The turbulent sea waters prevented much boat travel between the two towns. The mountain range blocked Grand Anse residents from seeing the beautiful sunsets visible in St. Pierre, and it blocked the sunrises for St. Pierre residents. Hearn noted the features of everyday life that distinguish the two towns. Because of the roughness of the sea, receiving and sending supplies and merchandise at Grand Anse depended on the strength and skill of swimmers who pushed barrels of merchandise from ships to shore or from shore to ships. Hearn's prose provides a vivid picture of these swimmers in action.

"Wonderful surf-swimmers these men are," he writes. "They will go far out for mere sport in the roughest kind of sea, when the waves, abnormally swollen by the peculiar conformation of the bay, come rolling in thirty and forty feet high. Sometimes, with the swift impulse of ascending a swell, the swimmer seems suspended in air as it passes beneath him, before he plunges into the trough beyond. The best swimmer is a young *capre* who cannot weigh more than a hundred and twenty pounds. Few of the Grand Anse men are heavily built; they do not compare for stature and thew with those longshoremen at St. Pierre who can be seen any busy afternoon on the landing, lifting heavy barrels at almost the full reach of their swarthy arms."[32]

While in Grand Anse, Hearn was invited to spend part of a day at one of the old colonial estates on a hill outside Grand Anse. He received a tour of the estate, which included a sugar mill and a rum distillery. The host pointed out to him birds and plants that were uncommon elsewhere on the island. One was a bird that suspended its nest, like a hammock, under the leaves of a banana tree. For Hearn, the most exciting part of his visit to the estate occurred when one of the Black workers in the settlement played on a drum made from a quarter-barrel. As the man pounded African rhythms on the drum with his hands, Hearn took his photo—one of his few successful photos with this camera.

Soon after Hearn returned to St. Pierre, wrote his story about Grand Anse and sent it to Alden, he planned his next trip. This new adventure would make his Grand Anse trip seem like a stroll on a sandy beach. Hearn arranged to hike to the top of Mount Pelee with Leon Sully, a couple of friends and native guides. The slopes of the 4,800-foot high Mount Pelee or Bald Mountain are dense with trees and vegetation. Climbing to the summit of Pelee, the most dominant geographical feature of Martinique, involved trekking for hours on paths covered with slippery moss-covered tree roots through dense forests inhabited by deadly snakes. To leave Martinique without climbing Pelee would be like visiting France without going Paris. Hearn knew his book on the French West Indies wouldn't be complete without a chapter about majestic and powerful Pelee. "As the culminant point of the island," he writes, "Pelee is also the ruler of its meteorologic life,—cloud-herder, lightning-forger, and rain-maker. During clear weather you can see it drawing to itself all the white vapors of the land,—robbing lesser eminences of their shoulder-wraps

---

[32]Hearn, *Two Years in the French West Indies*, 135.

and head-coverings…"[33]

At 5 a.m. on September 12, 1888, Hearn, his friends and Sully left St. Pierre in hopes of reaching the summit by early afternoon, a part of the day they were mostly likely to have a clear view. Most days, clouds covered Pelee's peak. They took the shortest route to Pelee, heading north from St. Pierre along the beach and after a half-hour, turning up a winding mountain road that lead to sugar plantations. Their horse-drawn carriage stopped at the last plantation, owned by one of Hearn's friends accompanying him on the climb. The friend provided for their horses, let the men change clothes at his house and arranged for two of his field hands to serve as their guides. The group set out on foot to begin the rugged ascent.

The two guides walked bare foot, carrying a cutlass in one hand and the group's provisions and photographic equipment on their heads. They brought the cutlasses to clear paths and to kill snakes. After walking on a path that led them through wild cane and guava and guinea-grass, they reached the entry to the primitive forest, where the path was overrun with tree roots. Hearn, slipping on the roots, fell so often that one of the guides, without taking the load off his head, cut and trimmed a staff with his cutlass and gave it to Hearn to help steady himself as he walked. Later, the forest became less dense, but the path continued to be steep and slippery. As they neared the Crater of the Three Palmistes, their path began to be broken by gaps about two feet wide. To prevent any member of the party from falling to his death in one of the gaps, the guides insisted on holding hands as they crossed.

Around 11:30 a.m., they reached the crater, which was filled with a shallow lake about 200 yards in diameter. The men stripped and swam in the lake, which Hearn said wasn't as cold as the Roxelane River in St. Pierre. After this pleasant interlude, they resumed their climb and reached Pelee's peak about 1 p.m. During their climb, they had enjoyed some spectacular views. But they were disappointed to find that moving masses of clouds engulfed the peak, allowing them to see no more than 50 feet except for brief gaps in the clouds. They decided to wait there for a while in hopes the clouds might clear away. As they sat waiting, they received a momentary scare. The mountain

---

[33] Ibid., 259.

peak suddenly vibrated to a booming sound from below. Could it be the rumblings of a volcanic eruption? They soon realized the noise was merely the thunder accompanying a rain storm soaking the forest below them. The clouds blocking their views never left, and they began their long descent. They arrived in St. Pierre at 9 p.m., 16 hours after they had departed.

The climb provided Hearn with a wealth of material for his sketch and some good photos, even though the clouds had prevented Sully from taking photos from the mountain's peak. Despite the daunting physical challenges of the climb, Hearn didn't regret doing it. But he had no intention of doing it again, no matter how clear the view might be from the top. "Today I feel as if I had been 'broken on the wheel'—cannot move,' he wrote to Henry Alden the day after the trip. "It was beyond any question the most terrible journey I ever made:— we had to climb up through seven or eight miles of tropical forest, and descend the same path,—always over roots of trees covered with a green slimy moss, slippery as ice. I think I must have fallen more than 200 times. The native guides, barefooted, never tripped or fell, although heavily loaded with provisions, and Mr. Sully's photographic instruments. For them the journey was nothing; I never saw such men!…I have done the best I could; will complete articles in a few days and send you. But I would not undertake the journey again;—it is atrocious!"[34]

In early1889, some of the Martinique residents who had left the island years before to work on the failed French Panama Canal returned home. Many didn't survive the working on the project. Hearn witnessed first-hand the terrible toll suffered by some of the surviving laborers Martinique. Begun in 1881, the project attracted workers from islands throughout the Caribbean. Hundreds of men from Martinique had emigrated to Colon, Panama, to work on the canal. But the project turned into an engineering, health and safety nightmare. Construction was suspended in 1889 because of financial, engineering and, most of all, health issues. More than 22,000 workers died from diseases or accidents. In a letter to Annie Alden, Hearn described the canal workers who returned to Martinique as "broken down in health, and looking more like swollen corpses than men…One Creole engi-

---

[34]Hearn to Henry Alden, September 13, 1888, *New Hearn Letters*, 91.

neer, employed upon a special mechanical construction, found all his aids,—graduates of the Ecole Polytechnique,—die one after the other, faster than he could replace them, and had to finish the work alone. How he survived himself is a mystery."[35]

His relationship with Henry Alden became strained at times, just as it had with most of his editors. His precarious finances made him anxious. He felt Alden should be more prompt in publishing Hearn's Martinique sketches in *Harper's Magazine* because he didn't get paid for his sketches until they appeared in print. Hearn's sense of isolation on Martinique caused him to magnify his grievances with Alden. In one letter, Hearn launched into a bitter diatribe about not being permitted to read his articles in proof. "Proofreading to me means more than a rewriting: it is the finish, the polish, the correction of all faults that cannot be judged in MS…I am an ex-professional proof-reader; and by polishing a proof, I do not mean giving the printer the trouble of resetting even a single page. It is a particular touching, and retouching of text, which totally changes the effect,—just as one touch to the outlines of a drawn profile changes all the expression and character of a face."[36] In a later letter, he all but apologized for his haughty complaints and acknowledged that it was impractical to send proofs to Martinique for him to edit and send back.[37]

The lifting of Martinique's quarantine in early 1889 provided a solution for this proofreading issue. Hearn decided he should leave Martinique and go to New York, where he could finish writing the Martinique articles he was planning to include in his book and read the proofs for these articles that would be running in the magazine and for his forthcoming book. Besides, he believed he had extracted as much writing material from the island as he could. Hearn borrowed money from his friend in Martinique, Leopold Arnoux, to pay off his debts and to buy passage on a ship to New York.

As much as he loved the natural beauty and the people of Martinique, he increasingly missed the intellectual discourse and companionship he had enjoyed in New Orleans with Page Baker, Elizabeth Bisland, Rudolf Matas and other friends. He also found it difficult to

---

[35]Hearn to Henry Alden, *New Hearn Letters*, 100.
[36]Hearn to Henry Alden, September 5, 1888, *New Hearn Letters*, 88-89.
[37]Hearn to Henry Alden, *New Hearn Letters*, 95.

concentrate on his work and feared that the lack of opportunities to read and speak English on the island could impair his writing ability. He complains of these deficiencies in a letter to Dr. George M. Gould, a Philadelphia ophthalmologist who had become one of Hearn's most valued correspondents since writing Hearn a letter praising *Chinese Ghosts*: "The resources of the intellectual life are all lacking here—no libraries, no books in any language;—a mind accustomed to discipline becomes like a garden long uncultivated, in which the rare flowers return to their primitive savage forms, or are smothered by rank, tough growths which ought to be pulled up and thrown away, Nature does not allow you to think here, or to study seriously, or to work earnestly; revolt against her, and with one subtle touch of fever she leaves you helpless and thoughtless for months."[38]

Despite Hearn's illnesses, struggles with the heat and bouts of depression, his two years in the Caribbean had been extraordinarily productive. His novella, *Chita*, had run in serial form in *Harper's Magazine* and was published by Harper & Brothers in 1889 to strong critical acclaim. *Two Years in the French West Indies* included "A Midsummer Trip to the Tropics," 12 Martinique articles and two tales. This book, published in 1890 by Harper & Brothers and dedicated to Arnoux, represents a new literary plateau for Hearn, a work that serves as a classic portrait of daily life in the Caribbean in the late 19th century. Through vivid prose and skillful story-telling, he brings to life the people and places he writes about.

At the plantation he had visited near Grand Anse, someone told him a presumably true story about the fate of slave girl in Martinique who was responsible for the care of a white child during the 1848 slave revolt. Hearn developed this story into a suspenseful novella, *Youma*. *Harper's Magazine* published *Youma* in its first two issues of 1990. Harper & Brothers issued it as a book the next year. Hearn dedicated it to his friend, Joseph S. Tunison.

The prose isn't as poetic as in *Chita* because it's a much different kind of story. *Chita* centers on the impact of the forces of nature on human life, while *Youma* explores the effect of social forces on individuals. Hearn examines the relationship between the whites and the slaves in a realistic and insightful manner, free from stereotypes of

---

[38]Hearn to George Gould, June, 1888, *Life and Letters,* vol. I, 423.

either race. His account of the slave riot itself is forceful and dramatic. A crowd of angry rioters gather outside a slaveowner's large house, where he, his family, some neighbors and Youma, a higher-ranking slave, hide in fear.

"Almost in the same instant," Hearn writes, "a stone shot by some powerful hand whirred by the head of the younger De Kersaint (adult son of the slaveowner), and crashed into the furniture of the apartment. Vainly the shutters were bolted; a second missile dashed them open again;—a third shivered those of the next window. Stone followed stone. There were several persons severely injured;—a lady was stricken senseless;—a gentleman's shoulder fractured. And the cry of the crowd was for more stones—"*Ba nou ouoches! ba ouoches!*—because the central pavement before the house was a rough cement, affording scanty material for missiles. But the lower cross-street was paved with rounded rocks from the river-bed;—a line of negresses formed from the point of attack to the corner at the cry of "*Fai lachaine!*"—and the disjointed pavement was passed up along the line by apronfuls. There was perfect order in this system of supplying projectiles: the Black women had been trained for generations to "make the chain" when transporting stone from the torrents to the site of a building, or the place of a protection-wall. Then the stone shower became terrific,—pulverizing furniture, bursting partitions, shattering chamber doors."[39]

Hearn hadn't yet completed *Youma* when, with some sadness, he boarded a ship in early May 1889 and sailed out of Martinique, the island where he had once contemplated spending the rest of his life. During his stay on the island, he believed that by writing about Martinique, he was preserving a vital record of its people, its landscape and its culture before some of its most attractive features began to fade. He had felt the same way when he was writing about the Creoles in New Orleans.

Tragically, an important piece of Martinique vanished on May 8, 1902. That morning, Mount Pelee erupted and completely destroyed St. Pierre, "the Little Paris of the West Indies," the city of fine architecture and picturesque streets. An inundation of volcanic rocks, white-hot ashes and poisonous gases reduced St. Pierre to rubble and

---

[39]Hearn, *Youma: The Story of a West Indian Slave*, in *Hearn: American Writings*, 603.

killed 29,000 people. The only survivor was a man who had been arrested the night before for public drunkenness and was protected by the thick stone walls of his underground jail cell. The city eventually was rebuilt, but the charm and beauty that had so captivated Hearn was gone. Hearn was living in Japan when he learned about the eruption of the volcanic mountain he had climbed 22 years earlier. The destruction of St. Pierre and its people devastated him. "But all this was—and is not!," he writes. "Never again will sun or moon shine upon the streets of that city;—never again will its ways be trodden;—never again will its gardens blossom—except in dreams."[40]

---

[40]Hearn, from a previously unpublished autobiographical fragment quoted in *Life and Letters,* vol. I, 101.

CHAPTER 9

Rapture in Japan

*W*HEN HEARN arrived in New York City on May 8, 1889, he looked forward to completing *Youma* and editing the proofs for *Two Years in the French West Indies*. But he had already decided he would leave New York, which he repeatedly referred to as "hell," as soon as this work was done. He didn't know yet where he might go—just that it would not be anywhere in the United States or any other industrialized Western country. He told Gould in a letter he felt "an unutterable weariness of the aggressive characteristics of existence in a highly organized society. The higher the social development, the sharper the struggle. One feels this especially in America,—in the nervous centres of the world's activity."

He collected the proofs for *Two Years in the French West Indies* from the publisher and stopped at the apartment of his old Cincinnati friend Joseph S. Tunison. When he discovered Tunison was out of town, he wrote him a letter mostly filled with an over-the-top diatribe against New York. "This city drives me crazy, or, if you prefer, crazier; and I have no peace of mind or rest of body till I get out of it. Nobody can find anybody, nothing seems to be anywhere, everything seems to be mathematics and geometry and enigmatics and riddles and confusion worse confounded…I think an earthquake might produce some improvement." He tells Tunison he would try to find him at some point in the summer, and he closes his rant with an incongruous "Best affection."[1]

In his letters to Hearn in Martinique, Gould had told him several times that when he returned to the United States, he was welcome to stay at his Philadelphia home for an extended period. No dates had

---

[1]Hearn to Joseph R. Tunison, 1889, *Life and Letters,* vol. I, 444.

been specified. But they had developed such a warm, intimate friendship through letters that Hearn decided to show up with his suitcase at Gould's door without advance warning. He had very little money and he didn't want to keep scouting around New York for cheap apartments. Gould was delighted to see him and immediately offered him a room, a gesture that didn't please his wife, Helen. Hearn had trusted the young ophthalmologist enough to write to him about many personal aspects of his life, including his convoluted family history and his eye problems. Hearn had barely settled into his room when Gould insisted on examining Hearn's good eye. He recommended wearing eyeglasses to ease the strain on the extremely nearsighted right eye. But Hearn refused, believing eyeglasses would have the opposite effect on his eye. He continued to rely on the magnifying glass and the folding telescope he had carried with him for years. Gould, who concocted eccentric theories about the impact of eyesight on one's intellect and personality, became interested in Hearn less as a friend and more as an object of scientific study. He believed all Hearn's virtues and faults and good and bad physical attributes stemmed from his eyesight. Arrogant and moralistic, Gould regarded Hearn as a special reformation project. At first, Hearn felt in awe of Gould because he was a doctor and knew about medical issues and other topics Hearn knew little about. He became so worshipful of Gould that he began idealizing their friendship, often deferring to Gould's opinions and calling him "Goolie." He took his daily meals with the Goulds, who sometimes unnerved him by staring at him while he ate.

Hearn had a private room for working on his proofs and his novella, *Youma*. After a few weeks, he began to feel uncomfortable about imposing on the Goulds' hospitality and asked Alden if he could find him part-time work so he could pay for his own apartment. But Alden didn't come forward with anything. Hearn tried to compensate Gould for allowing him to stay in his house rent-free by trying to interest Alden and other editors into publishing some of Gould's writings. Gould aspired to be a writer as well as a nationally prominent eye specialist. So Hearn sent Alden Gould's pamphlets and writings, touting his friend's genius. He also helped Gould edit a medical dictionary and wrote an article for him which Gould sold under his own name and kept the payment. The longer Hearn stayed with the Goulds, the more he wanted to escape an environment that he felt had become stifling. He and Gould were still on very good terms, but the initial enchantment had worn off for Hearn. After five months in the Goulds' house, he finally went to New York in October 1889. He checked into the hotel he had stayed out previously, the United States Hotel near the Battery. Then Alice Wellington Rollins, whom he had corresponded with after she reviewed *Some Chinese Ghosts*, invited him to stay at her house with her family. But when Hearn found out that he would be displacing Rollins' son from his room, he decided he needed to continue his search for a cheap room. At Tunison's suggestion, he looked at a room in the building where Tunison lived. But he didn't move in because the landlord told him the room could not be heated during the winter. Tunison unenthusiastically invited him to stay at his place. Perhaps Tunison was wary of Hearn after the bizarre letter blasting New York or maybe he just didn't want to share his living space with someone indefinitely.

Although Hearn struggled financially, his name had become known to the New York literati. Several stories had run in *Harper's* in the past year, *Chita* had just been published, and *Youma* was scheduled to run as a serial in *Harper's* and then be issued in book form. Henry Alden told him *Two Years in the French West Indies* would be published in 1890. Henry S. Harper, director of Harper & Brothers, invited Hearn to attend a dinner he was giving at the Union League Club to honor the painter Edwin Abbey. Hearn agreed to attend. But, knowing Hearn's aversion to fancy social affairs, he told Alden to accompany Hearn to the dinner. Though he was unaccustomed to formal dress—especially after spending two years in the Caribbean— Hearn showed up at the dinner wearing a nice suit. As he sat uncomfortably at the long banquet table, Hearn ate sparingly and said very little. Suddenly, William Dean Howells, a giant in American letters, got up from his seat and walked over to Hearn, shook his hand, told him how glad he was to meet him and praised his work. The encounter pleased Hearn greatly and made him relax. As the evening wore on, Hearn continued talking easily with Howells and other writers and editors. Hearn and Alden were the last ones to leave the dinner.[2]

Unfortunately, another social event didn't go so well for Hearn. Alice Rollins invited him to a dinner at her apartment. She conceived

---

[2]Elizabeth Stevenson, *Lafcadio Hearn* (New York: Macmillan, 1961), 185-186.

it as a welcoming party for Hearn. Elizabeth Bisland was among the guests. But Hearn got lost on his way there, wandering around for more than an hour before he found her apartment building. The doorman thought Hearn was some sort of service employee and sent him upstairs in the service elevator. He stumbled into the kitchen, where some guests stared curiously at this man dressed in outdated trousers and a pea jacket and carrying a big sombrero. Hearn never recovered from his embarrassment at being so late. He sat in a corner and spoke only when someone was introduced to him. One of the guests, Ellwood Hendrick sympathized with Hearn and, with Rollins' approval, asked him if he wanted to take a walk with him. Hearn readily agreed. "It seemed as though I were saving his life," Hendrick recalled years later in an article about Hearn.[3] Hendrick, 28, was a chemist by training, but worked at that time as an insurance agent and had a strong interest in literature.[4] As they walked down Sixth Avenue, the two man fell into a pleasant conversation and wound up hanging out at a beer cellar until 3 a.m. Hendrick went to Hearn's apartment late the next morning to resume their talk. Hendrick became one of Hearn's closest friends. They met nearly every day during Hearn's stay in New York that winter and spring.

While gaining Hendrick as a friend, he nearly lost Gould's friendship. He learned that Gould had given a series of lectures to local clubs and civic organizations based on notebooks and manuscripts Hearn had left behind at the house. In a telegram, Hearn scolded him for using the material without his permission and asked, "Are you a humbug, too?"[5] Helen Gould sent Hearn an indignant letter accusing him of being ungrateful for all they had done for him during his long stay in their house. She demanded a formal thank-you letter from him. Hearn obliged, sending a conciliatory letter admitting that he "wore out his welcome at your home, and made a good many clumsy mistakes." He expressed his gratefulness to her and closed with "Your horrid, horrid little friend, Lafcadio Hearn."

During his months in New York, his friendship with Elizabeth Bisland deepened. She replaced Gould as Hearn's chief confidante.

---

[3] Ellwood Hendrick, "Lafcadio Hearn," *The Nation,* Vol. 116 (April 11, 1923), quoted by Elizabeth Stevenson in *Lafcadio Hearn,* 192.

[4] Hearn to George Gould, 1889, in Stevenson, *Lafcadio Hearn,* 188.

[5] Hearn to Helen Gould, November, 1889, in Stevenson, *Lafcadio Hearn,* 188-189.

She held a certain romantic allure for him, but their relationship remained platonic. Hearn marveled at her talent, her work ethic, her social adeptness and her beauty. But he also felt a little intimidated by her and observed that "some of her best (male) admirers are afraid of her. One told me he felt as if he were playing with a beautiful dangerous leopard, which he loved for not biting him."[6] She introduced Hearn to many people in her career and social sphere and helped him cope with the labyrinthine world of New York City. He never wavered from his desire to leave New York for a distant, simpler and more tranquil civilization.

Before Hearn had decided where he would go next, he received a letter from Daniel James Hearn, the brother he hadn't seen or heard from since they were separated as young children. James told Lafcadio he had no idea of his whereabouts until he recently saw his name and photo in a Cleveland newspaper. When their parents divorced, 6-year-old Lafcadio was sent to live with his father's aunt, Sarah Brenane, and 2-year-old James was sent to a boarding school in Alton, England, run by a Scotsman named Dr. Stewart. He came to the United States in 1871 when he was 16, a move he later regarded as a mistake because it ended his formal education. He went to Wisconsin to stay with friends who had a market-gardening business in Madison.[7]

At the suggestion of Dr. Stewart, James returned to England five years later. He planned to enter the tea business in India with the help of Dr. Stewart's son, a civil engineer who worked for a tea company. The younger Stewart told him that before traveling to India, James should return to the United States to learn about the tobacco industry. For the next few years, James worked with a tobacco grower in Connecticut until he learned that the younger Stewart had died.

James decided to abandon his tobacco plans and traveled west, stopping in northern Ohio to work at a mill in Gibsonburg, a small town about 30 miles southeast of Toledo. Unbeknownst to 24-year-old James, a remarkable series of coincidences had placed him within 200 miles of Lafcadio, the brother he hadn't seen since he was a toddler. At the time, Lafcadio was working as a reporter in Cincinnati.

---

[6]Hearn to George Gould, November, 1889, in Stevenson, *Lafcadio Hearn*, 191.

[7]Tracy Kneeland, "An Interview with James Daniel Hearn—Lafcadio Hearn's Brother," *Atlantic Monthly*, January Henry, 1923, 20-27. Accessed through http://www.lafcadiohearn.net/index.html.

James bought one-third interest in the mill. But after only a year, he had developed asthma from the mill's flour dust. For health reasons, he left the mill and bought a farm in the Gibsonburg area. James' farm produced so little that he lost it when he couldn't keep up with payments. He continued farming in the Gibsonburg area, but worked on rented land.

Hearn responded cautiously to James' letter. Since achieving a degree of fame, he had received letters from others falsely claiming some connection with him, wanting only his autograph, he believed. He tested James by asking him questions about their family. In his next letter, James answered the questions correctly and sent Lafcadio photographs of himself and of their father. Lafcadio had lost his only photo of his father when a landlord confiscated his possessions in Cincinnati for overdue rent. Convinced that the letter writer was indeed his brother, Lafcadio wrote a warm letter to him and apologized for the terseness of his first letter. While Lafcadio was in New York, they exchanged several more letters, filling each other in on the key events in their lives and trading information and conjecture about their parents' troubled lives. James invited Lafcadio to visit him, but his work and his plan to leave the country prevented him. Lafcadio promised to send James the address of his residence when he moved to Japan, but he never did. "I'd like to have met him," James said in a 1922 interview with Henry Tracy Kneeland, who published a story about the Hearn brothers in the January 1923 issue of the *Atlantic Monthly*. "I offered to pay his expenses to Ohio, but he went off to Japan in a great hurry. Queer tenderhearted sort of a fellow he was, I believe."[8]

Asia had piqued Hearn's interest for many years. He had been exposed in his Cincinnati days to Chinese pottery and Japanese art at special exhibits and had viewed the large Japanese exhibit at the World's Industrial & Cotton Centennial Exposition in New Orleans. He was so enamored with it, he revisited it many times, writing that "a week's study is not too much to devote to this department."[9]

China also held a certain fascination for Hearn. He had written a book of stories based on Chinese folklore, *Some Chinese Ghosts*.

---

[8]Kneeland, "An Interview with James Daniel Hearn—Lafcadio Hearn's Brother."
[9]Hearn, "Some Oriental Curiosities," *Harper's Bazaar*, March 28, 1885, in *Occidental Gleanings*, ed. Albert Mordell (New York: Dodd, Mead and Company, 1925), 226.

He also considered going to Greece and writing stories based on the folklore of the Greek islands, which would have enabled him to explore his birthplace. But Japan held a special appeal for him. For years, Hearn had been collecting English and French translations of books by Japanese writers as well as scholarly studies of Japan by Western writers. While in Martinique, Hearn had read Percival Lowell's *Soul of the Far East* and was immensely impressed by it. The book deepened his desire to visit Japan some day. He gave a copy of the book to Gould, telling him, "Every word is dynamic. It is the finest book on the East ever written."[10] When Hearn was living at Gould's house in Philadelphia, Gould suggested he travel to Japan for his next long adventure. But Hearn was so busy preparing *Two Years in the French West Indies* that he couldn't devote much serious thought to his next trip. Hearn hadn't received any writing job offers in New York that would have given him a decent living wage. Even if he had, he might not have accepted them. New York, he felt, would stifle his creativity and eventually kill his soul. He wanted to move to a foreign land far from Western civilization. But he hadn't decided where yet.

During his New York stint, he became good friends with fellow Japanophile, William Patten, an art editor at *Harper's*. Patten had a large collection of rare books about Japanese art and literature. Patten lent some of these books to Hearn, and Hearn frequently went to Patten's apartment, where they discussed them. Patten encouraged him to think about going to Japan and writing about it. Patten told him he would try to arrange the trip for Hearn if Hearn would write him a letter explaining how he would approach a writing assignment in Japan and listing topics he might cover. Hearn enthusiastically agreed to do it.

"In attempting a book upon a country so well trodden as Japan," Hearn wrote in his November 28, 1889, letter, "I could not hope— nor would I consider it prudent attempting,—to discover totally new things, but only to consider things in a totally new way, so far as possible. I would put as much *life* and *color* especially into such a book, as I could, and attempt to interpret the former rather through vivid sensation given to the reader, than by any account or explanations such as may be found by other writers, whether travelers or schol-

---

[10]Hearn to George Gould, 1889, *Life and Letters,* vol. I, 460.

ars...The studied aim would be to create, in the minds of the readers, a vivid impression of *living* in Japan,—not simply as an observer but as one taking part in the daily existence of the common people, and *thinking their thoughts*."[11]

Patten thought illustrations would enhance Hearn's writing. He asked Harper's artist C.D. Weldon if he would be interested in being a part of the project and accompany Hearn to Japan. Weldon consented. With a writer and an artist lined up, Patten showed Hearn's letter to Alden, who was delighted with the proposal. "...there is no writer of English," he wrote to Patten, "so capable as he of fully appreciating and of adequately portraying with the utmost charm and felicity every shade, however quaint and subtle, of the life of strange people. The result of close studies by him in Japan will be a revelation to all readers."[12]

Patten helped secure free transportation to Japan for Hearn and Welden, persuading the Canadian Pacific Railway to provide rail service from Montreal to the West coast of Canada and a steamer from Canada to Japan in exchange for Hearn's writing an article about the trip. But during the ensuing weeks, Hearn began to fret about having enough money for staying in Japan up to a year and for traveling within the country. He seemed on the verge of backing out of the trip. Memories of his impoverished first months in Cincinnati and New Orleans and his serious illnesses in Martinique haunted him. It unsettled him to think of scuffling for lodging and food in a country whose language he didn't know while trying to research and write a book. He voiced his grave concerns in a letter to Alden. Under the existing financial arrangements, Hearn figured he would land in Japan with only $200 in his pocket.

"Money worries impair creative work exceedingly," he wrote. "But to face the uncertainties of climatic possibilities of sickness, inevitable delay in moving about the country (for no movement will be possible until the second remittances come in), on $200 means more than worry...I do not see how I shall be able to do anything more than waste time or ever be able to get back again. To be only able to live

[11] Hearn to William Patten, November 28, 1889, in *Lafcadio Hearn's American Days*, Edward Larocque Tinker (New York: Dodd, Mead and Company, 1924), 328, 330.
[12] Henry Alden to Patten, 1889, in *Lafcadio Hearn's American Days*, 332.

means to be unable to do anything else…The conditions are grossly unfair; if another will tackle the job, I shall not be sorry."[13]

Even though *Harper's* wouldn't have to pay for the trip, Alden had serious reservations about committing a lot of money to this venture. He knew Hearn had a penchant for running into unforeseen difficulties and conflicts, sometimes caused by his impulsive, volatile temperament. Hearn certainly had given Alden his share of headaches during his two years in Martinique. Alden specified in writing what he expected Hearn to produce on this trip and what he would be paid for articles if they were acceptable. There would be no contract and no advance payment. Infuriated at these terms, Hearn complained that he had debts to pay and couldn't go to Japan without enough money to establish himself and start working. To help him out, Alden arranged for him to earn some money by translating Anatole France's novel, *Le Crime de Sylvestre Bonnard* for the Harper publishing house and to prepare two magazine supplements for future issues of *Harper's Magazine*. He translated the novel in two weeks and quickly wrote a four-page introduction. With the money for the translation and the supplements, Hearn was able to pay off his debt to Leopold Arnoux and buy clothes, a few books and a supply of yellow paper.

Near the end of the preparations for his trip, he remembered that he had left a pair of shoes at Henry Krehbiel's apartment during his visit to New York almost two years ago. A maid who hadn't worked there during his previous visit answered the door and told him the Krehbiels weren't there. Because she didn't know Hearn, she refused to let him in to retrieve the shoes and eventually shut the door in his face. Hearn was so incensed that he wrote Krehbiel a caustic letter complaining about his treatment by the maid and told him if he wanted to see him before he left for Japan, he would have to come to him. Krehbiel sent him a curt note saying, "You can go to Japan or you can go to hell." The two men, who had been kindred spirits for much of their adult lives, never communicated with each other again.[14]

His parting with Bisland was much happier. He saw her just before she left on her trip around the world funded by her magazine, *Cosmopolitan*, in a race with Nellie Bly, who was backed by her news-

---

[13] Hearn to Alden, February 12, 1890, *Lafcadio Hearn's American Days*, 335-336.
[14] Stevenson, *Lafcadio Hearn*, 193.

paper, The *New York World*. Besides competing with each other, the two women were trying to beat the fictitious 80-day journey of Phileas Fogg in Jules Verne's *Around the World in Eighty Days*. Bisland, who had never been outside the United States before, and Bly left New York on November 14, 1889. As it turned out, Bisland lost the race around the world to Bly, who completed the trip in 72 days. But Bisland did score a victory of sorts, finishing in 76 days and beating Phileas Fogg's time.[15] Shortly after she began her adventure, Hearn wrote her a letter telling how much he had enjoyed all the times they had spent talking at her apartment during the past few months. "...I must tell you," he wrote, "that I looked forward to such visits as to something very delightful, that helped me to forget the great iron-whirling world and everything in it but yourself. You made a little circle of magnetic sunshine for me; and you know I liked to bask in it so much that I used to be quite selfish about it."[16]

On March 8, 1890, Hearn left New York for a trip of his own. It wouldn't come close to Bisland's round-the-world extravaganza, but it would be the longest trip of his life. He and Weldon would travel 8,000 miles in three weeks, from Montreal, Canada to Yokohama Japan. When they arrived in Montreal, they received their free train tickets and the $250 advance the railroad company had agreed to give them. They boarded a Canadian Pacific Railway train called "Yokohama" for a cross-continental trip to Vancouver. In frigid winter weather, the train rumbled through snow-covered fields. At the midpoint of its journey, the train stopped for an hour in Winnipeg. During the pause in travel, some passengers got out to board sleighs or stove-warmed streetcars to see some of the city. But the 25-degree-below-zero temperature and a bone-freezing southerly wind, Hearn and Weldon decided to stay on the train.

The next day, the train stopped at a station where Hearn noticed four snow-covered flower beds, each bordered by 50 buffalo horns. That sight led Hearn to sadly contemplate the annihilation of the buffalo herds that once lived in these prairies. During this stretch, the train passed Indian tents clustered near the stations. At one station,

---

[15]Matthew Goodman, "Elizabeth Bisland's Race Around the World," *The Public Domain Review*, October 16, 2013. Accessed through https://publicdomainreview.org/2013/10/16/elizabeth-bislands-race-around-the-world/

[16]Hearn to Bisland, November, 1889, *Life and Letters*, vol. I, 471.

several Indian women wearing brightly striped blankets boarded the train to try to sell a pair of buffalo horns. "There seems to me," Hearn writes in "A Winter Journey to Japan," an article published in November 1890 issue of *Harper's Magazine*, "a strange pathos in this little incident,—the spectacle of the survivors of a vanishing race offering for sale as curiosities some relics of their own God-given wild cattle, which, for unknown thousands of years, yielded them food, warmth, and shelter. The wanton destruction of the buffalo was the extermination also of a human race."[17]

The next part of the trip took them through the Rocky Mountains. Hearn marveled at their magnitude and the dizzying height of their peaks. The temperature warmed as the *Yokohama* wound through canyons that eventually opened into wide valleys leading to the Pacific Ocean. The train finally arrived in Vancouver, its final destination, and Hearn and Weldon boarded the steamship *Abysinnia* on March 17, 1890.

For more than three weeks, the ship sailed across the Pacific Ocean, arriving at the Bay of Japan on April 12, 1890. As it approached the city of Yokohama. Hearn stood on its deck and saw a sight that nearly took his breath away. In the distance, snow-capped Mount Fuji rose majestically above the horizon, an ancient sacred site and an indispensable symbol of Japan's national identity. For centuries, Japanese citizens from all levels of society felt a spiritual need to climb it at least once. As with everyone who saw it for the first time, Hearn looked with joy and excitement at this perfectly cone-shaped volcanic mountain.

It was an auspicious introduction to Japan. Only 40 years earlier Japan had been a feudal society ruled by shoguns and shut off from the outside world for more than 200 years. That began to change in 1853 when Commodore Matthew Perry of the U.S. Navy sailed into Tokyo's harbor and, with the American government's support, forced Japan to open its ports to U.S. merchant ships and permit trade. Since then, the United States and other Western nations developed a fascination with Japanese culture and daily life. By the time of Hearn's arrival at Yokohama, Japan had begun to influence the Western fine arts, decorative arts, performing arts and architecture. The West had

---

[17] Hearn, "A Winter Journey to Japan," *Harper's*, November, 1890.

a huge appetite for information about this bewitching, mysterious country. Hearn, who had developed a passion for Japan's arts and an interest in Buddhism, planned to write about its ancient traditions and the ordinary people and daily cultural rituals he encountered.

A sampan, a long flat boat propelled by two oars, took Hearn, Weldon and their baggage to the landing in Yokohama. Hearn's excitement grew during first full day in Japan. Hearn had developed an aversion for Weldon during their long journey, and he and Weldon had agreed to explore Yokohama separately. Hearn spent the entire cool spring day touring the city in a rickshaw, a small, two-wheeled, cart-like carriage with a fold-down top pulled by a man on foot who wore straw sandals and a white, wide-brimmed hat. Hearn was charmed by the little, blue-roofed houses, the shops with their raised matted floors, the streets filled with fluttering flags and blue draperies and the gold, black, blue or white Chinese and Japanese lettering that adorned signs, buildings, doorposts and paper screens. He felt an immediate kinship with the colorfully costumed Japanese people walking along the streets. He noticed that many of them were smiling and most of them were short, like him, a mere 5-foot-three.[18]

In his first day, he crammed in as much sight-seeing as he could. Hearn absorbed the varied streetscapes as his rickshaw driver, Cha, raced all over Yokohama, his mushroom-shaped hat bobbing up and down. Because Cha understood no English and Hearn spoke no Japanese, Hearn was content to let Cha take him wherever he wanted. Everything Hearn saw was new to him and captured his interest. He stopped in countless little shops to look at their wares. He delighted in the beauty of the simplest objects—a pair of wooden chopsticks in a bag with a drawing on it and a package of cherry-wood toothpicks bound in paper bearing colorful lettering. He even admired the small blue towel adorned with drawings of flying sparrows that Cha used to wipe the sweat off his face.

In mid-day, Hearn returned to his hotel so that one of the employees could tell Cha in Japanese that he wanted to visit Buddhist temples. Hearn had been an agnostic since he rejected Catholicism

---

[18]Lafcadio Hearn, "My First Day in the Orient," *Glimpses of Unfamiliar Japan,* vol. I (Boston and New York: Houghton, Mifflin and Company/Cambridge: Riverside Press, 1895), 1-28.

when he was a teenager. Through his readings about Buddhism, he believed that the religion appealed more to people's hopes than to their fears and shared similarities with the ancient Greek gods, which he had been attracted to since childhood. He also wanted to learn more about Shinto, Japan's ancient nature religion that, to some extent, became absorbed into Buddhism.

Cha stopped the rickshaw at the bottom of a hill and pointed to a long flight of stone steps leading to a temple. Hearn dismounted and began walking up the steps. On the way up, he passed through a large gate topped by a tilted roof. Its two open doors feature carvings of dragons and gargoyles with lions' heads. After walking through the gate, Hearn turned around and admired a striking panoramic view of Yokohama—an expanse of bluish roofs extending to the bay, with green wooded hills to the sides. In the distance stood the snow-capped top of Mount Fuji. Suddenly he had an eerie feeling of being in a dream, inhabiting a strange, beautiful world he had glimpsed only in picture-books.

A young attendant who spoke English guided Hearn through the temple. Hearn insisted on making a small offering to the shrine of Buddha even though the attendant told him he didn't have to do it. The attendant asked Hearn why he made the offering if he wasn't a Buddhist. "I revere the beauty of his teaching, and the faith of those who follow it," Hearn replied.[19] The attendant introduced Hearn to the chief priest, who invited him to have tea and sugar cakes with him, two young priests and the attendant. This was the first of many temples Hearn visited in his first weeks in Yokohama.

After only one day in Japan, this nomadic, rootless writer born of a Greek mother and an Irish father, fell asleep that night in a state of exhausted bliss. Hearn happily dreamed about his rickshaw ride through Yokohama, peering over Cha's bobbing straw hat. In the ensuing days, his affinity for Japan deepened. Ashamed of his face that was disfigured by his blind, whitish left eye and suffering the sting of rejection from his family, Hearn had felt like an outsider everywhere he had lived—Dublin and London in Europe; Cincinnati, New Orleans and New York City in the United States; and the French-speaking island of Martinique in the Caribbean. But as Hearn got his bearings in Japan,

---

[19]Hearn, *Glimpses of Unfamiliar Japan,* vol. I, 15.

he began to feel more at home there than he had anywhere else and he believed this island-nation could provide him with an almost endless supply of rich writing material, perhaps enough to last his lifetime.

"What I love in Japan is the Japanese,—the poor simple humanity of the country," he wrote in a letter to his friend, Elizabeth Bisland, shortly after his arrival there. "It is divine. No book ever written has reflected it. And I love their gods, their customs, their dress, their bird-like quavering songs, their houses, their superstitions, their faults."[20]

In one of the temples he visited on his first day in Yokohama, Hearn met a Buddhist student, Akira Manabe. The young man offered to be his guide. With a reliable guide and interpreter, Hearn spent almost every daytime hour exploring the streets, shops, neighborhoods and temples of the city. From reading books about the Orient over the years, he had learned a little about Buddhism and Shinto, Japan's ancient nature religion, and felt they had many attractive features. But exploring their temples in Japan, talking with the priests and observing the worshippers, seeing the Shinto shrines with their traditional symbolic gates called *toriis* added a new dimension to his understanding, and he became even more enamored with them. To Hearn, they seemed more welcoming and less somber than the Western religions. "What impresses me is the seeming joyousness of popular faith," he writes. "I have seen nothing grim, austere, or self-repressive. I have not even noted anything approaching the solemn. The bright temple courts and even the temple steps are thronged with laughing children, playing curious games; and mothers, entering the sanctuary to pray, suffer their little ones to creep about the matting and crow. The people take their religion lightly and cheerfully…Blessed are they who do not too much fear the gods which they have made!"[21]

Hearn stayed at a cheap but clean waterfront hotel run by an American named Carey. Most of the clientele of Carey's Hotel were sailors, sealers and crews of small boats. The commonplace, casual atmosphere suited Hearn just fine.

One day, Hearn and Akiri boarded a train to visit the hamlet of Kamakamura, which had once been a magnificent city that was the seat of feudal power under the shogunate, and the sacred island of

---

[20]Hearn to Bisland, 1890, *Life and Letters,* vol. II, 3.
[21]Hearn, *Glimpses,* vol. I, 34.

Enoshima. When they arrived in Kamakamura, about 20 miles south of Yokohama, they hired two rickshaws to take them to decaying remains of the temples and shrines that for hundreds of years drew countless pilgrims to pay homage to the gods. The temples that retained most of their beauty—especially on the interior—were those at the top of hills, where they had been protected from the destructive fires of the 15th and 16th centuries. In one of those temples hung a great 650-year-old bell almost double the height of Hearn. One of the ancient legends connected with the bell involved a man who died and went before the god Emma, the Judge of Souls. Emma told him that he still had some years allotted to him and that he should return to his world. The man protested that he couldn't find his way back in the darkness. Emma told him to follow the sound of the great bell. He did as he was told, and the bell guided him back to his world.

The great bell was rung by setting in motion a large wooden beam suspended from the ceiling. The beam would strike the side of the bell like a battering ram. A priest in the temple gave Hearn permission to ring the bell. Hearn pulled hard on a rope that swung the beam toward the bell. "—a sound deep as thunder, rich as the bass of a mighty organ,—a sound enormous, extraordinary, yet beautiful,—rolls over the hills and away," Hearn writes. "Then swiftly follows another and lesser and sweeter billowing of tone; then another; then an eddying of waves of echoes. Only once was it struck, the astounding bell; yet it continues to sob and moan for at least ten minutes!"[22] In another temple, a priest dramatically revealed a gigantic statue of a golden-robed god in a pitch-dark room by pulling on ropes attached to two swinging lanterns. As the pulley squeaked, the lanterns slowly ascended from the feet of the statue up to its tiara.

Hearn and Akira were able to get to the island of Enoshima by foot. The tide was out, leaving a narrow swath of sand from a village on the shore to the island. After reaching the island, they walked through a charming village, saw a beautiful bronze torii. With difficulty, they descended slippery stone steps to the Dragon cavern, so named because it was in the shape of a dragon. The cavern had been one of the islands prime attractions for pilgrims. There wasn't much left to see in the cavern, but Hearn felt a vague thrill in walking

---

[22]Hearn, *Glimpses,* vol. I, 66.

through a place that generations of pilgrims had considered sacred. Later, at the shrine of the goddess Kishibojin, Hearn also was moved when he saw the votive offerings left by mothers asking for blessings for their children. Hundreds of plain baby dresses made by the mothers hung from strings stretched between bamboo poles. "And the sight of all those little dresses," he writes, "each telling so naively its story of joy and pain,—those tiny kimono shaped and sewn by docile patient fingers of humble mothers,—touches irresistibly, like some unexpected revelation of the universal mother-love. And the tenderness of all the simple hearts that have testified thus to faith and thankfulness seems to thrill all about me softly like a caress of summer wind."[23]

Despite Hearn's blissful immersion in the Japanese culture in his first weeks in the country, his anger with Henry Alden and Harper & Brothers grew. His litany of grievances included: Harper's refusal to give him a contract or an advance for his Japan and West Indies projects; the objectionable editing of his magazine stories; his discovery that Weldon would be paid more per page than he would; his intense dislike for Weldon; his belief that Alden hadn't shown enough concern about him when he was ill in Martinique; and his contention that he was cheated out of $37 for his work on the magazine supplements.

In a letter filled with snide comments about Alden and Harper's, he directed Alden to send his book collection to Gould. Alden had been storing them for him in his house and was happy to be rid of them. The transfer of these books led eventually to a permanent break between Gould and Hearn. Gould believed Hearn was giving him the books in exchange for the five months of room and board at his house. After he had been in Japan for a while, Hearn asked Gould to send him some of the books. Gould refused and ignored his subsequent requests. Another of Hearn's close friendships had ruptured. Gould exacted his revenge by writing a disparaging biography of Hearn after his death. The most valuable part of Gould's biography was a comprehensive bibliography of Hearn's writings that was compiled by Laura Stedman. Gould generally praised his writing, but maligned his character at every opportunity. Ironically, Hearn's literary idol, Edgar Allen Poe, had suffered the same fate after his death at the hands of a physician who was his literary executor, Rufus Griswold.

---

[23]Hearn, *Glimpses*, vol. I, 98.

Griswold wrote numerous articles smearing Poe's character with exaggerations and outright lies. In Cincinnati, Hearn had written a story for the *Cincinnati Commercial* repudiating Griswold's writings about Poe. In another Poe-Hearn parallel, after Gould's book was published in 1908, Bisland, Tunison and Henry Watkin wrote letters to the editor to New York newspapers defending Hearn and criticizing Gould.

Hearn sent several more increasingly vitriolic letters to Alden, who responded to each one with letters intended to calm Hearn. Finally, Hearn's insults became too much even for the patient Alden. In Hearn's last letter to Alden, he said he wanted nothing more to do with him or *Harper's*. "Please understand," Hearn wrote, "that your resentment has for me less than the value of a bottled fart, and your bank-account less consequence than a wooden shithouse struck by lightning."[24]

His break with the publisher placed him in the same precarious situation he was in when he came to Cincinnati and New Orleans— no income and no job prospects. He was in worse shape in Yokohama. He was desperately poor in a foreign country whose language he didn't understand. He wrote to Elizabeth Bisland, asking her to help him get a job in the United States. "I am so very tired of being hard-pushed, and ignored and starved."[25]

He earned some money from tutoring a 15-year-old student at an English-language school in Yokohama. He had walked into the school unannounced and asked the headmaster for work. His student, 15-year-old Edward Clarke, son of an English father and a Japanese mother, needed remedial help in English. Years later, the adult Clarke recalled the psychological ploys Hearn used to prod him into working harder: "…I do remember a trick of his…he would burst out in praise, as I fancied, but even as I was mentally patting myself on the back, he would come down with a crusher, and lay me out flat! This sort of thing: 'Aha, this is *very* good, ve-ry good, my boy! You have surpassed yourself! The words are well-chosen, the manner quite elegant, the grammar superb, but (a slight pause, then) *it is not English!*'"[26]

He also wrote to Basil Chamberlain, who taught Japanese lit-

---

[24]Hearn to Alden, *Lafcadio Hearn*, 205.
[25]Hearn to Bisland, 1890, *Life and Letters*, vol. II, 4.
[26]Stevenson, *Lafcadio Hearn*, 209.

erature at Tokyo Imperial University and was among the foremost
Japanophiles of his day and asked him for his assistance in getting a
full-time job. Through a letter of introduction Hearn had secured, he
had met Chamberlain shortly after arriving in Japan. With Chamberlain's intervention, Hearn was hired as an English teacher at the
Shimane Prefectural Common Middle School and Normal School in
Matsue, a city in southwestern part of the country along the Sea of
Japan. After isolating itself from foreigners for more than two centuries under shogunate rule, Japan reluctantly opened its borders in the
1850s under pressure from Western countries anxious for Asian trade
and commerce. When Hearn arrived in Yokohama, the nation had
entered its modern Meiji era. It was trying hard to catch up with the
technological advances of the West. In conjunction with that effort,
Japanese high schools were required to teach English.

Even in Hearn's darkest moments in Yokohama, when he was
worried about running out of money, his enthusiasm for Japan never
wavered. Before moving to Matsue, he wrote a letter to Bisland telling her of his excitement about exploring Japan. "I feel indescribably
towards Japan. Of course Nature here is not the Nature of the tropics,
which is so splendid and savage and omnipotently beautiful that I feel
at this very moment of writing the same pain in my heart I felt when
leaving Martinique. This is a domesticated Nature, which loves man,
and makes itself beautiful for him in a quiet grey-and-blue way like
the Japanese women, and the trees seem to know what people say
about them,—seem to have little human souls...And I believe that
their art is as far in advance of our art as old Greek art was superior
to that of the earliest European art-gropings—I think there is more art
in a print by Hokusai or those who came after him than in a $10,000
painting—no, a $100,000 painting. *We* are the barbarians!"[27]

In Matsue, a city of 40,000 in the Izumo Province, Hearn would
have the good fortune of living in a part of Japan that was remote
enough to protect it from most Western influences. In Matsue and its
surrounding region, the people still clung to most of the traditions of
the pre-Meiji period. Hearn could see people living and worshipping
as they had for generations, practicing the daily rituals and ceremonies of their ancestors and holding the age-old festivals. This is the

---

[27]Hearn to Bisland, 1890, *Life and Letters,* vol. II, 3.

Japan Hearn most wanted to see and absorb.

Akiri asked to accompany Hearn to Matsue to be his translator during his journey and to help him get settled once they arrived in the city. They rode a train from Yokohama to Kobe. Then they took a four-day rickshaw trip on a route that wound around mountains, through valleys and over hills to Matsue. During their journey, they stopped overnight at an inn in the village of Kami-Ichi. Having seen hardly any foreigners, the village residents regarded Hearn with great curiosity. Many of them, mostly women and children, gathered around the rickshaw to get a close look at him. Shyly smiling, some of them even touched his clothes.

Hearn and Akiri soon learned that this was the first day of the three-day Bon Odori Festival, the Festival of the Dead. Through traditional music, dance and ceremonies, the Japanese remembered and honored their dead ancestors. At the inn, Hearn and Akiri heard the muffled sounds of the beating of a large temple drum and the rhythmic clapping of hands.

"Oh! We must go to see it," Akiri said. "It is the Bon Odori, the Dance of the Festival of the Dead. And you will see the Bon Odori danced here as it is never danced in cities—the Bon Odori of ancient days. For customs have not changed here; but in the cities all is changed."[28] Led that evening from the inn by a boy with a red paper lantern, they joined a crowd at the court of an ancient Buddhist temple that had been converted into a schoolhouse. In this moonlit open space, the solemn Dance of the Souls began. The female dancers, dressed in robes, move in a slow, trance-like manner, taking their cues from the tapping of the temple drum. "And always," Hearn writes, "the white hands sinuously wave together, as if weaving spells, alternately without and within the round, now with palms upward, now with palms downward; and all the elfish sleeves hover duskily together, with a shadowing as of wings; and all the feet poise together with such a rhythm of complex motion, that, in watching it, one feels a sensation of hypnotism—as while striving to watch a flowing and shimmering of water."[29] Hearn felt a haunting thrill as he thought about the long-gone generations being commemorated who, when they were alive,

<hr>

[28]Hearn, *Glimpses*, vol. I, 131.
[29]Hearn, *Glimpses*, vol. I, 134.

had witnessed this very same dance.

The next day, Hearn and Akiri boarded a small ship that took them from Yonago to Matsue, located on Lake Shinji, which was connected to Nakuma Lagoon by the Ohashi River. An inlet from the lagoon led to the Sea of Japan. Divided by two rivers, Matsue contained many canals that people crossed by small curved bridges. Matsue's feudal past was still recent enough that thousands of residents still remembered the shogunate's rule. Its feudal caste system was still evident in the distinctive architecture of each of Matsue's three districts—merchant, temple and shizoku (formerly samurai). The Shinto and Buddhist priests lived in the temples. The houses in the merchants district usually were two stories high, while houses in the old samurai district were large single-story houses. Many of the old samurai houses were clustered around the base of the hill where the Matsue Castle stood. According to legend, as a sacrifice to the gods, a Matsue maiden was buried alive inside the walls of the castle during its construction from 1607 to 1611. Soon after this, a law had to be passed prohibiting girls from dancing in the city streets. It was said that whenever a maiden danced, the castle's hill would shudder and cause the castle itself to shake from top to bottom.[30] Hearn loved hearing these kinds of legends. As he did in Cincinnati, New Orleans and Martinique, he collected as much folklore as possible during his years in Japan.

Hearn, who had turned 40 during his first summer in Japan, began his teaching assignment on September 2, 1890. Sentaro Nishida, the school's dean, introduced him to his students and helped him through the students' roll call. Hearn, the only foreign teacher in the school, knew no Japanese and had difficulty pronouncing some of the names. Nishida stayed for part of the class to help him get settled. Hearn's students were boys between 12 and 16 years old. All had been studying English since early childhood and understood whatever Hearn wrote on the blackboard. Hearn made a point of speaking slowly and using simple words. The relationship of the Japanese teachers and students consisted of mutual respect and kindness. Corporal punishment was forbidden, and teachers seldom scolded or criticized their students. Students generally behaved so well that

---

[30]Hearn, *Glimpses*, vol. I, 162-164.

discipline wasn't an issue. If students misbehaved, they usually were punished by being kept inside during outdoor recreation period. This genial, relaxed atmosphere contrasted sharply with Hearn's boyhood school experiences. Hearn's students quickly took a liking to him and told him that he was much different than a former foreign English teacher they once had.

One day one of his students said to him," I saw you bow before our Emperor's picture at the ceremony on the birthday of His Majesty. You are not like a former English teacher we had."

"How?," Hearn said.

"He said we were savages."

"Why?"

"He said there was nothing respectable except God,—*his* God,— and that only vulgar and ignorant people respect anything else."

"Where did he come from?"

"He was a Christian clergyman, and said he was an English subject."

The boy asked Hearn what he thought about the former teacher's regarding his Japanese students as savages.

"I think, my dear lad, that he himself was a savage,—a vulgar, ignorant savage bigot. I think it is your duty to respect your Emperor, to obey his laws, and to be ready to give your blood whenever he may require it of you for the sake of Japan. I think it is your duty to respect the gods of your fathers, the religion of your country,—even if you yourself cannot believe all that others believe. And I think, also that it is your duty, for your Emperor's sake and for your country's sake, to resent any such wicked and vulgar language as that you have told me of, no matter who uttered it."[31]

In these first weeks in Matsue, Hearn traveled on weekends as much as possible. One of his first trips was to the village of Kitzuki, about 20 miles west of Matsue. He and Akiri stayed at a very comfortable inn whose owner and staff welcomed them warmly. Nishida had sent a letter of introduction for Hearn to Senke Takamori, a Shinto priest whose family has been in charge of the temple for 82 generations. The morning after Hearn arrived in Kitzuki, a messenger from Senke came to the inn and informed Hearn that Senke would meet

---

[31] Hearn, *Glimpses,* vol. II, 471.

with him at the temple that day. Senke and the attendant priests, wearing their ceremonial costumes, escorted him into the temple's inner shrine of the chief deity, an honor no other European had ever received. Reports of this event raised Hearn's status in Matsue. As a foreign teacher and a respected writer, he became well known in Matsue. The local newspaper covered his activities, and various groups asked him to give talks at their meetings or other events. Hearn returned to Kitzuki many times and stayed at the same inn, whose staff became quite fond of him and helped him any way they could.

Since his arrival in Matsue, he had been staying at the Tomitaya Inn. But a quarrel with the proprietor prompted Hearn to move out at the end of October. The innkeeper's daughter had a disfigured eye, a condition Hearn felt great sympathy for. When Hearn talked to the father about getting medical treatment for his daughter, the man told him he had no intention of doing it. Hearn angrily admonished him and told the man he refused to stay under the same roof with such a cruel father. Hearn moved into a small rental house on Lake Shinji. He later gave the innkeeper money for medical treatment for his daughter's eye.[32]

Akiri went back to Yokohama soon after the school year began, leaving Hearn without a companion. Nishida helped fill this void. Besides assisting Hearn at school, Nishida, a friendly, kind-hearted man, invited Hearn for visits to his house. The two men developed a close friendship that lasted until Nishida's death in 1897. Between classes at school, Hearn enjoyed smoking with other teachers while sitting around a hibachi in the faculty room. Hearn bought a long Japanese pipe, like the others had. Hearn wore Western clothes at school but changed into traditional Japanese garb at home. He found a loose-fitting kimono and sandals much more comfortable than his shirts, trousers and hard-leather shoes.

The only disturbance to his contentment with his new life in Matsue was the weather. Hearn, who hated the cold, didn't anticipate the severity of winters in Matsue. Hearn's first winter there proved to be worse than normal. The temperature never dipped into single digits, but strong winds blew in from the lake and five feet of snow

---

[32]Setsuko Koizumi, *Reminiscences of Lafcadio Hearn* (Boston: Houghton, Mifflin Co. 1918), 8-9.

piled up around his house. The coal-burning porcelain hibachi didn't provide nearly enough heat in this house with paper-thin walls. Hearn became very ill with a respiratory infection that confined him to bed for a few weeks. "I fear a few more winters of this kind will put me underground," he wrote in a letter to Chamberlain.[33] As Hearn recovered from his illness, Nishida suggested that he should have a wife to take care of him. Hearn, feeling lonely and vulnerable, agreed that being married would be in his best interests. Traditional arranged marriages were perfectly acceptable in Japan in the late 19th century, although marriages with foreigners were unusual. With Hearn's consent, Nishida acted as a go-between in negotiating a marriage contract with 22-year-old Setsu Koizumi, the daughter of an impoverished samurai family. The demise of the feudal system had ended her family's source of income. Like other samurai families, they had no skills for earning a living in the Meiji Era. The marriage between Setsu and Hearn would help them both. Hearn would have the companionship and care of a wife, and Setsu and her family would live in a financially stable household. Hearn accepted the responsibility of supporting not only Setsu but also her parents and her grandparents. The family servants would live with them as well.

Hearn and Setsu were married in a traditional Japanese ceremony in January 1891 and began their life together in his house on the lake. When she first walked into the house, she was astonished at how little it contained—a table, a chair, a few books, one suit of clothes and one set of Japanese kimono. Although young, Setsu was very sensible, diplomatic, practical and orderly—qualities Hearn had never been known for. She realized early in their marriage that she must learn how to cope with her husband's impatience and sometimes prickly personality. "Hearn had a peculiar temperament, and it caused me much trouble," she writes in her 1918 memoir, *Reminiscences of Lafcadio Hearn*.[34] She became most upset with him when he would vent his anger or be rude to someone without justification. A new neighbor came to Hearn's house and asked to borrow a screwdriver. When the man mentioned that he was a friend of the hotel proprietor whose daughter had the disfigured eye, Hearn quickly rebuffed him.

---

[33] Hearn to Basil Chamberlain, *Life and Letters*, vol. II, 25.
[34] Setsuko Koizumi, *Reminiscences*, 8.

"I dislike you," Hearn said, "because you are that strange and unsympathetic fellow's friend. Syonara. Good-bye!" Hearn turned and went inside the house, leaving the embarrassed Setsu to try to explain the situation to the puzzled neighbor.[35] When Hearn would write a caustic letter to a publisher or editor in a fit of anger and ask her to mail it, she learned to hold onto it for a few days before mailing it. Usually, in a day or two, he would ask her if she had mailed the letter yet. When she told him she hadn't, he would ask for it back. Setsu followed the role of the traditional submissive Japanese wife, handing him his clothes in the morning, preparing three meals a day, walking a few paces behind him in public, restricting the housecleaning to when he was at school teaching so he wouldn't be disturbed by the noise when he was at home writing. Yet she didn't shy from criticizing him—usually gently and tactfully—when she felt he warranted it.

For all his rough edges, Hearn settled very comfortably into domesticity. For the first time in his life, he had a real family. He enjoyed living with Setsu's elders and was especially fond of her grandfather, who had once served as a tutor in the family of the lord of the castle in Matsue. He often invited Nishida and two or three other teachers from his school to his house for social visits. Hearn and Setsu, who knew little English, developed their own special baby-talk communication that utilized Japanese and English words. Hearn's Japanese friends facetiously called it the "Hearnian dialect." Since his arrival in Japan, Hearn encouraged people to tell him ancient Japanese folk tales and legends. Akiri had told him about many legends during their travels. Now Setsu became his prime source of these tales of the supernatural or ghost stories. As he had once savored the eerie tales of Edgar Allen Poe, he now listened intently to his wife tell ancient legends of the macabre. "On quiet nights, after lowering the wick of the lamp, I would begin to tell ghost stories," she recalls in her memoir. "Hearn would ask questions with bated breath, and would listen to my tales with a terrified air. I naturally emphasized the exciting parts of the stories when I saw him so moved."[36] He also encouraged his students to tell him Japanese folk tales. Hearn would take the bare bones of these stories, flesh them out, embellish them, and write them

---

[35]Ibid., 8-9.
[36]Ibid., 36.

in his own rich literary style.

In Japan, Hearn's writing underwent as profound a change as his private life had. When he lived in Martinique, he began to feel he needed to tone down some of the gaudy, overwrought aspects of his writing. He made a conscious effort in Japan to adopt a more simple, lucid style that embodied the power and compression of good poetry. The stark simplicity of much Japanese art and the conciseness of haikus and other forms of Japanese poetry influenced Hearn's writing. This change is evident not only in his retelling of Japanese folk tales but also in his travel writing.

A good example is Hearn's description of a ceremony that occurs on the third night of the Festival of the Dead. It is the Segaki, the ceremony of farewell. According to legend, the souls of the dead come by sea to this festival honoring them, and when the festival is over, they depart by sea. Hearn writes: "All that the living may to do to please the dead has been done; the time allotted by the powers of the unseen worlds unto the ghostly visitants is well-nigh past, and their friends must send them all back again. Everything has been prepared for them. In each home small boats made of barley straw closely woven have been freighted with supplies of choice food, with tiny lanterns, and written messages of faith and love. Seldom more than two feet in length are these boats; but the dead require little room. And the frail craft are launched on canal, lake, sea or river,—each with a miniature lantern glowing at the prow, and incense burning at the stern. And if the night be fair, they voyage long. Down all the creeks and rivers and canals the phantom fleets go glimmering to the sea; and all the sea sparkles to the horizon with the lights of the dead, and the sea wind is fragrant with incense."[37]

Hearn's passion for exploring unfamiliar cultures intensified with age. For him, no trip was too difficult or dangerous if he thought it would provide him with fascinating writing material. With its inexhaustible treasure of ancient myths, legends, lore and sacred places, Japan offered Hearn far more than New Orleans or any of the Caribbean islands had. When he learned about a sacred sea-cave where children's ghosts were said to build mounds of stones at night in homage to Jizo, the gentle and smiling Buddhist god who protects

---

[37]Hearn, *Glimpses,* vol. I, 109.

children's souls, Hearn arranged to visit it—even though it required venturing into hazardous waters.

He and Setsu traveled the first leg of the trip by rickshaw to the coastal village of Mitsu-ura, only seven miles from Matsue. But the route was so hilly that the journey took nearly three hours. At times, the hills were so steep that Hearn had to get out of the rickshaw and walk so that the man pulling it could get it to the hilltop. Because there was no hotel in Mitsu-ura, the Hearns stayed in a fisherman's house. Westerners were such a novelty there that while Hearn ate dinner inside, a crowd gathered in the doorways and climbed into the windows to get a good look at him. The embarrassed owner tried to shoo them away, but they wouldn't leave. So he slid the screens over the doors and windows. But there were holes in the paper panes, and the villagers took turns peeping through the lower ones.

The next morning Hearn, Setsu and his rickshaw driver and a couple climbed into a small boat manned by two scullers, a woman at the bow and a man at the stern. The water looked so inviting, Hearn couldn't resist jumping off the boat for a quick swim. The sea became rougher as they sailed near the base of a long line of towering cliffs. After two hours, they entered a sea-cave and glided for a long time in its caverns before reaching the cave of the children's ghosts, called Kyu-Kukedo-San or Ancient Cavern. They got out of the boat and put on straw sandals so they would be able to walk on the slippery rocks. They walked carefully between the many mounds of stones. The boatwoman warned Hearn and the others that if any of these were overturned, the children' spirits would cry. "So we move cautiously and slowly across the cave to a space bare of stone-heaps, where the rocky floor is covered with a thin layer of sand, detritus of a crumbling ledge above it," Hearn writes. "And in that sand I see light prints of little feet, children's feet, tiny naked feet, only three or four inches long,—*the footprints of the infant ghosts*."[38] Despite their care, Hearn knocked over two stone heaps and his rickshaw driver knocked over another. Buddhist principles required that two mounds be built for every one that was toppled. So Hearn and his driver had to build six stone mounds to replace the three they knocked down. Tiny children's straw sandals laid on some of the rocky ledges. Pilgrims had brought

---

[38]Ibid., 221.

them as offerings to the children's ghosts to protect their feet from the stones. Finally, Hearn's group came to the large granite statue of a seated Jizo, holding in one hand a mystic jewel that was said to fulfill all wishes and in the other, a staff. In front of this Buddhist god stood three articles associated with the Shinto faith—a small torii and a pair of gohei or wooden wands. "Evidently," Hearn writes, "this gentle divinity has no enemies; at the feet of the lover of children's ghosts, both creeds unite in tender homage."[39]

Because the Bon Odori dance was different in each village, Hearn tried to go wherever the dances had been highly recommended. One such place was Otsuka. He and 12 residents of the nearby village of Yabase went in Japanese costume to see the Bon Odori in Otsuka. Hearn encountered anti-foreigner hostility for the first time in his travels through Japan. The people interrupted their dance in Otsuka to pelt Hearn with little pellets of sand and mud. He and his group returned to Yabase.

That display of hostility surprised Hearn, but it didn't discourage him from traveling anywhere he wanted to explore Japanese cultural and religious traditions. Hearn was immediately intrigued when he heard about a community of rag-pickers who lived in a hollow along the hills at the southern end of Matsue. The rest of society shunned them, even though some became fairly wealthy by gathering and selling rags and waste paper and buying all kinds of trash. Rag-pickers had been treated as social pariahs for centuries. They could not work as servants or common laborers. In feudal times, samurai and aristocratic families paid them to perform songs and dances no one else knew and had been passed down in their families for generations. These special ancient songs and dances were called Daikoku-mai.

Hardly anyone ever went into the rag-pickers' communities. Always sensitive to any society's outcasts, Hearn persuaded a Japanese friend to take him into the community of rag-pickers just outside Matsue. These outcasts regarded Hearn with curiosity and wariness at first. But after they became convinced of his sincere interest in them and their culture, they performed the Daikoku-mai for him. "The singing lasted for more than an hour, during which the voices never failed in their quality," Hearn writes in a newspaper article. "And yet,

---

[39]Ibid., 222.

so far from being weary of it, and although I could not understand a word uttered, I felt very sorry when it was all over. And with the pleasure received there came to the foreign listener also a strong sense of sympathy for the young singers, victims of a prejudice so ancient that its origin is no longer known."[40]

Although Hearn was happy with his large extended family, he and Setsu decided they needed to move to a bigger house. The Hearns' two-story house on the lake provided beautiful views, but it was too small for their family. Hearn described it "as dainty as a bird-cage."[41] Early in the summer of 1891, the Hearns moved into an ancient 14-room samarai house near the castle. A samarai of high rank had once lived there. Besides the extra space the house provided, it also was in a quieter area than the one by the lake. Hearn loved the small walled garden areas surrounding three sides of the house. These gardens inspired him to write a brilliant essay in which he explained the nature and importance of gardens in Japan and described in eloquent language how his gardens reflected some of the qualities of a typical Japanese garden.

"I have already become a little too fond of my dwelling-place," he writes in his essay, "In a Japanese Garden," which was first published in the *Atlantic Monthly* and then in *Glimpses of Unfamiliar Japan*. "Each day, after returning from my college duties, and exchanging my teacher's uniform for the infinitely more comfortable Japanese robe, I find more than compensation for the weariness of five class-hours in the simple pleasure of squatting on the shaded veranda overlooking the gardens. Those antique garden walls, high-mossed below their ruined coping of tiles, seem to shut out even the murmur of the city's life. There are no sounds but the voices of birds, the thrilling of semi, or, at long, lay intervals, the solitary plash of a diving frog. Nay, those walls seclude me from much more than city streets. Outside them hums the changed Japan of telegraphs and newspapers and steamships; within dwell the all-reposing peace of nature and the dreams of the sixteenth century. There is a charm of quaintness in the very air, a faint sense of something viewless and sweet all about one; perhaps the gentle haunting of dead ladies who looked like the ladies of the

---

[40]Hearn, *Kokoro* (New York: Houghton Mifflin Company, 1896), 334.
[41]Hearn, *Glimpses*, vol. II, 343.

old picture-books, and who lived here when all this was new. Even in the summer light—touching the gray strange shapes of stone, thrilling through the foliage of the long-loved trees—there is the tenderness of a phantom caress. These are the gardens of the past. The future will know them only as dreams, creations of a forgotten art, whose charm no genius may reproduce."[42]

Hearn also developed a fascination with the insects of Japan. He was interested in all forms of life and had long been captivated by the insect world. During his first year in New Orleans, he would sit for hours and watch the movements of a colony of ants that had invaded his apartment.[43] To him, they weren't unwanted pests, but life forms to be studied.

The Japanese loved the distinct chirping of various kinds of insects, each different in tone and texture. In Hearn's time, people kept certain singing insects in tiny cages as pets in their homes so they could enjoy the music they made. Hearn notes in his essay, "Insect-Musicians,"[44] that Japanese poets had been praising the aesthetic value of insects' chirping for hundreds of years. People would go to rural areas on insect-hunts, eager to capture and bring into their homes varieties of insects that were noted for their beautiful "voices." In Hearn's day, the selling and breeding of insects had grown into a lucrative industry. The Japanese admired the singing of insects to the same degree that Westerners admired the singing of birds.

Hearn believed the Japanese people's ability to appreciate the beauty of sounds made by insects as well as by a certain kind of frog, called a kajika, indicated a keen sensitivity to nature that the industrialized world was losing. Unlike the Japanese, most Westerners considered insects and frogs to be distasteful annoyances. "...the Japanese," he writes, "discover beauty where we blindly imagine ugliness or formlessness or loathsomeness,—beauty in insects, beauty in stones, beauty in frogs. Is the fact without significance that they alone have been able to make artistic use of the form of the centipede?...You should see my Kyoto tobacco-pouch, with centipedes of gold running

[42]Ibid., 382-383.

[43]McWilliams, Vera Seely. *Lafcadio Hearn* (Boston: Houghton Mifflin Co., 1946), 148.

[44]Hearn, "Insect-Musicians," *Exotics and Retrospectives* (Boston: Little, Brown, and Company, 1895), 39-80.

over its figured leather like ripplings of fire!"[45]

Hearn wanted to share with Westerners all his experiences in Japan—including the tragedies. One of the Hearn's best students, 17-year-old Yokogi Tomisaburo, fell seriously ill days in early November 1891 after giving the eulogy at another classmate's funeral. A blood vessel had burst in Yokogi's head, and he had lapsed in and out of a coma. The doctor attributed the burst blood vessel to studying too hard. As Yokogi lay dying, he told his parents he wanted to see the exterior of his school one more time. They arranged for him to be carried the short distance from their house to the school. "I can remember all now," Yokogi said faintly. "I had forgotten—so sick I was. I remember everything again."[46]

The boy died not long after that. Hearn included an account of Yokogi's last days and of his funeral in his chapter about teaching in Matsue in *Glimpses of Unfamiliar Japan*. Heart-rending without being mawkish, it's one of the most touching and beautifully written parts of this book. He describes the funeral in meticulous detail, explaining the reasons for different aspects of the funeral rite. "For the last time," Hearn writes, "I see his face again, as he lies upon his bed of death,—white-robed from neck to feet,—white-girdled for his shadowy journey,—but smiling with closed eyes in almost the same queer gentle way he was wont to smile at class on learning the explanation of some seeming riddle in our difficult English tongue. Only, methinks, the smile is sweeter now, as with sudden larger knowledge of more mysterious things. So smiles, through dusk of incense in the great temple of Tokoji, the golden face of Buddha."

A memorial service was held for Yokogi about a month after the funeral. In two sentences, Hearn captures the sadness of the boy's family, friends, schoolmates and teachers who fill the temple: "The great bell of Tokoji is booming for the memorial service...slowly and regularly as a minute-gun. Peal on peal of its rich bronze thunder shakes over the lake, surges over the roofs of the town, and breaks in deep sobs of sound against the green circle of the hills."[47]

Hearn had become so attached to the people, sights and traditions

---

[45] Hearn, "Frogs," *Exotics*, 172.
[46] Hearn, *Glimpses*, vol. II, 481.
[47] Ibid., 485.

in and around Matsue that this seemed the perfect place for him to abandon his wandering ways and settle for many years. He was 41, after all, an age when most people have set down their roots. Setsu and her family gave his life stability and a sense of permanence.

But Matsue presented two major problems for Hearn. His teaching salary and his royalties from his published books weren't enough for him to support his wife and her elders. He also didn't think he could survive another severe winter in Matsue. He asked Basil Chamberlain, who had helped secure his teaching job in Matsue, to assist him in finding another teaching job with a higher salary in a warmer climate. Not long after, Hearn accepted a teaching position with a large government college called the Fifth Higher Middle School or Government College, located in Kumamoto, a city on Kyushu, Japan's southernmost island. He would teach English and Latin. The climate was warmer than in Matsue and Hearn would double his salary. With money being less a worry in Kumamoto, he could concentrate on writing his book about his first year in Japan.

CHAPTER 10

Life and Labor in Kumamoto and Kobe

*T*he depth of Hearn's impact on the people of Matsue and his students became poignantly clear in his final weeks there. Government officials, his school and community groups honored him with banquets and gifts. His fellow teachers sent him a pair of three-foot-high vases made in feudal times at Rakusan. The vases were adorned with paintings of birds, flowering trees at a beach where pink crabs were scurrying around. With the vases came a scroll with the names of the 32 donors in Chinese text. A committee from the Middle School brought to his house a gift from the students: a Japanese sword from the feudal period. The committee members asked Hearn to accompany them to the college assembly room. When he arrived there, the room was filled with students waiting to bid him their heart-felt goodbyes.

Masanabu Otani, representing all the students, read a short letter expressing their appreciation for his instruction and sorrow for his pending departure. "You have been one of the best and most benevolent teachers we ever had," he said. "We entreated our Director to find some way to keep you, but we discovered that could not be done." In thanking the students, Hearn said, "I am not less sorry to leave you, I think, than you are to see me go. The more I have learned to know the hearts of Japanese students, the more I have learned to love their country."[1] The students at the Normal School gave Hearn a farewell banquet. The captain of each class read in English letters of thanks

---

[1] Lafcadio Hearn, *Glimpses of Unfamiliar Japan,* vol. II (Boston and New York: Houghton Mifflin Company/Cambridge: The Riverside Press, 1894), 685-686.

and good wishes and sang their school songs for him. They promised to march with him to the steamer that would take him.

But four days after this banquet, tragedy struck. Cholera broke out in various parts of Matsue, including at the Normal School. Several teachers and students who had lauded Hearn at the banquet died from the cholera. The outbreak caused the Middle schools and the adjacent elementary schools to close. Hearn told the school's director he didn't think it would be healthy for the students to come to the wharf in the chilly morning air to say goodbye to him and his family before they boarded the steamer. But the director just laughed. An hour after sunrise on November 15, 1891, about 200 students and some teachers gathered in front of the gate of Hearn's house and escorted him to the wharf near the long white bridge where his steamer awaited. A throng of people—other students, students' parents, friends, merchants and townspeople—had already gathered at the wharf for Hearn's sendoff. Izumo's governor sent his secretary to deliver a kind message to Hearn, and the Normal School's president rushed down to shake Hearn's hand. Hearn's close friend, Sentaro Neshida, couldn't be there because he had been seriously ill for the past two months. But Neshida's father came to the wharf and gave Hearn some souvenirs and a letter his son wrote in his sickbed. Hearn boarded the steamer and, from its small deck, gazed at the riverfront with its long white bridge, the old houses near the water, the junks with their sails golden in the morning sun.

"Magical indeed," Hearn writes in his account of last day in Matsue in *Glimpses of Unfamiliar Japan*, "the charm of this land, as of a land veritably haunted by gods; so lovely the spectral delicacy of its colors,—so lovely the forms of its hills blending with the forms of its clouds,—so lovely, above all, those long trailings and bandings of mists which make its altitudes appear to hang in air. A land where sky and earth so strangely intermingle that what is reality may not be distinguished from what is illusion,—that all seems a mirage, about to vanish." As the steamer backed into the middle of the Ohashigawa River and turned away from the bridge, the students yelled and waved their caps. Hearn scrambled to the roof of the deck cabin, waved his hat and shouted, "Good-bye, good-bye!" They shouted back to him, "*Mainzai, mainzai!*" meaning "Ten-thousand years to you! Ten-thousand years!"[2]

---

[2]Ibid., 691-692.

After crossing Lake Shinji, Hearn and his family disembarked and climbed into rikshaws for a long, arduous journey across mountains to Hiroshima, where a steamer took them along the Honshu coast to the extreme southwestern tip of the main island, crossed the Straits of Shimonoseki and docked at Moji. After a long trip by train, they reached Kumamoto. Hearn immediately realized that a lot more than an immense geographical distance separated Matsue and Kumamoto. They were starkly different in architecture, ambiance and culture. Kumamoto was a sprawling garrison city filled with soldiers and drab-looking buildings. With most of its old town having been destroyed by fire during the 1877 Saigo Rebellion, this partly-Europeanized city had none of the charm, magic and mystery that Matsue possessed. Hearn was extremely disappointed and called Kumamoto "the most uninteresting city I was ever in, in Japan."[3] There were no great temples, magnificent gardens, interesting curio shops or alluring sights. The Government College consisted a collection of large stone and red-brick buildings on a rambling campus. Hearn lived in a house about two miles from the Government College. The people of Kumomoto and of the entire island of Kyushu took pride in their long history of spartan conservatism and samurai traditions. Their dress was plain and simple and their manner was straight-forward and direct. The house was about the same size as his samurai house in Matsue, but it had a lackluster garden. On the positive side, the Government College provide him with a salary that was almost triple what he had earned in Matsue. For the first time in their brief married life, he and Setsu could save money.

Hearn was the only foreign teacher at Government College, although several teachers spoke English and two spoke French. He had difficulty at first making friends with the other teachers. With the teacher's lounge a good distance from his classes, he usually didn't go there during the 10-minute breaks between classes. When he did go there, he usually sat in a corner and smoked his pipe. His students were different in many ways than his students in Matsue. They were older—18 to 25—and they all took the mandatory military training. In its zeal to protect itself from being subjugated by foreign nations, Japan emphasized military training and readiness. It was a key part of

---

[3]Hearn to Sentaro Nishida, 1891, *The Life and Letters of Lafcadio Hearn,* vol. II, Elizabeth Bisland (Boston: Houghton Mifflin Co., 1906), 65.

the nation's adaption to the modern, industrialized world it had reluctantly and cautiously entered only a few decades earlier. Contributing to the school's military atmosphere, bugle calls, not bells, signaled the beginning and ending of classes. Hearn found the textbooks to be of little use. He taught English and Latin primarily by writing on the blackboard, telling them legends and mythical tales from their own and other cultures and assigning them to write essays that he would correct and grade, often reading the best ones in class. In keeping with Kyushu's military spirit, his students displayed little emotion. "For a long time," Hearn writes, "I used to wonder in vain what feelings, sentiments, ideas might be hidden beneath all that unsmiling placidity."[4] Through his gentle manner of teaching and thought-provoking essay assignments, Hearn coaxed them into revealing more of their personalities and expressing their emotions in writing.

Hearn once asked his students to write an essay that answered the question, "What do men remember the longest?" One student wrote that painful events lingered the longest in a person's memory. "When I was only four years old, my dear, dear mother died," he wrote. "It was a winter's day. The wind was blowing hard in the trees, and round the roof of our house. There were no leaves on the branches of the trees. Quails were whistling in the distance,—making melancholy sounds. I recall something I did. As my mother was lying in bed,—a little before she died,—I gave her a sweet orange. She smiled and took it, and tasted it. It was the last time she smiled…. From the moment when she ceased to breathe to this hour more than sixteen years have elapsed. But to me the time is as a moment. Now also it is winter. The winds that blew when my mother died blow just as then; the quails utter the same cries; all things are the same. But my mother has gone away, and will never come back again."[5] Hearn said he never changed a word of this essay, but the presence of his trademark comma-dash indicated he probably changed the punctuation a little. At any rate, this essay illustrates how skillful and perceptive a teacher he was.

One day when Hearn had an hour between classes, he decided to climb to the top of a hill behind the college to see what was there. After walking up through the tiny terraced farm fields, he discov-

---

[4]Hearn, *Out of the East* (Boston and New York: Houghton Mifflin Company/Cambridge: The Riverside Press, 1895), 33.
[5]Ibid., 35-36.

ered an ancient village cemetery no longer in use. An ancient statue of Buddha sat in a lotus position among the cemetery's gravestones and weeds. This secluded spot became Hearn's little sanctuary from the modern buildings on campus and the grind of teaching. In good weather, he went there almost daily, quietly reading or meditating. "Then the Stone Buddha and I look down upon the college together," he writes, "and as we gaze, the smile of the Buddha—perhaps because of a change in the light—seems to me to have changed its expression, to have become an ironical smile. Nevertheless he is contemplating the fortress of a more than formidable enemy. In all that teaching of four-hundred youths by thirty-three teachers, there is no teaching of faith, but only teaching of face,—only teaching of the definite results of the systematization of human experience. And I am absolutely certain that if I were to question, concerning the things of the Buddha, any of these thirty-three instructors (saving one dear old man of seventy, the Professor of Chinese), I should receive no reply. For they belong unto the new generation, holding that such topics are fit for the consideration of Men-in-the-Straw-Raincoats only, and that in this twenty-sixth year of Meiji, the scholar should occupy himself only with the results of the systematization of human experience. Yet the systematization of human experience in no wise enlightens us as to the Whence, the Whither, or, worst of all!—the Why."[6]

In Kumamoto, Hearn realized how much Japan had succumbed to the 19th century Western philosophy and way of life. He often found himself arguing for the preservation of the ancient Japanese traditions with Japanese natives who wanted their country to move into the modern industrial world. They greatly feared Western dominance and believed Japan needed to adopt Western ways to retain its sovereignty. He said in a letter to Chamberlain that he loved the Japanese people the better he knew them but "I detest with unspeakable detestation the frank selfishness, the apathetic vanity, the shallow vulgar skepticism of the New Japan, the New Japan...that ridicules the dear old men of the pre-Meiji era and that never smiles, having a heart as hollow and bitter as a dried lemon."[7] He also hated the missionaries who

---

[6] Ibid., 178.

[7] Hearn to Chamberlain, January 17, 1893, *The Japanese Letters of Lafcadio Hearn*, ed. Elizabeth Bisland (Boston and New York: Houghton Mifflin Company/Cambridge: The Riverside Press, 1910), 38.

came to Japan to convert the populace to Christianity and undermine Shinto and Buddhism, which he considered morally superior because they emphasized sacrifice of the self for others. He told Chamberlain "the Japanese are better than the Christians, and Christianity only seems to corrupt their morals."[8] He succinctly summed up his feelings about Christian missionaries by telling Chamberlain, "Personally, of course I think the missionaries ought to be put on a small ship, and the ship scuttled at a reasonable distance of one thousand miles from shore."[9] He believed Christianity had degenerated into something far from what Christ had intended. Although he couldn't accept intellectually every aspect of Shinto and Buddhism, Eastern religious thought touched him emotionally in a way that Christianity did not.

Since his years in Cincinnati years, Hearn had embraced Herbert Spencer's theory of the evolution of all life forms, particularly the human race's continual progress toward perfection. Hearn saw striking similarities to Spencer in Buddhism. It seemed to Hearn that Buddhists' profound reverence for their ancestors and the knowledge passed down from one generation to the next meshed with Spencer's view of human spiritual and intellectual advancement. Although Hearn didn't necessarily believe in reincarnation, he did feel strongly that the human race progressed by building upon the achievements and knowledge of previous generations and upholding the virtues that had sustained them. In this way, he believed, the human race uncovers more of life's mysteries.

"Out of the unknown darkness," Hearn writes in "About Ancestor-Worship" in *Kokoro*, "we rise a moment into sunlight, look about us, rejoice and suffer, pass on the vibration of our being to other beings, and fall back again into darkness. So a wave rises, catches the light, transmits its motion, and sinks back into sea. So a plant ascends from clay, unfolds its leaves to light and air, flowers, seeds and becomes clay again. Only, the wave has no knowledge; the plant has no perceptions. Each human life seems no more than a parabolic curve of motion out of earth and back to earth; but in that brief interval of change it perceives the universe. The awfulness of the phenomenon is that nobody knows anything about it...I come out of mystery; I see

---

[8]Hearn to Chamberlain, January 19, 1893, *The Japanese Letters of Lafcadio Hearn*, 39.
[9]Hearn to Chamberlain, October 31, 1893, *The Japanese Letters of Lafcadio Hearn*, 190.

the sky and the land, men and women and their works; and I now that I must return to mystery; and merely what this not even the greatest of philosophers—not even Mr. Herbert Spencer—can tell me...All our knowledge is bequeathed knowledge. The dead have left a record of all they were about to learn about themselves and the world..."[10] In addition to the material world, he believed, human beings owe to their dead ancestors what they know about the immaterial world. "Whoever understands scientifically what human goodness is, and the terrible cost of making it, can find in the commonest phases of the humblest lives that beauty which is divine, and can feel that in one sense our dead are truly gods."[11]

Because of his break with Henry Alden, Hearn published nothing in America for almost a year after his last story appeared in *Harper's Magazine* in November 1890. In September 1891, the *Atlantic Monthly* published his article about the Festival of the Dead, the first of 21 Hearn stories the *Atlantic* would publish over the next six years. Around this time, Hearn repaired his strained relationship with Page Baker. Hearn wrote Baker a long, newsy letter updating him on his personal and professional life and acted as if nothing had ever come between them. Baker gladly responded, and their friendship resumed. Page Baker, who still was editor of the *New Orleans Times-Democrat*, offered to run some of Hearn's stories in the *Times-Democrat* and to set him up in syndication. Hearn accepted the offer, and his stories began appearing in the *Times-Democrat* and other American newspapers. Through his stories in the *Atlantic Monthly* and in the newspaper syndicate, Hearn began building a reputation as a compelling and perceptive interpreter of Japan for the English-speaking world. The United States and other Western countries had developed an intense fascination with Japan since it opened its borders to the outside world. In the last quarter of the 19th century, Japanese painting and pottery was in great demand, and Japanese aesthetics profoundly influenced Western art and decorative trends. Hearn began writing about Japan as the world's fascination with the Land of the Rising Sun was peaking. American periodicals like *Atlantic Monthly* were eager for stories about this bewitchingly beautiful and mysterious Asian nation.

---

[10]Hearn, *Kokoro*, 286-287.
[11]Ibid., 295.

The editors of the *Atlantic* soon discovered that Hearn didn't back down easily in editing disputes. Hearn used Japanese words in his articles when he thought it was appropriate. He would explain their meaning on first reference and then continue to use it throughout the rest of the article. The magazine's editors told him it would be less confusing to readers if he would eliminate the Japanese words and just use English substitutes. But Hearn wouldn't hear of it. He explained his reasoning in a June 5, 1893, letter to Chamberlain, who agreed with the *Atlantic* editors:

"Because they cannot hear the whispering of words, the rustling of the procession of letters, the dream-flutes and dream-drums which are thinly and weirdly played by words:

"Because they cannot perceive the pouting of words, the frowning and fuming of words, the weeping, the raging and racketing and rioting of words:

"Because they are insensible to the phosphorescing of words, the fragrance of words, the noisomeness of words, the tenderness or hardness, the dryness or juiciness of words—the interchange of values in the gold, the silver, the brass and the copper of words:

"Is that any reason why we should not try to make them hear, to make them see, to make them feel? Surely one who has never heard Wagner, cannot appreciate Wagner without study! Why should the people not be forcibly introduced to foreign words, as they were introduced to tea and coffee and tobacco?"[12]

This argument could also apply to his use of unfamiliar English words. He chose his words with painstaking care. He routinely rewrote an article or story four or five times over several days before he was satisfied with it. Hearn's themes and thoughts in them evolved and became more focused and refined with each rewriting. He explained this process in a different letter to Chamberlain: "In the course of four to five rewritings, the whole thought reshapes itself, and the whole style is changed and fixed. The work has done itself, developed grown; it would have bee very different had I trusted to the first thought. But I let the thought define and crystallize itself."[13]

Hearn's growing fame helped him connect with his three half-sis-

[12]Hearn to Chamberlain, June 5, 1893, *The Japanese Letters of Lafcadio Hearn*, 106-107.
[13]Hearn to Chamberlain, January 23, 1893, *The Japanese Letters of Lafcadio Hearn*, 43.

ters, children of his father and his father's second wife. He had never met or heard from them before. They saw his name or his picture in a newspaper or magazine and decided to write to him. Minnie Atkinson, a wife and mother who lived in England, was the only one of the sisters who received a reply from Hearn. He didn't want to became involved in a time-consuming correspondence with all three women. He responded to Atkinson because she had sent him a second letter and included a picture of herself and some family photographs. A small, pretty woman with blond hair, Atkinson impressed Hearn as a kind, considerate person who sincerely wanted to establish an intimate, sisterly relationship with him. In a series of letters to each other, they warmly exchanged information about themselves and what they knew about their parents and their family history. He sent her a photo of himself, typically showing only the right side of his face, not the left side with the whitish blind eye. He told her to teach her children to love him so they wouldn't be afraid of his face if he ever visited them. He wrote: "I send you a photo of one-half of it, the other is not pleasant, I assure you: like the moon, I show only one side of myself."[14]

Some of his former students in Matsue wrote letters to him, asking him to critique their English. He requested a few of his students to send him literal English translations of Japanese folk tales that he could add to his personal collection and possibly rewrite later in his own style. They gladly obliged.

Hearn also kept alert for daily events that might yield stories. He learned that a man who had killed a Kumamoto police officer four years earlier was being brought to the city the next day to stand trial. The man had tied up the members of a family in their home and robbed them. Within a day, he was captured by police. But on the way to the police station, he seized an officer's sword, killed him and escaped. Recently, a Kumamoto detective recognized the man at a prison in another city where he was being held for theft. He confronted the man, and he confessed to killing the police officer.

Hearn went to the Kumamoto railway station where the prisoner would be arriving. Because the murdered police officer had been highly respected and well-liked, Hearn anticipated an angry crowd

---

[14]Hearn to Minnie Atkinson, June 27, 1892, *Lafcadio Hearn*, Nina H. Kennard (New York: D. Appleton, 1912), 205.

would show up at the station and might try to attack the prisoner. But a very different scenario ensued. Hearn described it in simple but powerful language in a story, "At a Railway Station," later collected in his book, *Kokoro*:

"The train halted in the usual scene of hurry and noise,—scurry and clatter of passengers wearing *geta* (Japanese footwear),—screaming boys wanting to sell Japanese newspapers and Kumamoto lemonade. Outside the barrier we waited for nearly five minutes. Then, pushed through the wicket by a police-sergeant, the prisoner appeared,—a large wild-looking man, with head bowed down, and arms fastened behind his back. Prisoner and guard both halted in front of the wicket; and the people pressed forward to see—but in silence. Then the officer called out,—

'Sugihara San! Sugihara O-Kibi! is she present?'

"A slight small woman standing near me with a child on her back answered, 'Hai!" and advanced through the press. This was the widow of the murdered man; the child she carried was his son. At a wave of the officers hand the crowd fell back, so as to leave a clear space about the prisoner and his escort. In that space the woman with the child stood facing the murderer. The hush was of death.

"Not to the woman at all, but to the child only, did the officer then speak. He spoke low, but so clearly that I could catch every syllable:—

'Little one, this is the man who killed your father four years ago. You had not yet been born; you were in your mother's womb. That you have no father to love you now is the doing of this man. Look at him—[here the officer, putting a hand to the prisoner's chin, sternly forced him to lift his eyes]—look well at him, little boy! Do not be afraid. It is painful; but it is your duty. Look at him!'

"Over the mother's shoulder the boy gazed with eyes widely open, as in fear; then he began to sob; then tears came; but steadily and obediently he still looked—looked—looked—straight into the cringing face.

"The crowd seemed to have stopped breathing.

"I saw the prisoner's features distort; I saw him suddenly dash himself down upon his knees despite his fetters, and beat his face into the dust, crying out the while in a passion of hoarse remorse that made one's heart shake:—

'Pardon! pardon! pardon me, little one! That I did—not for hate was it done, but in mad fear only, in my desire to escape. Very, very wicked I have been; great unspeakable wrong have I done you! But now for my sin I go to die. I wish to die; I am glad to die! Therefore, O little one, be pitiful!—forgive me!'

"The child still cried silently. The officer raised the shaking criminal; the dumb crowd parted left and right to let them by. then, quite suddenly, the whole multitude began to sob. And as the bronzed guardian passed, I saw what I had never seen before,—what few men ever see,—what I shall probably never see again,—the tears of a Japanese policeman.

"The crowd ebbed, and left me musing on the strange morality of the spectacle. Here was justice unswerving yet compassionate,—forcing knowledge of a crime by the pathetic witness of its simplest result. Here was desperate remorse, praying only for a pardon before death. And here was a populace—perhaps the most dangerous in the Empire when angered—comprehending all, touched by all, satisfied with the contrition and the shame, and filled, not with wrath, but only with the great sorrow of the sin,—through simple deep experience of the difficulties of life and the weaknesses of human nature."[15]

During the summer of 1892, Hearn and Setsu took a long vacation that included Kyoto, Osaka, Nara and Kobe and ended in a trip to the Oki Islands, an archipelago in the Sea of Japan, about 100 miles from the coast of Izumo. Of its 16 islands, only four were permanently habitable. The sparsely populated Oki Islands were one of the most remote and least visited parts of Japan, features that made them especially appealing to Hearn. Fisheries were the islands' prime source of revenue. Hearn's transportation to the islands proved to be an unpleasant adventure. He boarded the Oki-Saigo, a small steamer

---

[15]Hearn, *Kokoro*, 2-6.

carrying live chickens, stacked baskets of squirming eels and other cargo as well as passengers. The steamer was so cramped, Hearn spent most of the voyage sitting on a watermelon on a cabin roof that was almost completely covered with watermelons.

The steamer stopped at a hotel in Urago, a village on Nishinoshima, long enough for dinner. It went on to Dogo, the largest and most populous Oki island. He stayed a month in the islands, first in the city of Saigo on Dogo, then in Urago and then in Hishi-ura on the island of Nakanoshima. The last three islands were part of a group known as Dozen. The residents of the islands were very friendly and respectful, similar to the people of Matsue. No one locked their doors because there were no thieves. The seacoasts of the islands were spectacular, with steep cliffs towering over the shores and waves smashing against the large rocks below. Small fishing villages, whose houses were covered with thatched roofs, were nestled in some of the coves. Hearn learned much ancient folklore from the residents and visited some Shinto shrines, although none were very noteworthy. He planned to see a celebrated shrine of Jizo on Dogo, but found out that it had burned down 20 years ago. He visited the simple tomb of Emperor Go-Toba, who had been exiled to the island of Nakanoshima in 1221 after staging an unsuccessful rebellion against the shogunate in an attempt to win back his throne. Go-Toba died there in 1239.

When Hearn stayed in Urago for three days, he found himself the center of much unwanted attention. Although he was the first foreigner ever seen on the islands, he escaped much attention in Dogo and Nakanoshima because he was short, dark-complexioned and wore Japanese clothing. But when the people of Urago found out a foreigner was staying in their village, they rushed to the hotel to see him. So many people swarmed outside the hotel, located on a corner, that they blocked the streets. No sooner than Hearn was shown to his large back room on the second floor, people began removing their sandals at the bottom of the stairs and quietly walking up the steps. They were too polite to walk uninvited into his room. But the first four or five people stuck their heads at once into the room to get a glimpse of him. They smiled at him, bowed their heads and then left to make way for the next group of gawkers. The line of spectators extended all the way down the stairs. People filled the upper rooms across the street and looked into his room from their windows. Men and boys packed the roofs of nearby buildings to see him. Boys climbed onto the awnings below Hearn's windows. "...all the openings of my room, on three sides, were full of faces,"[16] Hearn writes. Suddenly, some of the boys fell off the awnings, but they didn't get hurt. The frantic landlord called a policeman. The officer apologized to Hearn for the crowd's behavior, but asked him to excuse them because they had never seen a foreigner before. He asked Hearn if he wanted him to clear the street. Hearn said no, but he did want the boys, for their own safety, to stay off the awnings. The officer told the boys in a firm but low voice to keep off the awnings, and they obeyed. "And the queerest fact," Hearn writes, "was that during the performance of these extraordinary gymnastics there was a silence of death. Had I not seen the throng, I might have supposed there was not a soul in the street." Despite the heat, Hearn had to close his door and windows when he went to bed to prevent people from trying to watch him while he slept. Whenever he went outdoors, a silent, polite crowd of people followed him. Hearn good-naturedly endured their unending attention, but was relieved to leave Urago after three days. A much bigger annoyance for Hearn than the intrusion of his privacy was the frequent reek of cuttlefish entrails that Oki islanders used to fertilize their fields. But these shortcomings didn't weaken his deep affection for Oki.

"Once more, homeward bound," he writes at the end of his chapter about Oki in *Glimpses*, "I sat upon the cabin-roof of the Oki-Saigo,—this time happily unencumbered by watermelons,—and tried to explain to myself the feeling of melancholy with which I watched those wild island-coasts vanishing over the pale sea into the white horizon. No doubt it was inspired partly by the recollection of kindnesses received from many whom I shall never meet again; partly, also, by my familiarity with the ancient soil itself, and remembrance of shapes and places: the long blue visions down channels between islands,—the faint gray fishing hamlets hiding in stony bays,—the elfish oddity of narrow streets in little primitive towns,—the forms and tints of peak and vale made lovable by daily intimacy,—the crooked broken paths to shadowed shrines of gods with long mysterious names,—the butterfly-drifting of yellow sails out of the glow of an unknown horizon. Yet I think it was due much more to a particular

---

[16]Hearn, *Glimpses,* vol. II, 617.

sensation in which every memory was steeped and toned, as a landscape is steeped in the light and toned in the colors of the morning: the sensation of conditions closer to Nature's heart, and farther from the monstrous machine-world of Western life than any into which I had ever entered north of the torrid zone. And then it seemed to me that I loved Oki—in spite of the cuttlefish,—chiefly because of having felt there, as nowhere else in Japan, the full joy of escape from the far-reaching influences of high-pressure civilization,—the delight of knowing one's self, in Dozen at least, well beyond the range of everything artificial in human existence."[17]

One of the most unusual occurrences on Hearn's trip to Oki was his and Setsu's decision to take home with them a boy who was working in their hotel as a servant of people who had once been retainers of his family. They took a liking to the boy, who seemed intelligent and sensitive, and wanted him to be part of their household. Hearn planned to educate him. They told him they would take him to live with them in Kumomoto if he met them at the port on their day of departure. The boy did so. The Hearns sent him to school and treated him like a member of the family. Despite the family's efforts, the boy never connected emotionally with anyone in the household. He had an emotional shell no one could penetrate. Finally, Hearn sadly sent him back to Oki.

A few months after their trip to the Oki Islands, the Hearns moved into a better house with a more pleasing garden in December 1892. Early in the next year, Setsu became pregnant, which filled Lafcadio with excitement and anxiety. In the final weeks of her pregnancy, the Hearns had followed an old custom and borrowed a baby to prepare them for caring for one of their own. The experience seemed to calm everyone in the family except Lafcadio. He couldn't stop worrying about the health of Setsu and the baby.

On November 17, 1893, Setsu gave birth to a boy they named Leopold Kazuo Hearn. As two midwives tended to Setsu during her labor, Lafcadio knelt beside her and prayed that the baby, unlike him, would have good eyes. His prayers were answered. Kazuo was a healthy, strong baby with good eyes, and Setsu came through the birth in fine condition. At the age of 43, Hearn became a father for the first time. He was joyful and reflective about his new role.

---

[17]Ibid., 624-625.

"If ever you become a father," Hearn wrote to Ellwood Hendrick, "I think the strangest and strongest sensation of your life will be hearing for the first time the thin cry of your own child. For a moment, you have the strange feeling of being double; but there is something more, quite impossible to analyze—perhaps the echo in a man's heart of all the sensations felt by all the fathers and mothers of his are at a similar instant in the past..."[18] He vowed to raise his son as "a good little Buddhist. ..He will not have to go to church, and listen to stupid sermons, and be perpetually tormented by absurd conventions. He will have what I never had as a child,—natural physical freedom."

When Kazuo was one-and-a-half years old, Hearn wrote to Page Baker: "No man can possibly know what life means, what the world means, until he has a child and loves it. And then the whole universe changes and nothing will ever again seem exactly as it seemed before."[19] He told Baker he hoped Kazuo would become "a more sensible man than his foolish dad."

Although Lafcadio and Setsu had begun their life together in an arranged marriage, their feelings for each other deepened with time and evolved into love. She became accustomed to her husband's moods and to his total absorption in his writing. When he was hard at work writing, he seemed to fall almost in a trance and become completely oblivious to everything around him. Many times, Setsu would call his name from another room, and there would be no answer. Late one night she smelled smoke. She walked into the room where he was working. It was filled with dense smoke pouring from the oil lamp near him. "Hearn was almost suffocating," she recalls in her memoir, "but he was writing so enthusiastically that he noticed nothing, although he had a very sensitive nose for odors. I hurriedly opened the *shoji* (sliding paper window), and let in the air, and said, 'Papa-san! how dangerous it was that you did not know the lamp was on fire!' He exclaimed, 'Why was I so stupid!'"[20]

Hearn, who had frequented brothels in Cincinnati and New Orleans and had surrendered to the temptations of beautiful women in Martinique, had become a faithful, devoted husband in Japan. His

[18]Hearn to Ellwood Hendrick, November, 1893, *Life and Letters,* vol. II, 149-150.
[19]Hearn to Page Baker, April, 1895, *Life and Letters,* vol. II, 256.
[20]Setsuko Koizumi, *Reminiscences of Lafcadio Hearn* (Boston: Houghton Mifflin Co., 1918), 42-43.

Cincinnati journalist-friends never would have believed it. "One cannot dream or desire anything more after love is transmuted into the friendship of marriage," Hearn wrote to Hendrick. "It is like a haven from which you can see the dangerous sea-currents, running like violet bands beyond you out of sight."[21] In another letter, he writes: "The highest duty of the man is not to his father, but to his wife; and for the sake of that woman he abandons all other earthly ties, should any of these happen to interfere with that relation."[22] Nothing made him angrier than husbands who mistreated their wives and children or, worse, abandoned their families.

Setsu's father attempted to teach Hearn one of the skills of a Samurai warrior—shooting a bow and arrow. The Samurai bow wasn't the typical hand-held variety Westerners were familiar with. It stood about nine feet high. With the bottom of the bow on the ground, the shooter would grip the lower part of the bow, aim and fire. Hearn found it extremely difficult to control the path of the arrow. "I can scarcely do anything with it," he wrote in a letter to Chamberlain, "but he is teaching me. The target the first day was a metal wash-basin, covered with painted paper. His first arrow, though blunt, whistled through the basin and struck halfway through the fence. I am rather afraid of the trying,—for it would kill a man at once."[23]

Although his home life was happy, he had grown increasingly dissatisfied with his teaching job at the Government College. He hadn't made friends with any of the teachers, and the school had a new director who Hearn felt was standoffish with him. Hearn believed the school officials wanted to get rid of him. Considering his extreme sensitivity, it's difficult to know whether he was really being squeezed out or whether he had misjudged his bosses. On a train trip the Hearns took on a brief vacation, Setsu overheard a Kumamoto official telling others how much Hearn's students liked him. Hearn was pleased and surprised to hear this. "I am far more popular with the Kumamoto students than I imagined," he wrote to Chamberlain.[24] But he couldn't help

---

[21]Hearn to Ellwood Hendrick, November, 1992, *Life and Letters,* vol. II, 99.

[22]Hearn, *Books and Habits from the Lectures of Lafcadio Hearn,* ed. John Erskine (London: William Heinnaman, 1922), 2.

[23]Hearn to Chamberlain, April-May, 1894, *The Japanese Letters of Lafcadio Hearn,* 304-305.

[24]Ibid., 299.

wondering if Setsu or the official had been exaggerating. He did note that "the students have been coming very much closer to me, taking walks with me, and telling me wonderful things,—so it *may* be true."

Regardless, he had no doubts some school officials were plotting against him. So in the summer of 1894, he decided to look for a new job. He went to Yokohama, where he met W. B. Mason, a colleague of Chamberlain's at Tokyo Imperial University. Chamberlain had put Hearn in touch with Mason a couple of years earlier, and the two men had developed a friendship through letters. Hearn had a wonderful time in Yokohama with Mason and his family. He then went to Chamberlain's house in Tokyo. Chamberlain was vacationing for the summer in the mountains, and he had given Hearn permission to stay at his house. Hearn received first-rate treatment by Chamberlain's servants, who provided him with all the niceties he could want, including delicious meals. Hearn slept in a comfortable bed with a good mosquito net. He also made full use of Chamberlain's impressive personal library, poring over the literary works as well as the many books about Japan, folklore, languages and science. Hearn didn't find a new job during this trip. But he met with a publisher who printed books in English and reached a tentative agreement about issuing a series of elegantly bound fairytales.

More importantly, that same year, Houghton Mifflin published his first book about Japan, *Glimpses of Unfamiliar Japan*. Initially, the publisher had misgivings about the manuscript's extreme length. It included Hearn's stories that had appeared in the *Atlantic Monthly*, but most of the book consisted of new, unpublished material. Hearn convinced the publisher to issue it in two volumes, almost 700 pages in all. Hearn dedicated the book to Chamberlain and to Mitchell McDonald, Paymaster of the United States in Yokohama, whom Hearn had met in 1890 through an introductory letter from Elizabeth Bisland. McDonald, a genial, honest, down-to-earth man who loved literature, had helped Hearn in many ways. In Hearn's difficult early months in Japan, he had even lent him money. The book received good reviews in the United States and Great Britain. The most critical reviewer was Hearn himself. Most of the book had been based on notes he made of his experiences in his first year in Japan. Hearn believed many of his observations in the book about Japanese culture and daily life were superficial and naive. From the outset of his career, Hearn had a tendency to be too disparaging of his own work and that's the case with this book, which he said was "full of faults."[25] Actually, *Glimpses* is one of his finest books, a model of compelling, observant travel writing. It resonates with the passion and excitement of a man who is discovering a strange, beautiful world. He has remarkable talent for describing sights, sounds and people along with his immediate thoughts and feelings. There's a palpable, intimate quality to his writing that enables readers to see and feel what he does as he's experiencing it. The book is written in a lively, impressionistic style, and that's what gives it great depth and personality.

Shortly after returning home from his trip to Yokohama and Tokyo, Hearn received an offer to work full-time for an English-speaking newspaper in Kobe. The job involved writing editorials for the *Kobe Chronicle*. The offer came at an ideal time for Hearn. Just before he received it, an earthquake and a house break-in by thieves had shaken their sense of safety. They all had tired of living in Kumamoto. Setsu was excited about moving to a major city. Hearn quickly accepted the job offer. After wrapping up his teaching duties, Hearn moved to Kobe during the second week of October.

Kobe was an attractive major port city situated between Osaka Bay to the south and mountains to the north. In the years since Japan opened up to the West, a large colony of foreigners, protected by treaty rights that Japan had been forced to accept, had developed in Kobe. Although Hearn didn't like the presence of so many foreigners, he saw that Kobe still had many non-Westernized sections he could enjoy. Because of the large number of foreigners, Kobe had several foreign-language newspapers. The English-language *Kobe Chronicle* was run by a Scot, Robert Young, and his English wife. The newspaper's editorial stance was liberal, which Hearn liked. Young and Hearn found they agreed on major issues, and Young deferred to Hearn's viewpoint on a few minor ones they differed on. Hearn wrote all the editorials and had complete freedom in choosing his topics.

Hearn produced solid, competently written editorials that didn't require his best literary skills. The broad array of topics included Japanese education policies, the future outlook for Buddhism, Japan's na-

---

[25]Hearn to Chamberlain, January, 1895, *The Japanese Letters of Lafcadio Hearn,* vol. II, 198.

tional character and American racial issues. Young was impressed with Hearn's productivity and the quality of his work. "It was remarkable with what ease he could turn out an article," Young writes in a story about Hearn in a March 23, 1907, periodical called *The Living Age.*[26] The work during the day at the newspaper and his work on the evenings on his own writing projects strained his eyes so badly that he had to stop all activity for three weeks. For that period, he laid in a dark room with compresses over his eyes. His doctor told him he needed to choose between his newspaper job or his personal writing. He decided to quit the *Chronicle.* His second book, *Out of the East,* was published that year, and he was close to finishing his third book, *Kokoro.*

When his eyes recovered, he spent much his time at home reading. He missed the intellectual stimulation of teaching and the interaction with students and teachers. Those connections had helped him discover some of the topics he wrote about. Worrying about his eyes and brooding over the loss of his job at the newspaper, Hearn plunged into a depression. "I fear, however, my travelling days (except for business and monotonous work) are nearly over," Hearn wrote to Chamberlain in March 1895.[27] "I'm not going to get rich. Some day I may hit the public; but that will probably be when I shall have become ancient. I feel just now empty and useless and a dead failure." An eruption of anti-foreign sentiment in Kobe and other parts of Japan stemming from the country's wars with China and Korea and diplomatic pressures from Russia and Germany worsened Hearn's dark mood. In a letter to Chamberlain, Hearn complained that Japan "is going to become all industrially vulgar and industrially commonplace...In short the pendulum has swung the wrong way recently."[28]

When he walked the streets, boys would yell, "*Ijin! Tojin!*," words for foreigner. For someone who had been showered with kindness and affection from the Japanese people, the taunts stung Hearn deeply. It seemed to him the old Japan he loved was vanishing little by little, day by day. "I wish I could live somewhere out of the sight and the sound of all that is new," he wrote to Nishida.[29]

---

[26] Robert Young, "Lafcadio Hearn," *The Living Age, March 23, 1907,* quoted in *Lafcadio Hearn,* Elizabeth Stevenson, 272.

[27] From Hearn to Chamberlain, March, 1895, *Life and Letters,* vol. II, 219.

[28] Hearn to Chamberlain, July 7, 1893, *The Japanese Letters of Lafcadio Hearn,* 132.

[29] Hearn to Nishida, February, 1895, *Life and Letters,* vol. II, 291.

But one day something happened to lift his spirits. Two women came to his house selling ballads. One of the women, who was blind, began to sing, attracting a host of people in Hearn's tiny front yard. "Never did I listen to anything sweeter," Hearn told Chamberlain in a letter. "All the sorrow and beauty, all the pain and the sweetness of life thrilled and quivered in that voice; and the old first love of Japan and of things Japanese came back, and a great tenderness seemed to fill the place like a haunting. I looked at the people, and I saw they were nearly all weeping, and snuffing; and though I could not understand the words, I could feel the pathos and the beauty of things."[30]

When she finished singing, the Hearns invited the women into their house, gave them a meal and asked them their lives. The singer said she had been blinded by a bout with smallpox. Her husband was paralyzed. She sang and sold ballads to support herself, her husband and their son. Lafcadio bought two copies of the ballad she had sung. He had the lyrics translated into English and wrote a touching story about this encounter, "A Street Singer," which was published in his book, *Kokoro*.

Despite the increasingly hostile feelings toward foreigners in Japan, Hearn decided to become a Japanese citizen. His reason was purely practical. He wanted to protect his family's future financial security. If he died in Japan as a British citizen, Setsu would inherit nothing from him. The only way he could ensure that she would receive his money and property was for him to renounce his British citizenship and become registered as a Japanese citizen. When he became a Japanese citizen, he took the name Yakumo Koizumi. Koizumi was the name of his wife's family. Yakumo means "Eight Clouds." It's the first part of the most ancient surviving Japanese poem. He also chose that name because Yakumo is the poetic alternative for the name of his favorite part of Japan, Izumo, the province of his beloved Matsue.

"If all goes well," he wrote to Hendrick, "and I am not obliged to return to America, I shall next year probably return to Izumo, and make a permanent home there."[31] He figured he would travel to warmer climates during the winter.

---

[30]Hearn to Chamberlain, March, 1895, *Life and Letters,* vol. II, 220.

[31]Hearn to Ellwood Hendrick, *Life and Letters,* vol. II, 270.

CHAPTER 11

Ghost Stories and Journey's End in Tokyo

*A*S HEARN CONTEMPLATED a move back to Matsue, he began receiving overtures from Tokyo Imperial University, who was interested in hiring him to head its English Language and Literature Department. Basil Chamberlain had suggested Hearn to the president of the university's College of Literature as a possible candidate for the position. The inquiry indicated the extent of Hearn's literary reputation and stature in Japan. Wanting someone who was a distinguished writer and a respected teacher, the nation's most prestigious university turned to Hearn. The biggest sticking point was salary. Hearn was first contacted about the job in December 1895. At that point, the government was still processing his application for Japanese citizenship. As a matter of policy, foreign teachers in Japan generally were paid more than Japanese teachers. Hearn wanted his salary at the university to be what foreign teachers were paid. The university official who wanted to hire Hearn told him he thought the issue could be worked out. But Hearn didn't want to commit to the job until he knew exactly what his salary would be.

While Hearn waited for an answer, he continued to write. His second Japan book, *Out of the East*, had enhanced his reputation in the West as an authority on Japan. Among its highlights: "The Red Bridal," the true story of a double-suicide by two teenagers who were in love and wanted to thwart the pending arranged marriage of the girl to a widely hated wealthy older man; "The Dream of a Summer Day," in which Hearn ponders a haunting legend about a young man who falls asleep in his fishing boat and wakes up on an island where summer never dies; and "A Wish Fulfilled," an essay about Hearn's long, heart-felt conversation with a former student who came to his house to say goodbye before going off to war. The book, which Hearn dedicated to his dear friend, Sentaro Nishida, received laudatory reviews. In typical humility, he downplayed the critics' plaudits. He writes in a letter to Nishida: "Still, I am not foolish enough to take the praise for praise of fact,—feeling my own ignorance more and more every day, and being more pleased with the approval of a Japanese friend than with the verdict of a foreign reviewer, who, necessarily, knows nothing to speak of about Japan. But one thing is encouraging,— namely, that whatever I write about Japan hereafter will be widely read in Europe and elsewhere,—so that I may be able to do good."[1] His third book, *Kokoro*, was published in early 1896. Like *Out of the East*, *Kokoro* combined essays, stories and travel pieces, including "A Street Singer" and "At a Railway Station." In another story in *Kokoro*, "The Conservative," the son of a samurai succumbs to the Western influences permeating Japan and decided Christianity makes more sense than his family's and his country's Buddhist and Shinto faiths. But after living for a time in America and Europe, he sees his native country with different eyes. He finds deep meaning in the ancient Japanese traditions and returns to Japan, a prodigal son come home. In this story, Hearn deftly depicts in microcosm the clashing religious, cultural and social forces of the East and the West.

While Hearn's fame boosted his income and induced the job offer from Tokyo Imperial University, it also brought some unwanted consequences. He tells Page Baker in a letter: "The slightest success has to be very dearly paid for. It brings no friends at all, but many enemies and ill-wishers. It brings letters from autograph-hunters, and letters enclosing malicious criticisms, and letters requesting subscriptions to all sorts of shams, and letters of invitation to join respectable-humbug societies, and requests to call on people who merely want to gratify the meanest sort of curiosity..."[2] When autograph-seekers sent him postage stamps for return letters, Hearn would keep the stamps for his own use.

Questions about his salary at the university were still unanswered in March 1896 when Hearn became seriously ill. His doctor

---

[1]Lafcadio Hearn to Sentaro Nishida, April, 1896, *The Life and Letters of Lafcadio Hearn*, vol. II, Elizabeth Bisland (Boston and New York: Houghton Mifflin/Cambridge: The Riverside Press, 1910).

[2]Hearn to Page Baker, January, 1896, *Life and Letters*, vol. II, 286.

diagnosed a lung infection and also discovered heart problems and a hardening of the arteries. At age 46, Hearn already had concerns about his longevity. His health issues made his attempt to become a Japanese citizen even more critical for his family's financial security.

Hearn was still recovering from his illness when he, Setsu and Kazuo went to Izumo in June to see old friends and familiar sights in the region of Japan Lafcadio loved best. For him, it was not only a journey back to his past, but also to Japan's past, back to what Hearn considered an oasis in a nation in the ever-tightening grip of cataclysmic social and cultural changes. In Izumo, the Land of the Gods, the old ways and traditions still thrived. Happily, he saw that in the five years since he left Matsue, the city and its region hadn't changed much at all. At first, he thought the streets seemed more narrow and smaller than he remembered. But he figured that was because he had become accustomed to the larger streets of major cities, such as Kobe, Kyoto and Osaka. He went to his old samurai house in Matsue. The current owner welcomed him inside, and he saw his beloved gardens with its lotus-pond, the chrysanthemums and the little shrine of Inari. He went across the moat bridge to the old castle. It had undergone some exterior restorations. Hearn like some of them, but not all. He was disappointed that certain fish-shaped gable ornaments had been removed, and he preferred the former decaying colors of the roof and the exterior walls to their new colors.[3]

One day, Hearn toured the middle school where he had worked. As he was introduced in the classrooms he had once taught in, the new students stood and saluted him. He met another visitor, a soldier who had fought in the recently concluded Sino-Japanese War and had been one of the school's earliest students. He had served on a cruiser that sunk Chinese transport *Kowshing*, the first major Japanese battle victory in the war. That evening, Hearn attended a banquet given in his honor where he saw many old friends. One of the dancing girls he had known as a child entertained at the banquet. At Hearn's request, she performed the dance of Urashima, the youth of the ancient legend Hearn had recounted in "The Dream of a Summer Day."[4]

---

[3]Lafcadio Hearn, "Notes on a Trip to Izumo," *Atlantic Monthly*, May, 1897.
[4]Hearn, "The Dream of a Summer Day," in *Out of the East* (Boston and New York: Houghton Mifflin Company/Cambridge: The Riverside Press, 1895), 1-27.

A few days later, he visited many of the shrines and temples in Matsue. Many of these religious sites bore evidence of the war with China. Most of the temples contained spoils of the war left by Japanese soldiers and seamen offering homage to the gods. Items included Gatling and Armstrong guns, rifles, revolvers and Chinese banners, uniforms and lances. Hearn visited temples in the rural areas of Izumo as well as in Matsue. In the village of Sugata-mura, he stopped at O-Kyaku-San, a Shinto shrine with a thatched roof that overlooked an expanse of rice fields. Tresses of human hair, votive offerings, had been fastened to the granite torii at the entrance to the court. Mothers would come there to pray that their children would have beautiful hair, and girls with brown, curly hair would pray at the shrine for straight hair. Tied strands of hair and strands of help dyed to resemble real hair were hung from the shrine's grates. According to tradition, a beautiful woman named O-Kyaku-San, which means "Lady Guest," had lived in the area hundreds of years ago. Her beauty aroused extreme jealousy in many people, who criticized her for not having perfectly black hair. She became so distraught over the persistent taunts that she killed herself. Out of sympathy and atonement for her tragic fate, a temple was built for her spirit.[5]

For part of his trip, Hearn stayed at a two-story summer house near the edge of a high cliff overlooking a bay near ancient Mionoseki. The summer house provided its guests with sandals, a bathing dress, a large straw hat for shade, barley tea and cakes, a smoking box and a pillow. Guests had to bring their own food and towels. Hearn gloried in this bucolic setting where he could swim with Kazuo, relax, enjoy the view and fall asleep at night with a gentle sea breeze blowing into the room. "The summer-houses," Hearn writes, "are manifestations of something higher than the mere sense of beauty: they teach us also how fully Old Japan understood that the secret of happiness was to be found in content,—content with the sober necessaries of life, content with the simple pleasures that nature offers equally to all, content with what everyday humanity can give of unselfish companionship. Something of the old idyllic condition still lingers in Japan, despite the changes of the years of Meiji; and to one who has dwelt in it even but a little while, our trained Western notions about the 'battle for

---

[5]Hearn, "Notes on a Trip to Izumo," *Atlantic Monthly*, May, 1897.

existence,' the 'duty of struggle,' the 'obligation' of triumphing over our weaker brethren in the miserable striving for wealth and position, seem the doctrines of a monstrous social condition. Ages and ages ago, the Japanese discovered that the sole requirements for unselfish happiness were health, ability to earn a bare livelihood, and the natural cultivation of those moral and aesthetic sentiments possessed by every well-balanced mind. All else that made life worth living nature along could furnish,—joy, beauty, love, rest."[6] He believed his daily swimming in the bay helped him overcome his lung infection.

During this trip, Hearn found out that Tokyo Imperial University agreed to meet his salary demands and pay him what they would pay a foreigner. He received the news with mixed feelings. On one hand, he would be moving to Tokyo, a city he hated almost as much as New York City. On the other hand, he looked forward to teaching at the most prestigious university in Japan, where he would teach only 12 hours a week and have plenty of time to devote to his writing. He was painfully aware that in Tokyo, he would be at the crest of the massive changes sweeping Japan. "For me the New Japan is waiting; the great capital, so long dreaded, draws me to her vortex at last," he writes his *Atlantic Monthly* article. "And the question I now keep asking myself is whether in that New Japan I can be fortunate enough at happy moments to meet with something of the Old."

Not long after began teaching at Tokyo Imperial University, he found something of the old. He discovered some of his former students at Matsue and Kumamoto were enrolled there. They didn't hesitate to renew their relationship with their beloved former teacher. He had dinner with some Kumamoto students and invited some of his Matsue students to visit his house. Hearn enabled one of his Matsue students, Masanobu Otani, to enroll at the university by agreeing to employ him as an assistant. Otani gathered and translated material that Hearn might use in his classes. Most of his students were between 22 and 27 years old, the normal age range for Japanese university students at that time. Hearn quickly established a rapport with his students, just as he had at his previous teaching positions. He didn't lecture from detailed notes. His only cues for his lectures were pieces of paper containing names and dates. His lectures impressed his stu-

---

[6]Hearn, "Notes on a Trip to Izumo," *Atlantic Monthly*, May, 1897.

dents enough that some of them wrote down every word he said. He tried to convey to them the importance of literature's emotional dimension. One classroom visitor said he saw Hearn's students in tears after Hearn read a poignant poem in English.

The Hearns rented a newly constructed 10-room, two-story house in the Ushigome section of Tokyo that was a good distance from the university—45 minutes away by rickshaw. But nearby woods, open fields, farms with rice fields and a Buddhist temple hidden by tall cedar trees on a hill behind the house more than offset the inconvenience of the work commute. Tokyo's rapid growth in population and modernization created an unsightly, noisy and helter-skelter environment that Hearn hated. Roadways were torn up so the city could lay down water pipes underground, miles of telegraph poles and wires marred the streetscapes and squalid slums appeared in certain parts of the city. When Hearn complained about all this in a letter to Hendrick, he drew a line of telegraph poles with water pipes on the ground in front of them to give his American friend an idea of how ugly they were. He worried that living in Tokyo would impair his writing muse. He noted that many city dwellers captured or bought insects and kept them in little cages because the noises they made gave them the sense of being in the country. "In this horrid Tokyo I feel like a cicada," Hearn writes. "I am caged, and can't sing. Sometimes I wonder whether I shall ever be able to sing any more,—except at night?—like a bell-insect which has only *one* note."[7]

The little temple and its grounds on the hill behind his house was Hearn's patch of Old Japan. The temple's religious name was Ki-sho-in, but it was familiarly called Kobudera (Knotty Pine) because of the kind of wood from which it was built. The Kobudera and its grounds became Hearn's little haven. He and Setsu stopped in the temple each morning and evening and quickly became friends with the abbot, who often told them stories of Buddhist lore. Hearn loved walking in the shade of the cedar trees, sauntering through the temple's small cemetery surrounded by pine trees and looking at the Buddhist statues. Here Tokyo's noisy, unsightly helter-skelter environment seemed far away. He had always found solace in nature. But now Hearn also began experiencing a certain joy in the contemplation of Buddhism.

---

[7]Hearn to Hendrick, August, 1897, *Life and Letters*, vol. II, 335.

The Kobudera combined both elements.

Hearn once joked with Setsu about becoming a Buddhist priest so he could live in the temple.

"If you should become a priest, how funny you would look with your large eyes and high nose—a fine priest!," Setsu said.

"You could become a nun at the same time, and Kazuo a novice. How cute he would look! Every day we should read the scriptures and take care of the graves. That would be true happiness!"

"Pray that you may be born a priest in the next world," Setsu said.

"That is my wish," Hearn replied.[8]

But in the material world, writing was Hearn's greatest passion. Besides teaching and working on his books and magazine articles in Japan, Hearn produced loads of letters. Although he wrote his letters quickly and without revision, they usually were extremely well-written and thought-provoking. He carried on his most intense correspondence with Basil Chamberlain, his favorite intellectual companion. They discussed everything from the nuances of the Buddhist and Shinto faiths, the deficiencies of education in the West and in Japan, and ancient Japanese folk tales to the merits of the Romantic English poets, comparisons of various ancient and modern philosophers and an analysis of Russian novelists. Hearn tried in numerous letters to convince Chamberlain of the wisdom of his pet philosopher, Herbert Spencer. In Chamberlain, Hearn had a letter-writing partner of equal intellectual breadth, depth and curiosity.

Soon after Hearn moved to Tokyo, Hearn abruptly stopped answering Chamberlain's letters and didn't try to see him even though they taught at the same university. Chamberlain, who had recommended Hearn for the university job, was baffled by Hearn's sudden iciness toward him. After Hearn took the job with the *Kobe Chronicle*, he wrote a letter to Chamberlain scolding him and W. B. Mason for not sensing how badly he had wanted to get out of Kumamoto. "Well, I guess the two of you consulted over together (unfair!—two against one!) and concluded it was best to let me stick it out," he writes.[9] All Hearn would have had to do was ask Chamberlain to help him get

---

[8]Setsuko Koizumi, *Reminiscences of Lafcadio Hearn* (Boston: Houghton Mifflin Co. 1918), 27-28.

[9]Hearn to Chamberlain, October 14, 1894, *The Japanese Letters of Lafcadio Hearn*, 391.

another job and he would have done it. He had helped him get the teaching jobs in Matsue and Kumamoto when Hearn asked. Hearn's hypersensitivity and his unreasonable expectations of people once again caused him to end what had been a close friendship. Chamberlain took his place beside Henry Alden, George Washington Cable and Henry Krehbiel as former close Hearn friends he had lost through his petulance. Although he didn't contact Chamberlain any more, Hearn spoke favorably of him at home. Chamberlain understood Hearn's peculiar personality, accepted the situation and didn't hold any grudges against him. After Hearn's death, his family and Chamberlain became friends again.

Near the end of 1896, Setsu gave birth to her second son, Iwao, a healthy baby. Hearn was a little more relaxed with his second child and didn't fret over Iwao as he had Kazuo. As Hearn drew away from Chamberlain, he became closer to his friend, Mitchell McDonald, the paymaster of the United States Navy in Yokohama. Hearn relied on McDonald, who was honest and practical, for advice on personal issues. With a growing family, Hearn became increasingly concerned about long-term financial matters. McDonald suggested that Hearn invest some of his money in a business McDonald was involved with. McDonald agreed to serve as Hearn's his proxy at the investors' semi-annual meetings, which Hearn had no interest in attending. Hearn was delighted when his first attempt at capital investment turned out to be a beneficial one. McDonald became a regular Sunday visitor to the Hearn household, bringing toys and candy for the two boys and talking and laughing with Hearn for hours in the study.

After his successful first year of teaching at Tokyo Imperial University, Hearn decided to take his family on a vacation to seaside locale. He rejected more established, modern resorts and decided on a small fishing village called Yaidzu on Suruga Bay, about 120 miles southwest of Tokyo. Hearn, Setsu, their two sons and a nurse traveled by rickshaw. A friend arranged for the Hearns to rent four rooms from fish shop owner Yamaguchi Otokiochi. The rented rooms comprised the second story of Otokiochi's living quarters behind the fish shop. Despite the flies, the mosquitoes and the foul smells of fish entrails from the shop, Hearn loved staying there. Otokochi's wife cooked meals for the Hearns, and their children played with Kazuo. The beach consisted of mostly pebbles, but the cool, clear water was ideal for swimming. A sturdy sea wall protected the village from being slammed by high waves. Hearn impressed the village residents with his vigorous swimming style and with the way he floated on the water with ease. When the surf was running high, sometimes Hearn sat on the seawall for hours watching the waves crash against the lower part of the wall.

The Hearns were in Yaidzu during the Bon Odori, the Japanese Buddhist festival honoring the spirits of dead ancestors. On the night of the festival's last day, the villagers would launch dozens of lit paper lanterns on miniature model boats into the water from the shore, symbolic of the journey of their ancestors' spirits back to their resting place in the sea. Hearn assumed the launching would occur at midnight, as it did in most Japanese villages. But when he woke up just before midnight from his evening nap, he looked out the window and saw a swarm of tiny points of light moving out into the sea. He wanted to get a closer look at them. So he ran to the beach and plunged into the water. With strong, swift strokes, he caught up with the last few lanterns. He swam close to one without disturbing its course so that he could study it. "I watched those frail glowing shapes drifting through the night," he writes in the "At Yaidzu" chapter of *In Ghostly Japan*, "and ever as they drifted scattering, under impulse of wind and wave, more and more widely apart. Each, with its quiver of color, seemed a life afraid,—trembling on the blind current that was bearing it into the outer blackness…Are not we ourselves as lanterns launched upon a deeper and dimmer sea, and ever separating further and further one from another as we drift to the inevitable dissolution? Soon the thought-light in each burns itself out: then the poor frames, and all that is left of their once fair colors, must melt forever into the colorless Void…"[10] He swam back to the shore and was greeted by Otokichi and his wife, who had worried that he might not make it back.

Yaidzu became Hearn favorite vacation spot, a place he returned to year after year. He and his family were the only tourists in the little village. It made him yearn for Matsue and its simpler, more traditional life. Near the end of this first vacation, Hearn talked to Setsu about moving back to Matsue. But she immediately rejected the idea. She told him he wouldn't be able to support the family with the lower

---

[10]Lafcadio Hearn, *In Ghostly Japan* (Boston: Little, Brown, and Company, 1899), 232.

teacher's salary he would earn there. They wouldn't be able to consider such a move while raising their children. Hearn knew she was right and didn't argue.

He planned one more adventure before returning to Tokyo to begin the 1897–98 school year. Mount Fuji, Japan's most sacred mountain, wasn't far from Yaidzu. From the village, the majestic, snow-capped mountain, known as the Supreme Altar of the Sun, loomed on the northern horizon. One of his former students, Fujisaki, visited him at Yaidzu. With the encouragement of the young man, Hearn decided to climb to the summit of Mount Fuji with him before his summer vacation ended. Hearn, his former student, Setsu, her mother and Kazuo went to Gotemba, a town near base of Mount Fuji's south side. Hearn paid for two guides and rented a horse and rickshaw. Each year, hundreds of pilgrims from all parts of the nation climbed to the 12,500-foot-high summit of Mount Fuji, fulfilling what many Japanese believed was a religious duty.

While Setsu, her mother and Kazuo waited in Gotemba, Hearn, Fujisaki and their two guides set out on their two-day mountain trek. His guides came to his room at 3 a.m., August 25. Hearn thought he was properly dressed for the climb. But his guides insisted that he undress and put on heavy underclothing. They told him that even though it was hot at the foot of the mountain, it would be freezing cold at the top. Hearn did as he was told. His pilgrim outfit included a broad-brimmed straw hat, cleft stockings, sandals made of straw and a large staff. The slope was gradual enough that he would be able to ascend the first 5000 feet by rickshaw. There were three runners—two to pull the rickshaw and one to push it. After two hours, the grass disappeared and they had to travel over an expanse of black volcanic sand leading up to patches of snow. Discarded straw sandals laid on the ground ahead of them. The black grit quickly wore out the pilgrim's straw sandals. They had to replace them frequently during their ascent. It became so difficult to move Hearn's rickshaw through the black sand that the runners attached the horse to it. they reached the first of 10 rest stations on their route at 6:40 a.m. The large wooden house had meals to the pilgrims and contained a two-room shop selling hats, raincoats, sandals and staves. A photographer was selling inexpensive photos of the mountain.

After resting, Hearn proceeded on horseback because the rickshaw could go no farther. The horse wouldn't be able to go beyond the next station. But before he got there, an increasingly steep slope forced him get off the horse and walk. For the 42-year-old Hearn, the rest of the climb was sheer torture. Bracing against a cold, strong wind, they walked in zig-zag fashion through sand and cinders up a steep grade. To keep Hearn from falling, one guide pulled him using a cotton girdle as a rope while the other guide pushed him from behind. The footing became even more difficult when their walking surface became loose stones and cinders. "There is nothing firm, nothing re-sisting to stand on: loose stones and cinders roll down at every step," he writes. "If a big lava-block were to detach itself from above!…In spite of my helpers and of the staff, I continually slip, and am all in perspirations again. Almost every stone that I tread upon turns under me. How is it that no stone ever turns under the feet of the goriki (the guides)? *They* never slip,—never make a false step,—never seem less at ease than they would be in walking over a matted floor."[11]

With more than 4,000 feet to climb, they stopped overnight at a rest station. At 6:40 a.m. the next day, they resumed their ascent. At 8: 20 a.m., they finally reached the summit and saw the immense volcanic crater. Despite his aching, exhausted body, Hearn was able to enjoy the sunrise and the spectacular view. "But the view—the view for a hundred leagues,—and the light of the far faint dreamy world,—and the fairy vapors of morning,—and the marvelous wreathings of cloud: all this, and only this, consoles me for the labor and the pain…. Other pilgrims, earlier climbers,—poised upon the highest crag, with faces turned to the tremendous East,—are clapping their hands in Shinto prayer, saluting the mighty Day…. The immense poetry of the moment enters me with a thrill."[12] The descent by a different route proved much less arduous than the climb, and Hearn's family warmly welcomed him back to Gotemba. He felt happy that he had overcome the enormous physical obstacles to achieve his long-time goal of reaching the summit of Mount Fuji. But he had no desire to do it again. Like his climb to the top of Mount Pelee, once was enough.

Throughout his life, Hearn sought meaningful experiences that would provide insights into other cultures—such as, climbing to the

---

[11]Hearn, *Exotics and Retrospectives* (Boston: Little, Brown, and Company, 1898), 20.
[12]Ibid., 35-36.

tops of Mount Fuji and Mount Pelee, exploring the Louisiana bayous and little islands in the Gulf of Mexico and interviewing the seamstresses and washerwomen in Cincinnati. He believed he could learn more about a culture by communicating with the common people than with the educated. He had to explain this to Masananobu Otani, his student assistant at the university. Otani had collected hundreds of Japanese poems and song lyrics he thought Hearn could translate and use in his teaching or writing. In a letter to Hearn, Otani told him he knew Hearn didn't want "vulgar" songs, by which he meant songs written in the speech of the common people. But those were exactly the kind of songs Hearn wanted, and he explicitly pointed out why to Otani.

"They are just what I care *most* about," he writes. "The *refined* poetry of this era, and most of the poetry that you collected for me of other eras, is of little or no value. On the other hand, the "vulgar" songs sung by coolies and fishermen and sailors and farmers and artisans, are very true and beautiful poetry; and would be admired by great poets in England, in France, in Italy, in Germany, or in Russia…A great poem by Heine, by Shakespeare, by Calderon, by Petrarch, by Hafiz, by Saadi, remains a great poem *even when it is translated into the prose of another language*. It touches the emotion or the imagination in every language. But poetry which cannot be translated is of no value whatever in world-literature; and it is not even true poetry. It is mere playing with values of words. True poetry has nothing to do with mere word-values. It is fancy, it is emotion, it is passion, or it is thought. Therefore it has power and truth."[13]

Hearn was a folklorist at heart. He enjoyed waking up to the singing of the men who washed on a vacant lot next to his house. They sung as they whipped the wet clothes against big flat stones. Upon hearing a song that especially intrigued him, Hearn asked one of his students who lived there to translate it for him. At Hearn's urging, the student took on a project of gathering songs he heard on the streets sung by washerman, carpenters, blacksmiths, bamboo-weavers, rice cleaners and other common people. The student collected 47 songs and helped Hearn translate them into English. Hearn wrote an essay about these songs called "Out of the Street," which appears in his

---

[13]Hearn to Masananobu Otani, December, 1897, *Life and Letters*, vol. II, 343.

book, *Gleanings in the Buddha-fields*. "The real art of them, in short, is their absolute artlessness," he writes. "That was why I wanted them. Springing straight from the heart of the eternal youth of the race, these little gushes of song, like the untaught poetry of every people, utter what belongs to all human experience rather than to the limited life of a class or a time; and even in their melodies still resound the fresh and powerful pulsings of their primal source."[14] Hearn sensed the presence of the universal human spirit in those songs just as he had years ago in the songs of the Black dockworkers on the Cincinnati riverfront, of the Creoles in New Orleans and of the women washing clothes in the Roxelane River in St. Pierre.

All manner of people and all forms of life fascinated Hearn. He studied animals and plants with the same intensity and passion as he did human beings. He listened to many varieties of Japan's musical insects and wrote about the high esteem people in that country had for them. In "Insect-Musicians" in *Exotics and Retrospectives*, Hearn elucidates the different sounds and the appearances of these singing insects as if he were describing the musical instruments in an orchestra. The essay includes illustrations of many of the insects and cites examples of their presence in classic Japanese literature. Hearn writes that "in the aesthetic life of a most refined and artistic people, these insects hold a place not less important or well-deserved than that occupied in Western civilization by our thrushes, linnets, nightingales and canaries. What stranger could suppose that a literature one thousand years old,—a literature of curious and delicate beauty,—exists upon the subject of these short-lived insect-pests?"[15]

The Houghton Mifflin Company had published Hearn's first four books about Japan and was anticipating more. The company made the mistake of preparing a 19-page advertising biography of him without letting him know about it until the proofs were ready to be read. He was so angry at what he considered an invasion of his privacy that he tossed the proofs into his stove and arranged for Little, Brown and Company to publish his next book.

Hearn would have liked to give up teaching to devote all his work

---

[14]Hearn, *Gleanings in the Buddha-fields* (Boston and New York: Houghton Mifflin Company/Cambridge: The Riverside Press), 32.

[15]Hearn, *Exotics and Retrospectives*, 41.

time to his writing. But he needed the steady income to support his growing family. A third son, Kiyoshi, followed Iwao. Because Kazuo was the oldest and the most sensitive of his children, Hearn worried about him more than the others. He believed Kazuo had inherited some of his hypersensitivity and, like him, was easily hurt. Having suffered through most of his early years without a father, Hearn wanted to be sure he didn't neglect his own children. He felt Kazuo would learn more from him and from private tutors giving lessons at his house than he would by attending a public elementary school. When Kazuo was four years old, Hearn began teaching him English during their vacation at Yaidzu. During the first year of these lessons, Hearn drew pictures on old newspapers to teach Kazuo the English alphabet, numerals and simple words. Then he began using illustrated books for instruction. Kazuo's mother, grandfather and a student who was staying at their house taught him Japanese reading and writing. Hearn initially taught Kazuo English for an hour a day. But when Hearn decided Kazuo could learn more at home than at elementary school, his lessons stretched to three hours a day. Setsu and a student taught him Japanese and other subjects.

Kazuo found English a very difficult language to learn. Hearn sometimes lost his patience when Kazuo made too many mistakes. He sometimes scolded him severely and even slapped him. Japanese society, as in most parts of the world then, accepted corporal punishment as a part of child-rearing. When Hearn tried to strike Kazuo, the boy would turn toward the glass sash-door to evade his father's hand and lean against the door and cry. Once Kazuo walked in the room and saw his father wiping the stains from his tears off the glass with one of his socks. Not knowing Kazuo was there, Hearn touched the stains and said, "Don't think me cruel," and sighed sadly.[16] Once after spanking Kiyoshi at Setsu's request, the boy cried and rubbed his eyes so much that his eyelids swelled. Hearn felt terrible and said to Setsu, "There's no feeling so bad as after spanking the children. Every time I scold them, my life is shortened."[17]

Despite the spankings, Kazuo characterized Hearn as a loving, af-

---

[16]Kazuo Koizumi, *Father and I: Memories of Lafcadio Hearn* (Boston and New York: Houghton Mifflin Co., 1935), 144.
[17]Ibid., 201.

fectionate father who told them stories in his ungrammatical Japanese and joined in when the family sang together in the evenings. All the children, servants and maids participated these songfests. They all sat on mats on the floor. During the Russo-Japanese War, they sometimes sang war songs while marching around the dining room table. When Hearn came home from teaching, the children ran to him and stuck their hands in his pockets to grab the treats he often brought. In his book about Hearn, *Father and I*, he compares living with his father to living at the foot of a volcanic mountain. "Each morning and evening is displayed a new and charming aspect of the mountain," Kazuo writes, "but all at once it will send up huge columns of fire and emit voluminous heavy stones from its quiet cone…"[18]

Hearn believed knowing the English language was important for the future of all Japanese children. Part of his anxiety about making sure Kazuo learned to write and speak English stemmed from his feeling that he would die well before the boy reached adulthood. He felt he must teach him as much as he could as quickly as possible. When walking with Kazuo in their neighborhood, Hearn sometimes would look up at the crematory's tall chimney and say, "I will soon become a smoke and rise from that chimney," he would say." The remark always upset Kazuo. One day, he told his mother what his father said when they walked near the crematory.

"Papa-san, don't say such a thing to little Kazuo," she told her husband. "It's better not to. Nobody feels good in hearings such a thing."

Hearn apologized. "Pardon, pardon, but it's really so."

"No, it's not true," she replied. You must live a long time yet or we would be troubled."

"But I know my own body well. It will be hard for me to see Kazuo enter the middle school."[19]

His sense of imminent death drove him to work at a furious pace to write the books he had in mind so they could help support his family after he was gone. He worried especially about being able to provide a Western education for Kazuo. He believed Kazuo needed some schooling in the United States to speak English properly. With this in mind, Hearn began exploring future teaching possibilities at

---

[18]Ibid., 17.
[19]Ibid., 174.

universities in the United States. He asked his friend, Elizabeth Bisland Wetmore (who married Charles Wetmore in 1891), to help find a writing position for him.

Some days he became so absorbed in his writing that he wouldn't even hear his children calling him to dinner. When Setsu would come into his study and urge him to come to dinner, he would tell her he thought he had already eaten. His habit of daydreaming when walking alone became more dangerous in the last few years of his life. Once when preoccupied in his thoughts, he didn't realize he was about to walk into the path of a train. The warning yells of a woman behind brought him out of his reverie. He jumped back from the track just as the train roared past. After that frightening episode, his family made sure someone always accompanied him on his walks.

The Koizumis' portion of their neighborhood became increasingly unpleasant. Their street was torn up for months while a water main was being installed, and the nearby prison expanded. Guards marched the red-uniformed prisoners past Hearn's house in a line every morning and evening to work on the extension of the prison. Once in a while, a prisoner on the work detail would escape, causing residents to be fearful of break-ins and violent crime.

Hearn continued his daily walks on the Kobudera's grounds until the temple's friendly abbot, Archbishop Asakusa, had three tall cedar trees cut down so their wood could be sold for badly needed funds to repair the structure. When Hearn first came upon the three trees lying on the ground, he became as sad as if he had lost a member of his family. One of his great pleasures since moving to Tokyo had been walking and meditating among the grove of cedar trees. Two years before, he had hired a photographer from Izumo, Ichiro Hori, to take photos in Kobudera's cemetery that he included in his book, *Exotics and Retrospectives*. "He came out of the temple gate in a lifeless manner, as if some great event had taken place," Setsu writes in her memoir. "He sat down in the chair in his study, and was very much depressed."[20] He seldom visited the temple after that. The next year, 1901, a young abbot replaced the older one and soon had all the cedar trees cut down. By the time the Hearns moved to a different neighborhood in 1902, the temple's cemetery was gone. New tenements

---

[20]Setsuko Koizumi, *Reminiscences*, 29.

had replaced the grove of cedar trees and the graves. Hearn's private outdoor sanctuary, his little remnant of rural Old Japan, had vanished before his eyes.

When he and Setsu discussed moving, Hearn suggested building a house on one of the Oki islands. After Setsu quickly rejected that idea, he said they should buy a house in Izumo. They looked at lots, but Setsu decided she didn't want to live there, although Lafcadio loved it—except for the cold winters. They decided to buy a Japanese-style single-story house in the partly rural Tokyo neighborhood called Nishi-Okubo, the Gardener's Quarters. Before moving in, they added Hearn's study, Setsu's room, a dressing room and a parlor. Hearn asked that the addition to the house and other alternations should be in the Japanese style, that there be a room with a stove that he could light during the winter cold and that his desk be placed facing west. He let Setsu make all other decisions. During the construction of the addition, she went every day to inspect the work that was done. Hearn was delighted with finished product. The house had only Japanese sliding paper doors except for the glass doors in the room with the stove. Hearn also liked the bamboo grove in back of the house where the nightingales sang.

As he and Setsu arranged his books on shelves, he said suddenly said, "It hurts my heart."

Puzzled, Setzu said, "Why?"

"It is too pleasant to last," he said. "I pray that we may live here a long time."[21]

His pessimistic statement almost proved tragically prophetic. Not long after moving into the house, Hearn suffered bronchitis and a hemorrhage from a burst blood vessel in his throat. He wasn't permitted to talk for several weeks. This debilitating illness took a heavy physical toll on him. His hair and his mustache turned almost completely white, his cheeks appeared sunken and he could no longer lift the heavy dumb-bells he used for exercise. He looked much older than a man in his early 50s.

As if his health problems weren't enough to contend with, the officials at Tokyo Imperial University notified him in March 1903 that he would no longer receive a foreigner's salary when his contract

_____

[21] Ibid., 32.

was renewed. Because he was a Japanese citizen, his salary would be cut significantly so that it would be in line with the other non-foreign faculty members. The university also denied his request to take a year's sabbatical at this time, even though he was due to receive one. He wanted to take the sabbatical then because Cornell University had offered to pay him to deliver a series of lectures about Japanese civilization. Disappointed and angry, Hearn resigned from his teaching post. His students were so upset when they heard why he had quit, they lobbied to have him reinstated at the higher foreigner's salary. Some of them wanted to agitate more aggressively for his return, but Hearn persuaded them not to. Cornell wound up withdrawing its offer to Hearn because of an outbreak of typhoid fever on campus.

In the fall of 1903, Setsu gave birth to a girl, Setsuka, their fourth child. Hearn happily welcomed the new baby, but fretted that he wouldn't live long enough to help her have a secure future. "What a pain is in my heart!" he said as he looked at the infant.[22]

As his health improved, he resumed his intense writing regime. Since *Exotics and Retrospectives* was published in 1898, he had been remarkably productive. He wrote four books in four years: *In Ghostly Japan, Shadowings, A Japanese Miscellany* and *Kotto: Being Japanese Curios, with Sundry Cobwebs*. Each of the books contained a mix of essays about different aspects of Japan's spiritual, cultural and social life as well as ancient folk tales retold in Hearn's style. The topics include fireflies, Japanese female names, songs of Japanese children, Buddhist names and proverbs, incense, a translation of excerpts from the diary of an ordinary Japanese woman, silkworms and Hearn's own experiences. He finds significance and eerie beauty in seemingly mundane objects.

In a conversation Hearn has with a friend about silkworms in *In Ghostly Japan*, the friend remarks that the silkworm's eyebrows are beautiful. Hearn can't understand how that could be. But when the friend brings a silkworm to him, Hearn observes "that the antennae, very short and feathery, were so arched back over the two jewel-specks of eyes in the velvety head, as to give the appearance of a really handsome pair of eyebrows."[23]

[22]Ibid., 67.
[23]Hearn, *In Ghostly Japan* (Boston: Little Brown and Company, 1899), 60.

Hearn's friend explains that silkworms that are kept in captivity for spinning silk and for breeding lose the ability to fly and to care for themselves. They are totally dependent on their human caretakers for their continued existence. That leads Hearn to reflect on the parallels between total dependency of silkworms and humans' ideas about happiness. Many humans, he writes, believe that the ideal existence would be to have all their basic needs met without any pain or sweat on their part. Their ideal afterlife would be a state in which the gods provide all that's needed for their happiness. But Hearn wonders what would happen to such a totally dependent people before and after death. While alive, he concludes, they would become totally helpless. Their senses and mental faculties would diminish to the point that that would become "mere amorphous sacs, mere blind stomachs. Such would be the physical consequence of that kind of divine love which we so lazily wish for...Let pain and effort be suspended, and life must shrink back, first into protoplasmic shapelessness, thereafter into dust."[24]

The silkworm reminds Hearn of the Buddhist teaching that even in paradise, pleasure can't exist without pain and effort. He writes, "... all progress, whether moral or material, depends upon the power to meet and master pain...In a silkworm-paradise such as our mundane instincts lead us to desire, the seraph freed from the necessity of toil, and able to satisfy his every want at will, would lose his wings at last, and sink back into the condition of a grub."[25]

The sight of a single dewdrop hanging from the bamboo lattice of a window in his study at home inspires Hearn to write a meditation on the Buddhist concept of death and rebirth, which appears as "A Drop of Dew" in *Koto*.

In early 1904 he completed his most famous and perhaps his best book, *Kwaidan: Stories and Studies of Strange Things*. Kwaidan (pronounced Kay-dawn) is a Japanese word meaning ghost story. Almost the entire book is composed of ancient Japanese folk tales written in Hearn's poetic and potent style, based on the slim outlines of stories

---

[24]Ibid., 65.
[25]Ibid., 67.

furnished by his wife, his students and other sources. Several years earlier, Hearn had conceived the idea of writing a book of philosophical fairy tales. At his request, the Houghton Mifflin Company sent him four volumes by Hans Christian Andersen. He had loved Andersen's fairy tales when he had first read them years ago and wanted to read them again before he started his project. The second reading of Anderson impressed him even more than the first. Hearn was struck by the powerful simplicity of the writing and by Andersen's fertile imagination. But he didn't want to copy the Danish author. "To write like Andersen, one must be Andersen," he writes in a letter to Basil Chamberlain. "But the fountain of his inspiration is unexhausted, and I hope to gain by drinking from it."[26] In *Kwaidan*, Hearn writes in a spare yet expressive style that makes the macabre details of the tales even more chilling. Unlike Andersen, Hearn didn't write his tales principally for children. Their themes are more complex and adult in nature than Andersen's. Hearn's tales offer no simple morals. They have a spiritual and psychological depth that imbues them with layers of meaning and beauty. In these tales, Hearn captures the essence of the Japanese soul.

Demons, flesh-eaters, ghosts and goblins inhabit these stories. The injection of the supernatural into lives of ordinary human beings generate stories with suspenseful drama, powerful emotions and wide-ranging themes. They are unsettling partly because they emphasize the blurred boundaries between the spirit and the material worlds. People and objects are often quite different than what they appear to be. Dreams foretell reality.

In "Jikininki," Muso Kakushi, a priest of the Zen sect who's traveling late at night in a remote area, sees a small dwelling on a hill. The elderly priest who lives there directs him to a nearby hamlet for food and shelter. Later that night, he witnesses a vague and vast "Shape" devour a corpse he had agreed to sit with until morning. He discovers the Shape was the elderly priest, who was doomed to eat the flesh of the corpses in his district because he had failed to fulfill his priestly duties in his previous life.

In "Rokuro-Kubi," a different traveling priest accepts the hospitality of four people who invite him to eat with them and spent the

---

[26]Hearn to Chamberlain, *Life and Letters*, vol. II, 251.

night at their home. After hours of good food and pleasant conversation, everyone goes to sleep. The priest wakes up in the middle of the night and sees the headless bodies of his hosts lying on the floor. He realizes with horror that they are actually goblins who can detach their heads from their bodies and who eat human beings. He sees the heads outside talking about what a scrumptious meal he will make.

Two wood-cutters are stranded in a ferryman's hut in a fierce snowstorm in "Yuki-Onna." One of them watches a ghostly woman in white enter and blow her icy breath on his sleeping friend, killing him. She spares the life of the other wood-cutter because he's so young and tells him she would kill him if he ever told anyone about what he saw. Some time later, he falls in love with and marries a young woman. After they've been married a while, he tells her about the night in the ferryman's hut. She rebukes him and reveals that she is the snow demon who killed his friend. But instead of killing her husband, she disappears.

A young samurai falls in love with a woman of modest means who lives with her parents in "The Story of Aoyagi." He risks angering his lord by setting plans to marry the woman before asking his permission. But, seeing how in love they are, the lord forgives him and allows them to marry. After five happy years of marriage, the woman suddenly screams in pain and drops to the ground. As she lays dying, she tells her husband that she is in reality the soul of a willow tree at the place where they met and someone has just cut down that tree. He later goes to the spot they met and sees the stumps of three willow trees, two older ones which contained the souls of his wife's parents and a younger one that contained her soul. He realizes his dying wife spoke the truth, and he creates a memorial there for her and her parents.

Hearn's skillful descriptive writing gives the ancient folktales a narrative power that makes the supernatural beings and events in the stories seem harrowingly real. In "The Story of Mimi-Nashi-Hoichi," Hearn heightens the mystery by telling the first part of the story from the point of view of a blind man, Hoichi, who is famous for his public recitations. One night, when he is left alone in the temple he lives in, a deep voice of someone who says he's a samurai calls his name and tells him a person of high rank wants him to perform his famous recitation of a long-ago sea battle that wiped out the Heike clan. The person leads him to what he says is that official's house. Hoichi hears the voices of what appears to him to be a large assemblage of people.

Hearn writes: "Then Hoichi lifted up his voice, and changed the chant of the fight on the bitter sea,—wonderfully making his biwa (a four-stringed lute) to sound like the straining of oars and the rushing of ships, the whirr and the hissing of arrows, the shouting and trampling of men, the crashing of steel upon helmets, the plunging of slain in the flood. And to left and right of him, in the pauses of his playing, he could hear voices murmuring his praise: 'How marvelous an artist!'—'Never in our own province was playing heard like this!'"[27]

As Hoichi describes the deaths of the Heike women and children in the battle, voices wail loudly and sob. When he's finished, he receives more praise, and the person who led him to the house takes him back to the temple. But he instructs him to tell no one about this event. The next night, Hoichi is lured to the house again to give the same performance. Hearn's convincing, vivid rendering of Hoichi's experiences at these recitations make it all the more stunning to the reader when the temple priest's two servants follow the blind man on a third night and discover that he's under the spell of demons who plan to tear him to pieces at a later time. They observe Hoichi chanting his story of the battle while sitting alone in a seaside cemetery before the tomb of the Heike's infant king. No one else is there—only little candle-like fires of the dead surrounding him and the tomb, not the throng of people Hoichi thinks is listening to him.

This and the other stories in *Kwaidan* provide potent insights not just into ancient Japanese culture, religion and history but also timeless truths about human nature.

Kwaidan was published in April 1904 while Hearn was teaching at Waseda University in Tokyo. Waseda, a private liberal arts university, had hired him as a professor and had asked him to teach English literature in the last weeks of the spring semester to aspiring writers and journalists. Hearn, who planned to teach at Waseda in the coming fall, felt much more appreciated there than he had at Tokyo Imperial University. The atmosphere was friendlier, and it wasn't too far from his neighborhood. Another teaching option opened up for him around this same time. An official of the University of London sent a

---

[27]Lafcadio Hearn, *Kwaidan* (Boston and New York: Houghton, Mifflin & Co., 1904), 10.

letter asking him if he would be interested in presenting 10 lectures on Japanese civilization at some point during the coming school year. He didn't know if he would be able to do it but was flattered by the request.

By the summer, his health had improved to the point that he took Kazuo and Iwao to Yaizdu for several weeks. He had been too ill the previous summer to go there. For much of the vacation, Hearn was preoccupied with the developments of the Russo-Japanese War, which had broken out in February as a result of a dispute between the two nations over who would control Manchuria and Korea. Several of Hearn's students, dressed in military uniforms, had stopped by his house in Tokyo to say goodbye to him before heading off to war. Hearn wrote essays for Western newspapers and magazines explaining Japan's side of the conflict in hopes of generating support for his adopted country. In Yaidzu, he read the newspapers every day to follow the latest reports on the war. The residents of Yaidzu were intensely interested in the conflict because 17 young men from their small village had been set away to fight. The fishermen, the fish peddlers, shopkeepers and others would gather around Hearn outside in the evenings to ask him for his opinions about what might happen. On the evening of August 14, men selling special-edition newspapers appeared in the streets. The papers with banner headlines "Great Victory!" and "Banzai for Japan!" announced Japan's victory over Russia in an important sea battle. In celebration, Hearn paid for all the bottles of lemonade in Otokichi's shop and distributed them to everyone inside the shop and those gathered outside.

When he returned home from Yaidzu, he finished correcting proofs to *Japan: An Interpretation*, which contained 12 essays he had planned to present at Cornell, and sent them to the publisher, the Macmillan Company in New York. On the afternoon of September 19, when Setsu went into Hearn's study, he was walking around, clutching his chest in pain. He told her not to worry. But she immediately sent for a doctor. As they waited for the doctor, Hearn began writing a letter to a friend asking him to help his family if he died. "Perhaps, if this pain of mine increases, I may die," he told Setsu. "If I die, do not weep. Buy a little urn; you can find one for three or four *sen*. Put my bones in it, and bury it near a quiet temple in the country. I shall not like it if you cry. Amuse the children and play cards with them—how much better I shall enjoy that! There will be no need of announcing my death. If anyone asks, reply 'Oh, he died some time ago!' That will be quite proper."[28]

But a few minutes after giving her those instructions, he stood up and said the pain in his chest was gone. He took a cold bath and drank a glass of whiskey. When the doctor came, Hearn told him he was no longer ill. The doctor examined him and said he didn't detect anything seriously wrong with him. Over the next few days, Hearn resumed his normal activities.

When Setsu went into his study shortly after 6 a.m. on September 26, he was sitting by the hibachi smoking one of his pipes, as he did every morning. He told her about a dream he had that night. In the dream, he traveled a long distance, but he was not in Japan or Europe. It was somewhere he was unfamiliar with—"a strange place," he called it.[29] That afternoon, he looked for a book in his library to send to a former student who was fighting in the Russo-Japanese War. At dinner, he was in a jovial mood, laughing and talking with the children. But an hour after dinner, he came to Setsu, his hands on his chest, and said, "Mama-san, the sickness of the other day has come back again." She made him lie down. In a short time, Hearn died. "He died without any pain, having a little smile around his mouth," Setsu writes. "It could not be helped, if it was the order of Heaven."[30]

She disregarded his instructions about keeping a veil of secrecy around his death and burial. He had to know when he made the request that it would have been impossible to keep his death secret. Besides, his family, friends, students and those who knew him only through his writing wanted to honor his memory. Setsu decided to hold the funeral service at the Kobudera temple because of Hearn's love for it before the cedar trees were cut down. The former abbot there who had been such a good friend of Hearn and his family returned to conduct the Zen Buddhist ceremonies at Hearn's funeral. Besides his family and friends, the mourners included about 100 students, 40 professors and a few foreigners. The presence of the old abbot, who wore a gold brocade and cape, provided a great comfort to Hearn's wife and children, who were dressed in ceremonial white

---

[28]Setsuko Koizumi, *Reminiscences*, 74.
[29]Ibid., 79.
[30]Ibid., 82-83.

robes. Ten-year-old Kazuo was the first to step forward and offer incense before his father. He recalled later that he drew strength in knowing that the abbot who often had patted him on the head and had given him cakes when he was a small child, stood behind him, watching with compassion and reverence. "I felt as if I had come there, after a long absence, to visit the temple again with my father," he wrote.[31]

Hearn's family asked Otokichi, who had been Hearn's friend and landlord at Yaidzu, to participate in the ceremony of the gathering of Hearn's bones after his body was cremated. Otokichi paused while saying Buddhist prayers and picking up the bones to show a small flat and round bone to the crematory man and ask him, " What is it?" He told Otokichi it was a kneecap. "Then with this, Sansei-sama moved his leg and swam in our sea until just a little while ago, eh?," he said, and wiped tears from his eyes.[32]

Hearn had told Kazuo he wanted to have his remains placed in a simple urn and buried in the middle of a forest. But Hearn's bones were buried at Zoshigaya Cemetery in northern Tokyo, a pleasant site with many tall trees where he had enjoyed walking. His life's journey that began on a little Greek island in the Ionian Sea ended thousands of miles away in a rapidly growing city on a large island in the Sea of Japan. Patrick Lafcadio Hearn, the itinerant outsider, had found his true home and his final resting place in a foreign land that came to value him as a national treasure.

---

[31] Kazuo Koizumi, *Father and I*, 32.
[32] Ibid., 126.

Epilogue

*H*EARN'S SPIRIT didn't rest in peace for very long after his death. Controversy dogged him in death just as it had during his life. Two years after he died, Alethea "Mattie" Foley, the former slave he married in Cincinnati in 1874, filed a lawsuit claiming part of his estate. She said since she and Hearn had never divorced, she was his legal wife when he died and was entitled to inherit some of his money. In 1880, she said, she had received what she thought was reliable evidence that Hearn had died in Baton Rouge, Louisiana. A year later, she married an African-American man, John Kleintank. When learning shortly after this marriage that Hearn was still living, Foley said, she separated from Kleintank.

This salacious saga was the kind Hearn would have relished writing about during his Cincinnati years. The Cincinnati newspapers and others throughout the United States reported this court fight between a prominent author and a Black woman, focusing on the history of their relationship. In a July 14, 1906, *Cincinnati Enquirer* story, Foley said she voluntarily left Hearn because "she wearied of his peculiarities. Hers was not the morose, silent disposition that was his. Nothing ever suited him, she says."[1] The court battle didn't last very long. A judge ruled that whatever marital ceremony Hearn and Foley may have participated in was illegal because interracial marriages were banned at that time in Ohio. Therefore, the ruling said, Foley had no legal claim to Hearn's estate.

None of Hearn's four children became journalists. But in an ironic twist of fate, Foley's son, William L. Anderson, who briefly had been Hearn's illegal step-son, worked as a writer and editor of several Cin-

---

[1] "CLAIM: Made by a Negress that She is the Lawful Wife of Lafcadio P. Hearn," *Cincinnati Enquirer*, 8.

cinnati African-American newspapers. Anderson had been born in Dover, Kentucky in 1868 as the illegitimate son of Foley and a Scotsman named Louis Anderson. He was educated in public schools and worked as a newsboy, a porter and a blacksmith before becoming a printer, writer and editor. His editing stints included the *Cincinnati American Reformer* (1892–1894), the *Rostrum* (1897–1902) and the *Cincinnati Pilot* (1911–1912), according to the University of Kentucky Libraries' Notable Kentucky African Americans Database.[2] He served as an alternate delegate-at-large to the 1912 Republican National Convention in Chicago and was an unsuccessful candidate for Cincinnati City Council in 1939. He died in Cincinnati in 1940 at the age of 71.

Soon after Hearn's death, some of his former students began translating his books into the Japanese language. The eerie ancient Japanese folk tales he recast in his own style were especially popular and helped him become a literary icon in his adopted country. In many Japanese schools, Hearn's ghost stories became required reading. Besides helping the students learn English, the stories taught them about their own heritage. By the mid-20th century, Hearn was better known and more widely read in Japan than in the West.

His great friend Elizabeth Bisland wrote the first Hearn biography, published in 1908. Since then, there have been dozens of books about Hearn and his work written by Japanese, American and European writers. Over the years, his books have been published and republished, and many of Hearn stories and articles that originally appeared in newspapers or magazines have been collected in books. One of those books, "The Selected Writings of Lafcadio Hearn" (New York: The Citadel Press, 1941), included an appreciative introduction by renowned American literary critic Malcom Cowley. "Unlike many authors with broader talents," Cowley writes, "he had the métier, the vocation for writing, the conscience that kept him working over each passage until it had the exact color of what he needed to say; and in most cases the colors have proved fast…. Lafcadio Hearn at his best was independent of fashion and was writing for our time as much as for his own."

---

[2]"William Louis Anderson," University of Kentucky Libraries' Notable Kentucky African Americans Database. Accessed through https://nkaa.uky.edu/nkaa/items/show/679.

Three novels based upon his life have been written—even though his life was so unusual it didn't require fictionalization.[3] Japanese filmmaker Masaki Kobayashi made a classic movie, *Kwaidan*, in 1967 that presented four Hearn stories based on Japanese folklore. A Japanese miniseries about Hearn's life was filmed in 1984, with George Chakiris portraying Hearn. Chakiris had a bit of a geographical connection to Hearn. He was born in Norwood, Ohio, a small city surrounded by Cincinnati. In 2009, the Library of America published a broad selection of Hearn's writings from Cincinnati and New Orleans in *Hearn: American Writings*.

Many of the places Hearn lived have commemorated him in some way. His birthplace, the Ionian island of Lefkada, opened a Lafcadio Hearn Historical Center in 2014, the first museum in Europe dedicated to him. In Dublin, a plaque commemorating Hearn hangs near the front door of the house he had lived in as a boy with his great-aunt, Sarah Brenane. In Tramore, Ireland, where Hearn spent many happy summer vacations swimming in the sea, the Lafcadio Hearn Memorial Gardens opened in 2015. Cincinnati has no permanent marker for Hearn yet, but a small group of Hearn enthusiasts are working to raise enough money to pay a Cincinnati sculptor to create a large memorial plaque. The University of Cincinnati's Journalism Department offers an annual student writing award that bears Hearn's name, and the Public Library of Cincinnati and Hamilton County has an impressive Lafcadio Hearn Collection, including Hearn's signed copies of Ye Giglampz and four Hearn letters. The Japan Research Center of Greater Cincinnati, the Lafcadio Hearn Society/USA and the Japan America Society of Greater Cincinnati are working to erect a permanent memorial to Hearn in the city.

In New Orleans, an apartment building at 1565 Cleveland Avenue where Hearn lived has been restored, and a memorial plaque hangs outside. Tulane University's Howard Tilton Memorial Library has a Lafcadio Hearn Room. In St. Pierre, Martinique, museum documenting the 1902 volcanic eruption that destroyed the city and killed more than 30,000 people contains some artifacts recovered from the rubble.

---

[3] Harry S. Wedeck, *Mortal Hunger* (New York: Sheridan House Publishers, 1947; Roger Pulvers, *The Dream of Lafcadio Hearn* (Kumomoto: Kurodahan Press, 2011); Monique Truong, *The Sweetest Fruits* (Viking, 2020).

One of them is the city cathedral's master or "Bourbon" bell that was melted into a grotesque shape. That display includes a card bearing Hearn's description of the bell's beautiful sound from his book, *Two Years in the French West Indies*.[4]

No country celebrates Hearn like Japan and no city commemorates him more than his beloved Matsue. The samurai house he lived in has been restored and is open to the public. The garden he loved so much has is kept exactly as he described it in his brilliant essay about Japanese gardens. Next to this house is Lafcadio Hearn's Memorial Museum. It contains autographed manuscripts, his writing desk, his pipes, spectacles and many other personal items. Space is devoted to his Cincinnati years, with displays of *Cincinnati Enquirer* and the *Cincinnati Commercial* front pages with stories written by Hearn.

The University of Toyama in Toyama, Japan, houses Hearn's personal library of 2,433 books. The collection consists of 1,350 English books, 719 French books and 364 Japanese books as well as hand-written manuscripts of his last book, *Japan: An Attempt at Interpretation*. They include the books Hearn left in the care of George Gould in Philadelphia when he moved to Japan 1890. Gould, who felt he deserved to keep the books in compensation for allowing Hearn to stay at his house for five months, refused Hearn's requests to send the books to Japan. Hearn never saw those books again. But shortly after his death, they were sent to the Koizumi family.

An earthquake that devastated Tokyo in 1923 caused Setsu Koizumi to worry about the safety of her husband's library. She wanted to sell it to a library where it would be much safer than in her house. Ideally, it would be a library in the Tokyo region, near her and her family.

But, instead, it wound up at a high school in a city 155 miles from Tokyo that Hearn had never set foot in. Ryuji Tanabe, who had been one of Hearn's best pupils, was helping the Koizumi family find a buyer. He informed his brother, Nannichi Tsunetaro, the director of Toyama High School, that the Koizumi family was planning to sell Hearn's library. Tsunetaro wanted his school to have the collection. At his and Tanabe's request, Mrs. Haruko Baba, widow of a wealthy shipping merchant, made an offer for Hearn's library. It turned out to

---

[4]Lafcadio Hearn, *Two Years in the French West Indies* (New York: Harper & Brothers, Franklin Square, 1890), 50.

be the highest offer, and Setsu accepted it. In 1924, Baba donated the library to Toyama High School, which later evolved into the University of Toyama. The university has a permanent Hearn study group and hosts an annual Hearn symposium.[5]

Throughout Japan, Lafcadio Hearn Societies abound. Hearn's great-grandson, Bon Koizumi, a college folklore professor, serves as director of the Hearn museum in Matsue. He and his wife, Shoko, work to promote Hearn's legacy within and outside Japan with the help of Takis Efstathiou, a New York City art dealer and Hearn enthusiast. Efstathiou, a native of Greece, has donated his promotional talents, money and rare Hearn first-edition books to help establish permanent memorials to Hearn throughout the world.

When Hearn still lived in New Orleans, he said in a letter to Gould that he wished he worked at a profession such as physician or architect that would make him wealthy. "Then I think I would never settle down in any place; would visit all, wander about as long as I could," he wrote. "There is such a delightful pleasantness about the first relations with people in strange places—before you have made any rival, excited any ill will, incurred anybody's displeasure. Stay long enough in any one place and the illusion is over..."[6]

Hearn never really settled down. His restless spirit and his intense curiosity wouldn't let him. Even in Japan, his adopted homeland, he lived in five different cities in 14 years. This half-blind Greek-Irish orphan faced poverty and loneliness when he moved to Cincinnati, New Orleans, Martinique and Japan. He overcame those obstacles as well as the racial and cultural prejudices of his day to create a vibrant, varied and idiosyncratic literary canon. More than a century after his death, Hearn's writing continues to offer timeless insights into human nature and the many diverse worlds he explored.

---

[5]The Lafcadio Hearn Library Web site. Accessed through the University of Toyama, http://www.lib.u-toyama.ac.jp/chuo/hearn/hearn_index.html#hearn_en.
[6]Hearn to George M. Gould, 1887, *Life and Letters*, vol. I, 398.

Bibliography

Barel, Léona Queyrouze. *The Idyl: My Personal Reminiscences of Lafcadio Hearn*. Kanda, Tokyo, Japan: The Hokuseido Press, 1933.

Bisland, Elizabeth. *The Life and Letters of Lafcadio Hearn,* vols. 1 and 2. Boston: Houghton Mifflin Co., 1906.

_____. *The Japanese Letters of Lafcadio Hearn*, Houghton Mifflin Co., 1910.

Bronner, Milton, ed. *Letters from the Raven: Being the Correspondence of Lafcadio Hearn to Henry Watkin*. New York: Bretano's, 1907.

Cimprich, John. *Fort Pillow, a Civil War Massacre, and Public Memory*. Baton Rouge: Louisiana State University Press, 2011.

Cincinnati Enquirer and *Cincinnati Commercial* articles on microfilm at the Public Library of Cincinnati and Hamilton County, OH.

Cockerill, John A., "Lafcadio Hearn: the Author of Kokoro," *Current Literature*, vol. xix, June 1, 1896.

Cott, Jonathan. *Wandering Ghost: The Odyssey of Lafcadio Hearn*. New York: Knopf, 1991.

Erskine, John, ed. *Books and Habits from the Lectures of Lafcadio Hearn*. London: William Heinnaman, 1922.

Frost, Orcutt William. *Young Hearn*. Tokyo: Hokuseido Press, 1958.

Fuller, H. S. "Lafcadio Hearn: Some Interesting Recollections of His Cincinnati Associations." *Cincinnati Enquirer*, June 17, 1908.

Goodman, Matthew. "Elizabeth Bisland's Race Around the World," *The Public Domain Review*, Oct. 16, 2013. https://public domainreview. org/2013/10/16/elizabeth-bislands-race-around-the-world/

Gould, George M., M.D. *Concerning Lafcadio Hearn. With a Bibliography by Laura Stedman*. Philadelphia : George W. Jacobs & Company, 1908.

Hearn, Lafcadio. *Lafcadio Hearn/American Writings*, Christopher Benfey, ed. New York: The Library of America, 2009.

_____. *The Writings of Lafcadio Hearn,* vols. 1 and II. Boston and New York: Houghton Mifflin Co.,/Cambridge: The Riverside Press, 1923.

Henderson, Edwin. "Lafcadio Hearn: Cincinnati Man Not in Sympathy with Efforts of Literary Historians." *Cincinnati Enquirer*, Nov. 27, 1909.

_____. (under the pseudonym, Contour). "Origin of Hearn's Literary Career," *Cincinnati Enquirer*, April 17, 1921.

Hirakawa, Sukehiro, ed. *Rediscovering Lafcadio Hearn: Japanese Legends, Life and Culture*. Folkestone, UK: Global Oriental Studies, 1997.

Hughes, Jon Christopher, ed. *Period of the Gruesome: Selected Cincinnati Journalism of Lafcadio Hearn*. Lanham, MD: University Press of America. 1990.

_____. ed, *Ye Giglampz: A Weekly Illustrated Journal Devoted to Art, Literature and Satire, Edited by Lafcadio Hearn and Henry Farny*. Cincinnati: Crossroads Books with the Public Library of Cincinnati and Hamilton County, OH, 1983.

_____. The Tanyard Murder: on the case with Lafcadio Hearn. Washington, DC: University Press of America. 1989,

Keagy, Walter R. "Lafcadio Hearn—"Cincinnati's Stepchild," in *The Quarterly Bulletin*, Historical and Philosophical Society of Ohio, April 1950, Cincinnati 1950, 113-127.

Kennard, Nina H. *Lafcadio Hearn*. New York: D. Appleton, 1912.

Kneeland, Tracy. "Lafcadio Hearn's Brother," *Atlantic Monthly*, January, 1923. http://www.lafcadiohearn.net/jameshearn.html.

Koizumi, Kazuo. *Father and I: Memories of Lafcadio Hearn*. New York: Houghton Mifflin Co., 1935.

Koizumi, Setsuko. *Reminiscences of Lafcadio Hearn*. Translated by Paul Kiyoshi Hisada and Frederick Johnson. Boston: Houghton Mifflin Co., 1918.

LaBarre, Delia, ed. *The New Orleans of Lafcadio Hearn*. Baton Rouge: Louisiana State University, 2007.

The Lafcadio Hearn Library Web site. University of Toyama, http://www.lib.u-toyama.ac.jp/chuo/hearn/hearn_index.html#hearn_en.

Lemoine, Bernadette, "Lafcadio Hearn as an Ambassador of French Literature in the United States and Japan," *Revue de Litterature Comparee*, March, 2006. https://www.cairn.info/revue-de-litterature-comparee-2006-3-page-299.htm#.

Lewis, Oscar. *Hearn and His Biographers: The Record of a Literary Controversy*. San Francisco: The Westgate Press, 1930.

Loyola University's Monroe Library's digital archive.

Mather, Frank Lincoln, ed. *Who's Who of the Colored Race: A General Biographical Dictionary of Men and Women of African Descent, vol. 1*. Chicago: F.L. Mather, 1915.

McWhirter, Cameron and Findsen, Owen, eds. *Whimsically Grotesque: Selected Writings of Lafcadio Hearn in the Cincinnati Enquirer, 1872-1875*. Kanda, Chiyoda-ku, Tokyo, Japan: Do-Jidai Sha Company Limited, 2004.

McWilliams, Vera Seely. *Lafcadio Hearn*. Boston: Houghton Mifflin Co., 1946.

Milne, Andrew. "In the Footsteps of Empress Josephine in Martinique," Explore France Web site. https://us.france.fr/en/martinique/list/empress-josephine-martinique.

Moran, John, "Early Influences on Lafcadio Hearn." *Proceedings: International Symposium on "The Open Mind of Lafcadio Hearn: His Spirit from the West to the East, July 5-6, 2014."* Shingo Nagaoka, editor-in-chief. Tokyo: The Planning Committee for the Memorial Events in Greece to Commemorate the 110th Anniversary of Lafcadio Hearn's Death: 2014.

Mordell, Albert, ed. *Occidental Gleanings*. New York: Dodd, Mead and Company, 1925.

Murray, Paul. *A Fantastic Journey: The Life and Literature of Lafcadio Hearn*. Sandgate, Folkestone, Kent: Japan Library, 1993.

Nishizaki, Ichiro. *New Hearn Letters from the French West Indies*. Tokyo: Ochanomizu University, 1959.

Ohio Memory Collection blog, https://ohiomemory.org/digital/collection/ p267401coll36/id/21960/.

Prabook Web site. "Henry Mills Alden." https://prabook.com/web/henry. alden/3750327.

Richardson, Thomas J. "George Washington Cable, 1844-1925)," Encyclopedia of Southern Culture (University of North Carolina Press, 1989), Charles Reagan Wilson and William Ferris, eds. Accessed through "Documenting the American South" Website, https://docsouth.unc. edu/southlit/cablecreole/bio.html.

Sekita, Karol. *Letters and Correspondence Between Lafcadio Hearn and Mrs. Ellen Freeman.* Tokyo: Shohakusha, 2021.

Smith, Joanne. "John A. Cockerill." American Newspaper Journalists, 1873-1900. Ed. Perry J. Ashley. Detroit: Gale Research, 1983. Dictionary of Literary Biography Vol. 23. Literature Resource Center. Web. 28 Feb. 2013.

Stern, Joseph S. Jr., "Cincinnati's Butch Cassidy and the Sundance Kid" in *Queen City Heritage.* Summer 1992.

Stevens, George E. *The Queen City in 1869.* Cincinnati, OH: George S. Blanchard & Co., 1869.

Stevenson, Elizabeth. *Lafcadio Hearn.* New York: Macmillan, 1961.

Suess, Jeff. "Charming 'Old Main.'" *Cincinnati Enquirer,* January 19, 2004.

Tinker, Edward Larocque. *Lafcadio Hearn's American Days.* New York: Dodd, Mead and Company, 1924.

Tulane University Health Sciences Center Rudolph Matas Library's Web site. http://www.tulane.edu/~matas/historical/charity/charity5.htm.

Tunison, Joseph P. "Lafcadio Hearn," *Dayton Journal,* Dec. 25, 1906.

_____. "Lafcadio Hearn: An Appreciation of the Author by One Who Was Close to Him," *Cincinnati Enquirer,* Oct. 2, 1904.

_____. "Concerning Lafcadio Hearn," *Dayton Journal,* May 11, 1908.

_____. Unpublished article sent to *The Atlantic Monthly,* 1890s. From the personal research archives of Jon Christoper Hughes, ed., Period of the Gruesome (New York, University Press of American, 1990), who obtained a copy of this manuscript from the Library of Congress.

University of Kentucky Libraries' Notable Kentucky African Americans Database. "William Louis Anderson." https://nkaa.uky.edu/nkaa/items/show/679.

Williamson, Rodger Steele, *Lafcadio Hearn's Development and Realization of Fundamental Points of View during his Cincinnati Period.* EIHOSHA, October, 2005.

Woodson, Carter G. "The Negroes of Cincinnati Prior to the Civil War" in *The Journal of Negro History,* Vol. 1, January, 1916.

Young, Robert. "Lafcadio Hearn," The Living Age, March 23, 1907, quoted in *Lafcadio Hearn*, Elizabeth Stevenson (New York: Macmillan, 1961), 272.

Yu, Beongcheon, *An Ape of Gods: The Art and Thought of Lafcadio Hearn.* Detroit: Wayne State University Press, 1964.

Acknowledgments

I AM DEEPLY GRATEFUL to John Hughes, an author, photographer and retired University of Cincinnati journalism professor who generously gave me access to his research material concerning Lafcadio Hearn's Cincinnati years. Jon produced three Hearn-related books and expanded the bibliography of Hearn's Cincinnati newspaper articles. He gave me valuable suggestions as I worked on this book.

To Bon and Shoko Koizumi, who have helped and encouraged me in my writings about Bon's great-grandfather and who gave me access to the photos from the Koizumi Family Archive to use in this book.

To Kinji Tanaka, a Hearn scholar who shared his extensive research and wisdom with me. A native of Japan and a longtime resident of Cincinnati, he guided me during my trip to Japan in 2004 for the nine, four-city symposium commemorating the 100th anniversary of Hearn's death and even lent me some yen during that trip when I ran low on cash. He was a cherished friend who died in 2020.

To Jim DeBrosse, an author and my former *Cincinnati Enquirer* and *Cincinnati Post* colleague who read my manuscript and made valuable suggestions.

To Jim Ott, a writer and my journalism mentor in college whose advice helped improve this book's introductory chapter.

To Takis Efstathiou, a tireless promoter of Hearn's legacy who has helped and encouraged me during this project. A New York City art dealer born and raised in Greece, he has helped me make valuable connections with Hearn scholars throughout the world.

To Toshie Nakajima and Mariko Mizuno, professors at the University of Toyama in Japan who invited me to give a presentation in 2018 at the university's annual Lafcadio Hearn Symposium. They enriched my knowledge of Hearn and 19th century Japan by showing me his personal library, housed at the university, and taking me to historic sections of Toyama.

To Gary Eith, former president of the Lafcadio Hearn Society/ USA, with whom I've worked to produce issues of a Hearn online journal and to organize a Hearn symposium.

To Naomi Westcott, a Hearn aficionado and a native of Japan who aided me in navigating the 2004 Hearn symposium in Japan.

To my wife, Karen, who has given me unfailing encouragement and support in all my Hearn endeavors.

"Books to Span the East and West"

Tuttle Publishing was founded in 1832 in the small New England town of Rutland, Vermont [USA]. Our core values remain as strong today as they were then—to publish best-in-class books which bring people together one page at a time. In 1948, we established a publishing outpost in Japan—and Tuttle is now a leader in publishing English-language books about the arts, languages and cultures of Asia. The world has become a much smaller place today and Asia's economic and cultural influence has grown. Yet the need for meaningful dialogue and information about this diverse region has never been greater. Over the past seven decades, Tuttle has published thousands of books on subjects ranging from martial arts and paper crafts to language learning and literature—and our talented authors, illustrators, designers and photographers have won many prestigious awards. We welcome you to explore the wealth of information available on Asia at **www.tuttlepublishing.com**.

Published by Tuttle Publishing, an imprint of Periplus Editions (HK) Ltd.

www.tuttlepublishing.com

Copyright © 2023 by Steve Kemme

Library of Congress Cataloging-in-Publication Data is in progress

ISBN: 978-4-8053-1760-0

26 25 24 23
10 9 8 7 6 5 4 3 2 1   2304VP

Printed in Malaysia

TUTTLE PUBLISHING® is a registered trademark of Tuttle Publishing, a division of Periplus Editions (HK) Ltd.

Distributed by

North America, Latin America & Europe
Tuttle Publishing
364 Innovation Drive
North Clarendon
VT 05759-9436 U.S.A.
Tel: 1 (802) 773-8930
Fax: 1 (802) 773-6993
info@tuttlepublishing.com
www.tuttlepublishing.com

Japan
Tuttle Publishing
Yaekari Building, 3rd Floor
5-4-12 Osaki, Shinagawa-ku
Tokyo 141 0032
Tel: (81) 3 5437-0171
Fax: (81) 3 5437-0755
sales@tuttle.co.jp
www.tuttle.co.jp

Asia Pacific
Berkeley Books Pte Ltd
3 Kallang Sector #04-01
Singapore 349278
Tel: (65) 6741 2178
Fax: (65) 6741 2179
inquiries@periplus.com.sg
www.tuttlepublishing.com